SPIRITUAL JOURNEY

SPIRITUAL JOURNEY

AUGUSTINE'S REFLECTIONS
ON THE CHRISTIAN LIFE

Michele Cardinal Pellegrino

With a foreword by
Thomas F. Martin, O.S.A.

Edited by
John E. Rotelle, O.S.A.

Augustinian Press
1996

Cover design by Accent Communications.

Library of Congress Cataloging-in-Publication Data

Augustine, Saint, Bishop of Hippo.
   [Itinerario spirituale. English]
   Spiritual Journey: Augustine's reflections on the Christian life / by Michele Pellegrino; edited by John E. Rotelle.
   p. cm.
   Previously published: Give what you command. Catholic Book Pub. Co., 1972.
   Includes bibliographical references.
   ISBN 0-941491-98-6 (cloth). — ISBN 0-941491-97-8 (paper)
   1. Augustine, Saint, Bishop of Hippo. 2. Theology, Doctrinal — History — Early church, ca. 30-600. 3. Spiritual life — Christianity — Early work to 1800. I. Pellegrino, Michele. II. Rotelle, John E. III. Title.

BR1720.A9A3   1996   96-24008
248.4'814—dc20   CIP

Augustinian Press
P.O. Box 476
Villanova, PA 19085

CONTENTS

FOREWORD

There is no doubt that Augustine of Hippo touched something deep within the heart of Michele Pellegrino. Thus it was that, with profound admiration and yet critical intellect, this scholar and pastor both modeled and taught Augustine. The present volume is one of many works, some more popular, others techincal studies, that reflect his life-long adventure with the Bishop of Hippo. Born at the dawn of the 20th century, son of humble and hard-working parents, responsive early on to God's call, Michele Pellegrino became scholar, priest, pastor, and eventually Cardinal of Turin, Italy. Deeply committed to the Church, he was just as deeply committed to the serious search for truth — and saw neither commitment as incompatible with the other. Not surprisingly, his interventions at Vatican II supported freedom of research — as well as the education of the clergy.

The present work, with its suggestive title, reflects what Michele Pellegrino discovered to be at the heart of Augustine's genius — a tension and dynamism centered in the search for God. For Augustine this journeying was as interior as it was shared. It was radically Christological — but always a Christ discovered within the embrace of the Church. Love, humility, and truth were its hallmarks — all of which could be transformed into prayer. It did not take away one's humanity — but liberated it, healed it, and restored it. It was precisely for these reasons that Michele Pellegrino found Augustine to be a spiritual guide eminently suited for 20th century seekers after truth.

In an article written shortly after the II Vatican Council Cardinal Pellegrino reaffirmed why he saw such a profound linkage between this man of the ancient world and men and women of the 20th century. Augustine's sense of history, his probing into the real human situation, his call to discover the "within," his vision of the Church more as mystery than institution, his willingness to dialogue with his world — these were the values Michele Pellegrino found Augustine offering in his own day and continuing to offer today. Above all it was the Bishop of Hippo's own relentless and radical quest to view everything human

from the perspective of God that he found to be Augustine's greatest
challenge to the modern world. "We are not on this earth for ourselves, nor for the earth — but for God." (*Il messaggio di S Agostino al
mondo moderno*, 23). Yet this affirmation was never felt to be a dismiss-
al of humanity, but rather its ultimate validation.

A decade has past since the death of Cardinal Michele Pellegrino.
Much has changed in world and Church — and many eyes now cast
about to seek even a glimpse of what the new millennium heralds. Yet
his portrayal of Augustine the journeyer, reflected in the pages that
follow, are precisely what has prompted the Editor of this series to
make this work once again accessible to seekers of all kinds. In the
pages that follow Michele Pellegrino most often fades into the back-
ground and simple lets Augustine speak for himself. And Augustine
would ask the same for himself:

> Take it for absolutely certain that even if you can learn some-
> thing from me that is good, your true Master will always be the
> Interior Master of the interior person. It is he who enable you
> to understand in the depth of your being the truth of what is
> said to you. For the one who plants is nothing, nor the one who
> waters, for everything comes from God who gives the increase
> (*Letter* 266, 2).

Thomas F. Martin, O.S.A.

EDITOR'S NOTE

Cardinal Pellegrino's magnificent book *Itinerario Spirituale* appeared in Italian in 1964. It was truly considered a gem in Augustinian publications because for the first time we had a compilation of texts which gave Augustine's thought on the Christian life.

In 1972 Cardinal Pellegrino's book was published by Catholic Book Publishing Company under the title *Give What You Command*. At that time it was thought that the title *Spiritual Journey* would not be appreciated so we selected the famous phrase from Augustine's work the *Confessions* (X, 31, 45) which synthesizes his thought on Christian life and grace. Matthew O'Connell was the translator; I was the editor.

In this 1996 edition I use the original title of the Italian work. The original translator, Matthew O'Connell, reviewed and updated the 1972 translation. In this edition the new translations, thus far published or in preparation, of The Works of Saint Augustine have been included.

The presentation of this fine work is a bit difficult because, as Cardinal Pellegrino says, this book is a collection of Augustine texts. There is very little commentary written by the Cardinal. So all the lengthy texts of Augustine, that is more than nine lines, have been presented with an indented format. The shorter texts are not indented and are set in quotation marks. All direct quotes of sacred scripture are set in italics with the appropriate citation; all direct Augustine texts have the appropriate citation directly after the text.

It is hoped that the relaunching of this important work on Saint Augustine will benefit those who wish to know what Saint Augustine says on the Christian life. May the thought of Saint Augustine accompany believers on their own spiritual journey in God.

24 April 1996   John E. Rotelle, O.S.A.

CHAPTER 1

INTERIORITY

The spiritual teaching of Saint Augustine, like his personal experience, is dominated by a continual summons to interiority. The value of persons is measured by what they are before God who reads the heart; in the interior self dwells the truth which enlightens us, and there the Spirit builds God's temple. We must enter into ourselves if we are to transcend ourselves and encounter God. The Church indeed needs hands that toil, but it needs even more the interior activity of contemplation and love which is the goal of all external action. Augustine meditated on, preached, and lived these principles with an intensity of dedication that strikes anyone who reads what has been written about him and especially the pages in which he himself tells us his thought on these matters and sketches his own spiritual portrait for us.

Possidius says of Augustine:

He did not allow his heart to become attached to or entangled in the possessions of the Church. But while his attention and concern were focused rather on the more important things of the spirit, he did at times turn his thoughts from eternal things and bring them down to temporal affairs. Once these had been arranged in orderly fashion, he would withdraw from them as from stings and annoyances and return to the interior, higher things of the mind, either studying the things of God or dictating something of what he had discovered or correcting what had been written at his dictation. This he did in laborious days and nights filled with toil. In this he resembled that most devout woman, Mary, who is a type of the heavenly Church and of whom we read that she sat at the Lord's feet and listened intently to his words. And when her sister complained that though she had so much serving to do Mary did not help her, she was told: *Martha, Martha, Mary has chosen the better part, and it shall not be taken from her* (Lk 10:39) (*Life* 24, 10-12).

The biographer, a close associate of his hero for almost forty years, has here given felicitous, concrete expression to an essential trait of Saint Augustine's spiritual nature. In the latter's writings we find constant reference to the supreme value of interiority. Augustine is ever searching for its deeper meaning, outlining its various stages in the journey of Christian life, and indicating the means of attaining it.

Authentic Worth

Augustine loves to recall the essentially interior character of the Christian life, even when some aspects of this life are formulated in terms of outward observances. Thus, the precept of fasting is really aimed at the purification of the heart.

Here again we must be careful that the spirit of self-assertion and the desire for human praise do not creep in to divide the heart and prevent it from seeking God in naked simplicity. *When you fast, you are not to look glum as the hypocrites do. They change the appearance of their faces so that others may see they are fasting. I assure you, they are already repaid. When you fast see to it that you groom your hair and wash your face. In that way no one can see you are fasting but your heavenly Father who is hidden; and your Father who sees what is hidden will repay you* (Mt 6:16-18). These precepts evidently direct our whole attention to interior joys; we are not to follow this world's fashion by seeking our reward in external things and thus throw away the promise of a happiness that is all the more sure and substantial as it is the more interior. In that promise God *has predestined us to share the image of his Son* (Rom 8:29) (*The Lord's Sermon on the Mount* II, 12, 40).

The interiority to which the precept points is given special and even exclusive stress when Jesus says: *When you fast, see to it that you groom your hair and wash your face. In that way no one can see you are fasting but your Father.* For:

it would be unreasonable to ask that when we fast we not only wash our face, as we do every day, but perfume our hair as well. Everyone would find such a demand highly unsuitable. We must therefore take the command to perfume our heads and wash our faces as referring to the interior self. Anointing the head is a symbolic reference to joy; washing the face, to purity. We anoint our head when we rejoice within in soul and intellect (*ibid.* II, 12, 42).

We find Saint Augustine making a similar observation in connection with Paul's praise of love: *If I give everything I have to feed the poor and hand over my body to be burned, but have not love, I gain nothing* (1 Cor 13:3).

> The divine scripture thus summons us to interiority and away from all exterior and obvious ostentation; from the surface, where we display ourselves before others, it summons us to our interior depths. Enter into your conscience and question it. Do not look to the blossom which is seen but to the root which is deep in the earth (*Homilies on the First Letter of John* 8, 9).

It is God's own word, then, that teaches the essential value of interiority, over against the outward appearances which spur our pride and seduce us. The interior life is a source of indescribable joy: the joy which Ambrose experienced but which Augustine, then far from God, would never have suspected (*Confessions* VI, 3, 3).

Later on, Augustine himself did have the happy experience of these hidden joys:

> How sweet did it suddenly seem to me to shrug off those sweet frivolities, and how glad I now was to get rid of them — I who had been loath to let them go! For it was you who cast them out from me, you, our real and all-surpassing sweetness. You cast them out and entered yourself to take their place, you who are lovelier than any pleasure, though not to flesh and blood, more lustrous than any light, yet more inward than is any secret intimacy, loftier than all honor, yet not to those who look for loftiness in themselves (*Confessions* IX, 1, 1).

Some twelve years later, he tells us that such experiences shed light on his inner life:

> You, the Truth, are the unfailing Light from which I sought counsel upon all these things, asking whether they were, what they were, and how they were to be valued. But I heard you teaching me and I heard the commands you gave. Often I do this. I find pleasure in it, and when I can relax from my necessary duties, I take refuge in this pleasure. But in all the regions where I thread my way, seeking your guidance, only in you do I find a safe haven for my mind, a gathering-place for my scattered parts, where no portion of me can depart from you. And sometimes you allow me to experience a feeling quite unlike my normal state, an inward sense of delight which, if it were to reach perfection in me, would be something not encountered in this life, though what it is I cannot tell (*Confessions* X, 40, 65).

Deeper Meaning

In order to grasp the full significance of Augustinian interiority (which is concerned not with the problem of knowledge but with the orientation of the Christian life), we must go beyond Augustine's appeals to scripture and look more closely at the personal experience he describes. We know, of course, the part played in this experience by philosophical reflection, especially in his encounter with the Neoplatonists.

Enter into yourself

"Do not go outside but enter into yourself, for truth dwells in the interior self" (*True Religion* 72, 102).

As Augustine looks back on a youth spent far from God, he reproaches himself for having kept his eyes fixed on the external world. For, by so doing, he had kept himself from perceiving the light by which God intended to illuminate his inner self. "*You knew all my longings; the very light that shone in my eyes was mine no longer* (Ps 38:10-11). For the light of my eyes was not there at my command: it was within, but I was outside; it occupied no place, but I had fixed my gaze on spatially positioned things, and so I found in them nowhere to rest" (*Confessions* VII, 7, 11).

What he was experiencing was his own intellectual nature, but the discovery would have very important repercussions on the direction of his life as a whole. After all, the rescue of the prodigal son began with his return to himself. After citing the apostle's words: *People will be lovers of self and of money* (2 Tm 3:2), Augustine observes in a sermon:

> Now, you can see that you are outside yourself. Stay in yourself, if you can. Why go outside? Has money really made you rich, you lover of money? As soon as you began to love things outside yourself, you lost yourself. So when a person's love also reaches out from himself to what is outside, he begins to disintegrate with dissipation, and to squander his powers somehow or other like the spendthrift prodigal son. He empties himself, he pours himself out, he ends up penniless, he herds pigs. . . . *And he returned to himself.* If he returned to himself, it means he had gone away from himself. Because he had fallen from himself and gone away from himself, he first returns to himself in order to return to the one from whom he had fallen, in falling from himself (Sermon 96, 2).

The return to the self is not required only of those who have become lost in sin by pursuing empty dreams of a happiness far from God. It is also required of those who have gone about in search of God and restlessly questioned creature after creature. "I see the things my God has made, but I do not see him, my God, who made them. But since I am a flame with desire *as the hind longs for the running waters* (Ps 41:2) and the fountain of life is in God . . . *and the invisible realities of God are seen and recognized through the things he has made* (Rom 1:20), what shall I do in order to find my God?

> I shall look at the earth, but the earth was made. Earth's beauty is great, but it has a maker. Great marvels are to be found in seeds and beings that reproduce themselves, but all these have a creator. I turn my gaze to the immensity of the sea that surrounds us, and I am stunned with admiration; I seek its maker. I raise my eyes to heaven and the splendor of the stars; I am in admiration of the blazing sun that is able to bring forth the day, and the moon that relieves the darkness of the night. Wonderful and praiseworthy are all these things; they even strike us dumb, for they are no longer things of earth but of heaven. But they do not slake my thirst. I gaze at them in wonder and praise them, but I thirst for him who made them. I enter into myself and ask who I am that seek such things (*Expositions of the Psalms* 42, 7).

Toward the end of a long sermon on the Trinity, Augustine invites his hearers to enter into themselves and meditate on what they have heard:

> Let us leave a little room for reflection, room too for silence. Enter into yourself, leave behind all noise and confusion. Look within yourself and see whether there be some sweet hidden place in your consciousness where you can be free of noise and argument, where you need not be carrying on your disputes and planning to have your own stubborn way. Hear the word in quietness that you may understand it. Then perhaps you will say: *You will let me hear the sounds of joy and gladness, and my bones shall rejoice* — bones that *are crushed* (Ps 51:10), not standing proudly upright (Sermon 56, 22).

"Transcend yourself as well"

Some of the passages I have cited go on to explain that interiority is a leap taken by those who have turned from external things and entered into themselves, so that they may transcend themselves and reach God.

Do not go outside but enter into yourself, for truth dwells in
the interior self. Once you have found your own changeable
nature, then transcend yourself as well. But remember that
when you transcend yourself, you also transcend the reasoning
soul. Retrace your steps, then, to the point where the lamp of
reason itself derives its light. After all, does not every human
being who makes proper use of reason reach truth itself? . . .
Admit that you do not know what truth really is. Truth does not
go looking for itself, whereas you come seeking it, not by crossing space but through the questing desire of the heart, so that
the inner self may be enabled to become like the one who
dwells within, in a love that is no longer base and carnal but
sublime and spiritual (*True Religion* 39, 72).

I entered, and with the eye of my soul, such as it was, I saw the
Light that never changes casting its rays over the same eye of
my soul, over my mind. . . . It shone above my mind, but not in
the way that oil floats above water or the sky hangs over the
earth. It was above me because it was itself the Light that made
me, and I was below because I was made by it. All who know
the truth know this Light, and all who know this Light know
eternity. It is the Light that charity knows. Eternal Truth, true
Love, beloved Eternity (*Confessions* VII, 10, 16).

Even for the prodigal son, the return to himself implies a return to
his father, that is, to God.

You see, by falling from himself he had remained in himself. So
in the same way, when he returns to himself he must not remain
in himself, in case he again goes away from himself. On returning
to himself, what did he say in order not to remain in himself? *I
will arise and go to my father* (Lk 15:17-18). That's the place from
which he had fallen from himself; he had fallen from his father,
he had fallen from himself. He had gone away from himself to
things outside. He comes back to himself and sets off to his
father, where he can keep himself in the utmost security (Sermon 96, 2).

Turning away from the contemplation of visible things, Augustine
entered into himself, but in order to find God he had to transcend
himself.

I seek my God in the material things of heaven and earth, and I
do not find him. I seek the reality of him in my own soul, and I
do not find it. Yet I am determined to seek my God and, in my
yearning to understand and gaze upon the invisible things of
God by means of created things, *I pour out my soul within me* (Ps

41:5). I have no other purpose henceforth but to reach my God. The dwelling of my God lies above my soul. There he dwells; from there he gazes upon me; from there he created human beings and governs me; from there he rouses me and guides me and leads me to the goal (*Expositions of the Psalms* 42, 8).

Only by entering into ourselves in order to find God do we find the true happiness for which we long.

Now we may not only believe, but also begin to understand that it has truly been written on divine authority that we are not to call anyone on earth "teacher," because there is one teacher of all in heaven. But what "in heaven" means will be shown to us by him who guides us by means of human agents and external signs, so that we may learn to turn inward to him. To love him and to know him is the happy life; all claim to seek this, but so few ever rejoice at having found it (*The Teacher* XIV, 46).

God speaks to the heart

As the passage just cited has indicated, God is the interior teacher, the light that illumines the recesses of our being. We must welcome God into our heart, for this is his temple.

The soul of the just is the seat of wisdom. Where does God have his seat, except where he dwells? And where does he dwell, if not in his temple? *For the temple of God is holy, and you are that temple* (1 Cor 3:17). See, therefore, how you must welcome God. *God is spirit, and we must worship him in spirit and truth* (Jn 4:24). If God pleases, enter at last into your heart, the ark of the covenant, and topple Dagon from his place (see 1 Sm 5:2-5). Listen and learn to long for God; learn how to prepare yourself to see God. It is written: *Blessed are the single-hearted, for they shall see God* (Mt 5:8) (Sermon 53, 7).

The eye is but one part of the body, yet it alone enjoys the light; the other parts of the body may be bathed in light, yet they cannot perceive it; only the eye is penetrated by it and enjoys it. So too in our soul there is a power called the intellect. It is precisely this power, the 'intellect' or 'mind,' that is illumined by a higher light. Now that higher light, which illumines the human soul, is God. He was the true light that enlightens every human being who comes into the world (Jn 1:9). That light was Christ (*Homilies on the Gospel of John* 15, 19).

Within our hearts we speak to God, and God makes heard his voice that gives consolation and joy. "We also have within us, then, a mouth; within ourselves we pray, with that mouth we pray. If we prepare a house within ourselves to welcome God, therein we speak and therein we are heard" (*Expositions of the Psalms* 138, 2).

> Let them [those who set themselves apart from you] . . . turn back and seek you, for you do not forsake your creation as they have forsaken their Creator. Let them only turn back, see! there you are in their hearts, in the hearts of all those who confess to you, who fling themselves into your arms and weep against your breast after their difficult journey, while you so easily will wipe away their tears. At this they weep the more, yet even their laments are matter for joy, because you, Lord, are not some human being of flesh and blood, but the Lord who made them, and now make them anew and comfort them (*Confessions* V, 2, 2).

The Stages of the Journey

In its first meaning interiority is identical with a Christian life that is lived according to the basic requirements of Christianity. Here, too, we have the first stage in the journey that is the interior life. Built upon this there is a further, progressive interiorization that can reach the highest peaks of mystical union with God.

Christ, the interior teacher, is received into the heart when a person believes.

> *Enter, then, into your heart* (Is 46:8), and if you have faith, you will find Christ there. There he speaks to you. I, the preacher, must raise my voice, but he instructs you more effectively in silence. I speak in sounding words; he speaks within, by inspiring a holy fear. It is for him, then, to sow my words in your hearts. . . . Because faith, and Christ, are in your hearts, he will teach you what I seek to communicate to you through the sound of my words (Sermon 102, 1).

Interiority, an essential element in the Christian life

Here are a few more passages in which Augustine teaches us this truth.

> By abandoning God and loving yourself you have gone out of yourself, and now you set greater value on external things than on yourself. Return, then, to yourself. But when you do transcend and enter into yourself, do not lock yourself up within yourself. First, return from external things into yourself, and give yourself to him who made you, to him who, when you were lost, found you as you were fleeing and called you back from afar to himself. Return, then, to yourself and go to him who made

you. Imitate the younger son, for perhaps you are in fact like him (Sermon 330, 3).

"Gaze now upon heaven and earth; these material things, beautiful though they are, are not so precious to you that you can seek your happiness in them. What you seek is within your soul. Do you want to be happy? Then look and see whether there is not something better even than your soul" (Expositions of the Psalms 33, II, Sermon 2, 16).

"He who sees within us loves within us; he loves within us, let him be loved in return, for he brings beauty itself within us. What are the interior beauties? Those of conscience. There Christ sees and loves and speaks and punishes and crowns" (Expositions of the Psalms 45, 29).

The ascensions of the heart

The passage from a wholly external life to interiority, and the various stages that mark the journey, are summarized in a passage from True Religion:

> This self which I have described as old and external and earthly . . . some carry with them from the beginning of this life to its end. Others, on the contrary, though they must inevitably begin their earthly life in such a state, achieve an interior rebirth; then, by expending spiritual energy and through progress in wisdom, they destroy what is left of the old self until they have killed it and subjected it to heavenly laws; finally, after bodily death, they are totally renewed. The renewed self is called the new self, and it is interior and heavenly; it passes through spiritual stages that are distinguished not by calendar year but by progress made (True Religion 26, 49).

The description of the "ascensions of the heart" on the journey to increasing interiority reflects chiefly Augustine's personal experience. This is true not only in his Confessions, where we expect such confidences from him, but also in some of his sermons, where the inner fire flashes out uncontrollably.

A climactic point in the Confessions is the "ecstasy" at Ostia, which Augustine experienced in a moment of mysterious spiritual communion with his mother.

> But because the day when she was to quit this life was drawing near — a day known to you, though we were ignorant of it — she and I happened to be alone, through the mysterious workings of your will, as I believe. We stood leaning against a window which looked out on a garden within the house where we were staying at Ostia on the Tiber, for there, far from the crowds, we were recruiting our strength after the long journey, in prepara-

tion for our voyage overseas. We were alone, conferring very intimately. Forgetting what lay in the past, and stretching out to what was ahead, we enquired between ourselves in the light of present truth, the Truth which is yourself, what the eternal life of the saints would be like. Eye has not seen nor ear heard nor human heart conceived it, yet with the mouth of our hearts wide open we panted thirstily for the celestial streams of your fountain, the fount of life which is with you, that bedewed from it according to our present capacity we might in our little measure think upon a thing so great.

Our colloquy led us to the point where the pleasures of the body's senses, however intense and in however brilliant a material light enjoyed, seemed unworthy not merely of comparison but even of remembrance beside the joy of that life, and we lifted ourselves in longing yet more ardent toward *That Which Is*, and step by step traversed all bodily creatures and heaven itself, whence sun and moon and stars shed their light upon the earth. Higher still we mounted by inward thought and wondering discourse on your works, and we arrived at the summit of our own minds; and this too we transcended, to touch that land of never-failing plenty where you pasture Israel for ever with the food of truth. Life there is the Wisdom through whom all these things are made, and all others that have been and will be for ever. Rather should we say that in her there is no "has been" or "will be," but only being, for she is eternal, but past and future do not belong to eternity. And as we talked and panted for it, we just touched the edge of it by the utmost leap of our hearts; then, sighing and unsatisfied, we left the first-fruits of our spirit captive there, and returned to the noise of articulate speech, where a word has beginning and end. How different from your Word, our Lord, who abides in himself, and grows not old, but renews all things.

Then we said, "If the tumult of the flesh fell silent for someone, and silent too were the phantasms of earth, sea and air, silent the heavens, and the very soul silent to itself, that it might pass beyond itself by not thinking of its own being; if dreams and revelations known through its imagination were silent, if every tongue, and every sign, and whatever is subject to transience were wholly stilled for him — for if anyone listens, all these things will tell him, 'We did not make ourselves; he made us who abides for ever' — and having said this they held their peace for they had pricked the listening ear to him who made them; and then he alone were to speak, not through things that are made, but of himself, that we might hear his Word, not through fleshly tongue nor angel's voice, nor thundercloud, nor any riddling parable, hear him unmediated, whom we love in all these things, hear him without them, as now we stretch out and in a flash of thought touch that eternal Wisdom who abides above all things; if this could last, and all other visions, so far inferior, be taken away, and this sight alone ravish him who saw it, and engulf him and hide him away, kept for inward joys, so that this moment that left us aching for more — should there be life eternal, would not *Enter into the joy of thy Lord* be this, and this alone? (*Confessions* IX, 10, 23-25).

In the following passage, regret for a past spent far from God yields place to a cry of gratitude for the indescribable interior joys with which God now fills him:

Late have I loved you, Beauty so ancient and so new, late have I loved you! Lo, you were within, but I outside, seeking there for you, and upon the shapely things you have made I rushed head-long, I, misshapen. You were with me, but I was not with you. They held me back far from you, those things which would have no being were they not in you. You called, shouted, broke through my deafness; you flared, blazed, banished my blindness; you lavished your fragrance, I gasped, and now I pant for you; I tasted you, and I hunger and thirst; you touched me, and I burned for your peace (*Confessions* X, 27, 38).

This hind that feeds day and night upon its own tears and is carried away with longing for the springs of water, that is, for the interior sweetness of God; that pours out its soul within itself so that it may reach what is higher than its own soul; that walks in procession even to the house of God; that is drawn by the sweetness of the inner, spiritual word to despise all outer reality and lets itself be carried away to interior reality — this hind is still a human being; it still groans here on earth and carries the burden of the weak flesh; it is still in danger as it walks among the stumbling blocks of this world. . . . But we are saddened, for we have experienced the joy of a certain inner sweetness and at the pinnacle of the soul we have glimpsed, though but for a fleeting moment, a changeless reality (*Expositions of the Psalms* 42, 10).

In the following passage Augustine prays ardently that the wonderful work of interior transformation may be completed. "*I will give thanks to you, O Lord, with all my heart* (Ps 138:1). The Psalmist is saying: 'Let my whole heart be inflamed with love for you; let nothing in me belong to me and let me have no thought for myself; but let me burn and be wholly consumed in you, let me love you with my whole being as one set on fire by you'" (*Expositions of the Psalms* 138, 2).

Hence, when the interior life advances to a certain stage which is connatural to it, it becomes a fountain of peace and indescribable joy. Some further passages will confirm and clarify what we have already learned in this respect.

> See how the Psalmist praises interior things: *The children of men take refuge in the shadow of your wings* (Ps 36:8). See what it means to "enter," see what it means to take refuge under his protection. . . . What is it that is within? *They have their fill of the prime gifts of your house.* When you make them enter the joy of their Lord, they will *have their fill of the prime gifts of your house, from your delightful stream you give them to drink. For with you is the fountain of life* (Ps 36:9-10). The fountain of life is not outside you but within you. . . . Those who live a just and laborious life do not grow rebellious; they have within themselves what the wealthy do not have; therefore they are not cast down, they are not worried and do not become discouraged. The wealthy have money in their treasure-chests, but these have God in their hearts. Compare now the gold and God, the treasure-chest and the heart. . . . Therefore, we must enter in that we may live (*Homilies on the Gospel of John* 25, 17).

A life like Mary's, which was wholly interior, brings the soul the purest spiritual joys. "There are two lives: one is concerned with delight, the other with satisfying needs. . . . But enter into yourself and do not seek delight outside" (Sermon 255, 6). "Those who are nourished on the word of God within themselves do not seek their delight in the desert of this world" (*True Religion* 38, 71).

To live interiorly

While he knows that the one who works effectively within human beings is Christ, the only true teacher, Augustine also knows that it is up to them to prepare themselves for the divine action and to cooperate with it in a humble and faithful way. In this role which the human person plays we can distinguish a negative and a positive aspect.

The negative aspect

This consists in liberation and purification from whatever may hinder the action of the interior teacher. "*Blessed are the single-hearted* (Mt 5:8). Why do you take care of your bodily eyes? Anything that you see with them will be located in a place. But he who is wholly everywhere is not in any place. Cleanse therefore the organ with which he may be seen" (Sermon 53, 7-8).

Freedom from external things

If we seek to enjoy external things and consider them an end rather than a means, they cause us to forget God who dwells within. "In proportion as the soul centers its affections on external things, it goes out to what is outside itself, desiring to enjoy the creature, and it forgets the creator who is within" (*Notes on Job* 9).

Augustine cites Sirach 11:10: "*My son, why increase your cares?*" by way of comment on Jethro's words to Moses: "*Now listen to me, and I will give you some advice, that God may be with you*" (Ex 18:19), and he adds: "In my opinion this means that a soul which is too concerned with human affairs is, in a sense, emptied of God; on the other hand, the freer the soul is to rise up to heavenly and eternal things, the more it is filled with God" (*Questions on the Heptateuch* 68).

"You do not understand the blessings Christ has brought; you are filled by another, the enemy of Christ, to whom you have given a place in your heart. . . . You are full of evil desires; if I speak to you of the great blessings of Jerusalem, you do not understand. You must empty yourself of what fills you now, if you are to be filled with what you now lack" (*Expositions of the Psalms* 137, 9-10).

Therefore we have need of silence, which facilitates meditation whether on internal or external realities.

> *I consider the days of old* says the Psalmist (Ps 77:6). He does well. Notice, if you will, the object of his consideration. It is something interior; he thinks within himself of the days of old. . . . Let him continue thus to do well, and may God help him. Let him think of the days of old and tell us what he has done in that inner chamber of his, what point he has reached, what obstacles he has overcome, where he now stands. *I consider the days of old, the everlasting years I remember.* What are these *everlasting years?* What a vast conception! Ask yourselves whether such a conception does not require a deep silence. Those who wish to reflect upon these everlasting years must go apart from all external noise and from the confusion of human affairs. . . . Our own years are changeable things, and we must turn our thoughts to the years that last, not being made up of days that come and go, the years concerning which another passage of scripture says to God: 'You are the same, and your years have no end' (Ps 102:28). The Psalmist therefore passes over his own fleeting years and reflects, not in outward verbosity but in si-

lence: *The everlasting years I remember* (*Expositions of the Psalms* 77, 8).

Purification from what sullies the heart

"God says to you: 'When you persist in ruining yourself with drink, it is not just any house you are destroying, but mine! Where am I to dwell? In these filthy ruins? If you were receiving any of my servants as your guest, you would fix up and clean your house to welcome them. Will you not, then, clean your heart, where I want to make my dwelling?" (Sermon 278, 8).

I sought the Lord, and he answered me (Ps 34:5). Where did the Lord hear? Within. Where does he reply? Within. There you pray, there you are heard, there you are made happy. You prayed, you were heard, you have been made happy. Those standing near you know nothing of this, for everything happens in a hidden way, as the Lord indicates in the gospel: *Go to your room, close your door, and pray to your Father in private. Then your Father, who sees what no human being sees, will repay you* (Mt 6:6). Therefore, when you enter your room you enter your heart. Happy those who delight to enter their hearts and find no evil there! Listen carefully, my holy people! Men with crabby wives do not like to go home; they go to the city square instead and are content. When the time comes to go home, they are saddened, for they are going home to annoying complaints and bitterness and confusion. There is no order in a house in which husband and wife are at odds; it is indeed better for the man to wander about outside. If then those people are in a sorry state who anticipate that when they go home they will be upset by the continual disturbance there, how much more unfortunate those who are afraid to enter into their own consciences lest they be caught up in their conflicting sinful passions. So then, if you want to be glad to enter your own heart, cleanse it: *Blessed are the single-hearted, for they shall see God* (Mt 5:8). Take away the filth of sinful desire and avarice and superstition, take away the evil and sacrilegious thoughts, take away the hatred you have, and cease to hate not just your friends but even your enemies. Away with all of that! Then enter your heart, and you will be content (*Expositions of the Psalms* 34, Sermon 2, 8).

What more can they seek who have God with them? And what can be enough for those for whom God is not enough? We want to see God, we strive to see God, we ardently long to see God. Who does not? But note what is said: *Blessed are they single-hearted, for they shall see God* (Mt 5:8). Prepare, then, a heart that can see him. To use a material comparison: what is the point of looking forward to sunrise if your eyes are bleary? If your eyes are clear, the light is a pleasure; if they are not, the light is painful. So too you are not able to see with an unclean heart what it takes a clean heart to see (Sermon 53, 6, 6).

The bodily eye is made to see the light that shines in time; it is a heavenly light indeed, but also a material one, and it shines not only for human beings, but for even the lowliest of animals (indeed these are created so that they may see the light). Now if anything enters the eye and disturbs it, the eye is cut off from the light. Even though the light bathes the eye in its presence, the eye turns away and is absent from the light. In fact, not only does the disturbance in the eye render it absent from the light which is there, but that very light which the eye was made to see now becomes a source of torment. So too the eye of the heart, when disturbed and wounded, turns from the light of justice; it does not dare, indeed it cannot, contemplate that light. What is it that disturbs the eye of the heart? Covetousness, avarice, evildoing, worldly desires — these are what disturb and close up and blind the eye of the heart. When the bodily eye is disturbed, we seek out a doctor; there is no delay in having the eye opened and cleansed so that it may be healed and see the light. We run without delay if even a tiny speck gets into our eye. Now it is God who made the sun which we so desire to look upon with healthy eyes. But the maker himself is far more resplendent, and the light which illumines the eye of the mind is not of the same nature as material light. For the light that shines upon the mind is eternal wisdom. God made you, human beings, in his own image. Would he then give an eye to see the sun which he created, and not give you an eye to see him, the maker, although he made you in his own image? No, he gave you such an eye; he gave you both kinds of eyes. Yet you highly esteem the outer eyes, and you greatly neglect the inner eye (Sermon 88, 5-6).

Augustine knows from experience how painful the process of purification is when human beings are forced to enter into themselves and discover there their shameful sinfulness.

Ponticianus went on with his story; but, Lord, even while he spoke you were wrenching me back toward myself, and pulling me round from that standpoint behind my back which I had taken to avoid looking at myself. You set me down before my face, forcing me to mark how despicable I was, how misshapen and begrimed, filthy and festering. I saw shuddered. If I tried to turn my gaze away, he went on relentlessly telling his tale, and you set me before myself once more, thrusting me into my sight that I might perceive my sin and hate it. I had been aware of it all along, but I had been glossing over it, suppressing it and forgetting (*Confessions* VIII, 7, 16).

"I probed the hidden depths of my soul and wrung its pitiful secrets from it, and when I mustered them all before the eyes of my heart, a great storm broke within me, bringing with it a great deluge of tears" (*Confessions* VIII, 12, 28). They were cleansing tears.

Purification from pride

Pride, in Augustine's view, is the chief obstacle to our penetrating into the depths of our own heart and discovering God there.

Why are dust and ashes proud? (Sir 10:9). Tell us: Why are they proud? *Because during their life men and women have cast away what is within themselves.* What does *cast away* (*proiecit*) mean but to 'cast far off'? In other words: to go out. To enter within is to desire interior things; to cast interior things away is to go out of oneself. The proud throw interior things away; the humble seek them. Through pride we are cast out of ourselves; through humility we return to ourselves (*Homilies on the Gospel of John* 25, 15).

"The proud soul seeks to be pleasing in the sight of others; the humble soul seeks to be pleasing within, where God sees. Therefore, if the humble do please others by their good works, they rejoice with those who are thus pleased, but not with themselves. For themselves, it is enough to have done the good deed" (*Expositions of the Psalms* 19, Sermon 2, 16).

If sin is an insurmountable obstacle to the interior life, the reason is that sinning means going out of oneself and away from God and pouring oneself out in an undue and disordered way upon exterior things. "Where was I when I looked for you? You were there before my eyes, but I had deserted even my own self. I could not find myself, much less find you" (*Confessions* V, 2, 2).

Augustine recalls the "abominable things" of his past life. "For love of your love I shall retrace my wicked ways. The memory is bitter, but it will help me to savour your sweetness, the sweetness that does not deceive but brings real joy and never fails. For love of your love I shall retrieve myself from the havoc of disruption which tore me to pieces when I turned away from you, whom alone I should have sought, and lost myself instead on many a different quest" (*Confessions* II, 1, 1).

Along with sin (especially pride) went error, and the young Manichean was prevented from tasting the interior joys for which he longed.

> I was about twenty-six or twenty-seven when I wrote those volumes [*The Beauty and the Fitting*]. The materialistic images on which I was speculating set up a din in the ears of my heart, ears which were straining to catch your inner melody, O gentle truth. I was thinking about the beautiful and the harmonious, and longing to stand and hear you, that my joy might be perfect at the sound of the Bridegroom's voice, but I could not, because I was carried off outside myself by the clamour of my errors, and I fell low, dragged down by the weight of my pride. No joy and gladness from you reached my ears, nor did my bones exult, for they had not yet been humbled (*Confessions* IV, 15, 27).

The positive aspect

We must *question ourselves* and examine our own consciences. "I question you [the hearer], and I come in contact with you. Listen to my question as it sounds in your ears and then ask a silent question of yourself. . . . I ask you: 'If God were not to see you when you sin and if there were no one to accuse you at his judgment seat, would you go ahead and sin?' Examine yourself. You cannot answer right off to all my questions: look within yourself!" (Sermon 161, 8).

We must *contemplate God in his works*. Here we will find an unexpected source of interior joy.

> *I remember the works of the Lord* (Ps 77:12). See how the Psalmist walks about amid the works of the Lord. He had gone chattering about outside himself and grown sad and downhearted. Then he spoke with his own heart within and with his own spirit; he examined that spirit and remembered the everlasting years. He remembered God's mercy and how God does not reject forever. Then he began peacefully to rejoice and be glad in the Lord's works. Let us likewise listen to the Lord's works and rejoice. But let us also raise our affections beyond ourselves and not limit ourselves to joy in temporal things. We too have a chamber. Why do we not enter into it? Why do we not abide in silence and examine our own spirit? Why do we not reflect upon the everlasting years and find joy in the works of the Lord? . . . Who can live without joy? Do you think, brothers and sisters, that those who reverence and worship and love God have no joys? Do you really think that the arts and the theatre, and hunting and fowling and fishing, all bring joy, but God's works do not? Do you think that meditation on God does not

bring its inner joys when we look upon the universe and the spectacle of nature and seek out its maker and find a creator who is never displeasing but supremely pleasing? (*Expositions of the Psalms* 77, 13-14).

We must *listen to the voice of God.*

Let everyone be quick to listen, slow to speak (Jas 1:19), and let all, if possible, desire to have no need of speaking and discoursing and teaching. I am speaking to you, dear brothers and sisters, so that I may teach you something. But how much better it would be if we all had knowledge, and no one had to teach anyone else. Then we would not have one person speaking and another listening, but we would all be listening only to him to whom the Psalmist says: *Let me hear the sounds of joy and gladness* (Ps 51:10). . . . Let your joy, then, be to listen to God, and let necessity alone force you to speak. . . . Why do you like to speak and not listen? You are constantly going out of yourself and refusing to enter within yourself. He who truly teaches you is within; but when you yourself teach, you go out of yourself, as it were, to those who are outside. Let us listen to the truth from him who is within, and then speak from the heart to those who are without (*Expositions of the Psalms* 140, 15).

Listening to God who speaks within us is a source of joy. "When we listen to him teaching us or offering some suggestion within, we have peace and joy, for we are in the master's school, seeking his glory and praising his instruction. We find delight in his truth within us, where there is no one to make noise or hear it. There the Psalmist finds joy and gladness: *Let me hear the sounds of joy and gladness* (Ps 51:10)" (*Expositions of the Psalms* 51, 13).

Are the words of human beings useless, then? Not if they spur us on and help us hear the word of God. That is how Augustine understands the role of the preacher. That is how Adeodatus had understood the role of a human teacher, when, at the end of the dialogue *The Teacher*, he summed up the thoughts his father had been expressing: "I indeed have learned by the reminding of your words that words only remind a person, so that he may learn. Also, it is clear that speech reveals only a very small part of a speaker's thoughts. But whether what was said is true, I have not been reminded that only he who lives within us, but who is spoken of externally, can teach us" (*The Teacher* XIV, 46).

Moreover, human words help us to enter into ourselves only if God comes to our aid (see *Confessions* VII, 10, 16).

There must be *good will.*

But when we understand all these things, we do not consult the speaker who gives the outward expression, but the truth that rules within the mind itself, though perhaps the words reminded us to consult it. The one who is consulted is the one who teaches; he is Christ, who is said to dwell in the inner person. He is the unchangeable power of God and eternal wisdom, which every rational soul does indeed consult, although it is revealed according to each one's ability to accept it, depending on the evil or goodness of his or her will. If sometimes one is deceived, this is not because of some defect in the truth consulted, just as it is not because of some defect in the external light that the bodily eyes are often deceived; and we admit that we consult this light concerning visible things, so that it may show them to us, as far as we are able to perceive them (*The Teacher* XI, 38).

Good will inspires intense desire. "We hunger and thirst, then, for justice, that we may be filled by the justice for which we now hunger and thirst. . . . Let the inner self, too, hunger and thirst, for it also has food and drink" (Sermon 53, 4).

Similar thoughts occur in the sermon on Psalm 41, passages of which I have already quoted.

Run to the fountain, yearn for the running waters. In God is the fountain of life, a fountain that cannot run dry, and his light is a light that can never grow dim. Long for this light! It is a fountain and a light which your bodily eyes do not know. To see this light we prepare our inner eye; to drink of this fountain we need an inner thirst. Run to the fountain, yearn for it. But do not run in an indiscriminate way or like just any animal; run like the hind. What does it mean to run like a hind? It means that you must not run slowly; run energetically, desire the fountain with intense desire. For the hind is a symbol of swiftness (*Expositions of the Psalms* 42, 2).

There must be *prayer*. I shall have to speak at length of this subject in a later chapter. Here it will be enough to cite a few passages dealing with interiority.

I poured forth prayer within my bosom (Ps 35:13). In this verse we indeed see a *bosom*; may the Lord enable us to penetrate it. For a bosom means something secret or hidden. Brothers and sisters, we are rightly bidden to pray within our bosom, for it is there that God sees and hears. No human eye reaches into that place, and he alone sees who brings help to us. It was there that Susanna prayed, and though human beings did not hear her voice, God did (Dn 13:35, 42-44) (*Expositions of the Psalms* 35, Sermon 2, 5).

The interior teacher wants us to pray within our hearts so that he may enlighten us. Augustine says to his son Adeodatus:

> I think that you are unaware that the command to pray in our secret chambers, which means within the mind, was given to us only for the reason that God does not need to be reminded or taught by our speech in order to grant our wishes. For one who speaks announces his or her desire by a distinct sound. But God is to be sought and prayed to in the secrecy of the rational soul, which is called the inner person, for this he wished to be his temple. Have you not read in the apostle, *Do you not know that you are God's temple and God's spirit dwells in you* (1 Cor 3:16) and *Christ dwells in the inner person* (Eph 3:17)? And have you not noticed in the prophet, *Speak in your hearts and be sorry in your chambers. Offer a just sacrifice and hope in the Lord* (Ps 4:5-6)? Where do you think a just sacrifice is be offered, except in the temple of the mind and the chambers of the heart? And where one sacrifices, there one should also pray (*The Teacher* 1, 2).

In the interior light given by the one teacher all that a person can teach or learn becomes clear. Such is the thought that closes Augustine's lengthy letter "on the grace of the New Testament."

> Here, then, you have a book that is quite long but nonetheless useful, I believe. But also read carefully the ecclesiastical writings, and you will not have many more questions that need answering from me. As you read and reflect, you must also pray with a pure heart to God, the giver of every gift. Then you will learn everything worth knowing, or at least a very great deal of it; this through God's inspiration rather than through human instruction. Moreover, when we rightly approve someone who offers correct doctrine from outside of us, what are we doing but attesting to the presence within us of the interior light which is our true teacher? (Letter 140, 85).

The Life-Giving Spirit

The role Augustine assigns to the Holy Spirit in the genesis and development of the Christian's interior life is so essential, and therefore so continually emphasized by him, that it will not be out of place for me to devote a special section to it, though I must note that these ideas are already present in what I have been saying thus far.

The Holy Spirit gives rise to and nourishes our interior life by making us dwell in God.

> *In this we know that we abide in him and he in us, because he has given us of his Spirit* (1 Jn 4:13). So it is the Holy Spirit of which he has given us that makes us abide in God and him in us. But this is precisely what love does. He then is the gift of God who is love. Finally, after repeating this a little later and saying, *Love is God,* he immediately added, *and whoever abides in love abides in God, and God abides in him* (1 Jn 4:16), about which he had said above, *In this we know that we abide in him and he in us, because he has given us of his Spirit* (1 Jn 4:13). He then is the one meant when we read, *Love is God* (1 Jn 4:8.16). So it is God the Holy Spirit proceeding from God who fires man to the love of God and neighbor when he has been given to him, and he himself is love. Man has no capacity to love God except from God (*The Trinity* XV, 31).

The Holy Spirit causes human beings to be born to a new life. "*One must be reborn of water and the Holy Spirit for the sake of the kingdom of God. . . . Flesh begets flesh, Spirit begets spirit* (Jn 3:6). Our new birth, then, is spiritual, and we are born in the Spirit through word and sacrament. The Spirit is present so that we may be reborn. The Spirit is invisibly present at your birth because your birth itself is invisible" (*Homilies on the Gospel of John* 12, 5).

As Augustine observes in a passage in which neoplatonic reminiscences are given a higher meaning through reflection on revealed truth, the Holy Spirit, as the bond of union between Father and Son, brings us back from the scattered state into which sin and error had put us, and he unifies us.

> The Father and the Son willed that we be in communion with each other and with them, by means of that which is common to them. They wanted to unify us through this gift which belongs to both of them, that is, through the Holy Spirit, who is God and God's gift. In him we are reconciled with the godhead and find our delight therein. Of what use would it be to us to know the good if we did not also love it? Well, as we learn by means of truth, so we love by means of charity, that we may know even more fully and find blessedness in what we know. *The love of God has been poured out in our hearts through the Holy Spirit who has been given to us* (Rom 5:5) (Sermon 71, 18).

The Holy Spirit dwells in us in order to make of us the Body of Christ and to give our prayer the vitality of love.

> As John the apostle says, *The way we know that we abide in him and he is us is that he has given us of his Spirit* (1 Jn 4:13) *The Spirit himself gives witness with our spirit that we are children of God* (Rom

8:16). The Spirit is responsible for the fellowship in which we become the one body of the one Son of God. This is why we read: *If, then, there is any encouragement in Christ, any solace of love, any fellowship in the Spirit . . .* (Phil 2:1). The Son himself tells us that the Spirit is the Spirit of the Father: *he comes from the Father* (Jn 15:26), and, elsewhere, *You yourselves will not be the speakers; the Spirit of your Father will be speaking in you* (Mt 10:20). That the Spirit is also the Spirit of the Son we are told by the Apostle: *God has sent forth in our hearts the Spirit of his Son, which cries out 'Abba!'* ('Father') (Gal 4:6); that is, the Spirit makes us utter this cry. For it is we who cry out, but we do so in him; that is, he pours into our heart the love without which any cry would be empty and vain. This is why the Apostle also says: *Anyone who does not have the Spirit of Christ does not belong to Christ* (Rom 8:9) (Sermon 71, 28-29).

The classical text in Isaiah which provided theology with a basis for developing the doctrine of the seven gifts of the Holy Spirit is often quoted by Augustine, who likes to link it to the platonic doctrine of descent and ascent.

Human beings do not obey these ten commandments by their own power, but must be helped by God. If then they do not fulfill the law by their own power but must be helped by God through his Spirit, you will recall how the Holy Spirit is associated with the number seven. Thus the holy prophet says that we must be filled with the Spirit of God, that is, with wisdom and understanding, counsel and strength, knowledge and piety, and fear of the Lord (Is 11:2-3). These seven activities remind us by their number of the Holy Spirit who starts his descent as it were with wisdom and moves down to fear of the Lord. We, on the contrary, must begin our ascent with fear of the Lord, and we find our perfection when we reach wisdom (Sermon 248, 5; see also Sermon 250, 3).

The Spirit communicates holiness and joy.

In saying, *The runlets* [of the stream] *gladden the city of God* (Ps 46:5), the Psalmist shows what stream he means, namely, the stream of the Holy Spirit. What does he go on to say? *The dwelling of the Most High.* In thus speaking immediately of sanctification, the writer makes it clear that the runlets of the stream are to be taken as referring to the Holy Spirit who sanctifies all devout believers in Christ so that they may become citizens of God's city (*Expositions of the Psalms* 46, 8).

Augustine comments as follows on the third commandment:

The third commandment: *Remember the sabbath day to sanctify it.* This third commandment imposes a regular periodical holiday — quietness of heart, tranquillity of mind, the product of a good conscience. Here is sanctification, because here is the Spirit of God. Well, here is what a true holiday, that is to say, quietness and rest, means: *Upon whom,* he says, *shall my Spirit rest? Upon one who is humble and quiet and trembles at my words* (Is 66:2). So unquiet people are those who recoil from the Holy Spirit, loving quarrels, spreading scandals, keener on argument than on truth, and so in their restlessness they do not allow the quietness of the spiritual sabbath entry into themselves. Against such restlessness we are told to have a kind of sabbath in the heart, the sanctification of the Spirit of God: *Be meek in listening to the word, that you may understand* (Sir 5:11) (Sermon 8, 6).

Later on in the same sermon, Augustine explains God's rest on the seventh day:

The sabbath day, God's rest, is sanctified. . . . As far as I can see, as far as you too can tell, as far as we believe, there is no divine and true sanctification except from the Holy Spirit. It is not for nothing that the Spirit is properly called holy. While the Father is holy and the Son is holy, nonetheless the Spirit received this as a proper name, so that the third person in the Trinity is called the Holy Spirit. He rests upon the humble and the quiet, as though upon his sabbath. . . . Isaiah says that the Spirit of God comes upon the believer, the Christian, the member of Christ, the Spirit of wisdom and understanding, of counsel and courage, of knowledge and piety, the Spirit of the fear of God. If you have been counting, I have run through seven things, as though the Spirit of God were coming down to us from wisdom as far as fear, in order that we might climb up from fear to wisdom (Sermon 8, 17).

The Holy Spirit "gives his help in different ways according as he does not yet dwell within us or already so dwells; when he does not yet dwell in us, he gives his help so that men and women may become believers; when he already dwells, he helps them remain believers" (Letter 94, 18).

In conclusion, it may be said that the Holy Spirit effects a daily interior renewal in Christians. After citing two passages in which Saint Paul tells us of his trials (2 Cor 6:4; 11:24-33) and "of all the other dangers which might be mentioned and which cannot be borne without the help of the Holy Spirit," Augustine comments:

So he frequently had to undergo all the harsh and rough treatment he mentioned here, but of course he had the Holy Spirit with him to renew the inner self from day to day, while the outer self was wasting away, and to give him a taste of spiritual rest in the abundant delights of God, in the hope of future bliss, while smoothing away all the roughness of the present, and soothing its harshness. That just shows you how comfortable was the yoke of Christ he bore, and how light the load; that he could call all those dreadful, cruel experiences, which appall any listener who hears them read out, that he could call them a light affliction. With the inner eyes of faith he considered what temporal price must be paid for eternal life, for not suffering the eternal toils of the wicked, and for enjoying without the slightest anxiety the eternal happiness of the just (Sermon 70, 1-2).

A short prayer may provide a fitting ending for this chapter: "Merciful God, help those who study, and shed your interior light on those who seek the Truth" (*Answer to the Letter Known as "The Foundation"* 27).

CHAPTER 2

HUMILITY

In Augustine's view, the only way to reach an abiding, active knowledge of the truth is through humility. Dioscurus, a young pagan physician, had written to Augustine for the answer to some philosophical difficulties. His letter had manifested a somewhat ingenuous kind of presumption, and Augustine answers him as follows:

> My dear Dioscurus, I wish you would submit with sincere piety to him and not seek any other way to abiding truth but the one shown us by him who, being God, knows our weakness. This way consists, first, of humility, second, of humility, and third, of humility. No matter how often you put the question to me, I shall give the same answer. It is not that there are no other precepts to be mentioned. But, unless humility precedes, accompanies, and follows whatever good we do, unless it is a goal on which we keep our eye, a companion at our side, and a yoke upon our neck, we will find that we have done little good to rejoice in; pride will have bereft us of everything (Letter 118, 22).

God Comes in Humility

The essential foundation of our humility is the redemptive incarnation.

The duty and necessity for the Christian to be humble has its essential basis in the mystery of the incarnation, in which "God came in lowliness." Following Paul, Augustine looks at this mystery as a prelude to the abasement or humiliation of the cross.

> Because of this vice, this great sin of pride, God came in humility. This was the cause, this the great sin, this the frightful sickness of souls, that brought the all-powerful physician down from the heavens, humbled him into the form of a slave, covered him

with insults, and hung him from a cross, so that so powerful and salutary a medicine might be ours for healing such a wound. Let human beings at last blush at their own pride, since for their sake God lowered himself. Thereby, says the psalmist, *I shall be cleansed of serious sin* (Ps 19:14), for *God resists the proud but bestows his favor on the lowly* (Jas 4:6) (*Expositions of the Psalms* 19, II, 15).

So we have sung about Christ: *You are the Lord, most high above all the earth; you are exceedingly exalted above all gods* (Ps 97:9). Who, I mean to say, was exalted, but the one who had been humbled? See him humbled, and see him exalted. The apostle tells you about both. He was exalted, you see, from the beginning, because *in the beginning was the Word.* This exaltation is without beginning, without time, because *through him all things were made* (Jn 1:1.3). So what does the apostle say about it? *Since he was in the form of God,* he says, *he did not think it robbery to be equal to God* (Phil 2:6); because it was his nature, it wasn't robbery. He didn't, after all, put in a claim for equality with God, but he was always equal, because he was born equal. *So, since he was in the form of God, he did not think it robbery to be equal to God.* You have heard about his inexpressible exaltation; now hear about his humility. *He emptied himself.* . . . The emptying consisted of taking on a lowly state, not of losing a sublime one (Sermon 265E, 2).

The creator of man was subject to man because he showed himself as a man, the liberator of man. He was subject to man, but in the form of man, hidden as God, only discovered, however, because previously despised. For you see, he wasn't prepared to give you glory until he had first taught you humility (Sermon 20A, 4).

Nothing is more contrary to love than envy, and the mother of envy is pride. Therefore the Lord Jesus Christ, the God-man, is both the proof of divine love for us and the example of human humility among us, so that our swelling pride might be healed by the more powerful medicine of its contrary. A proud human being is a wretched thing, but a humble God is an even greater mercy (*The Instruction of Beginners* IV, 8).

My brothers, it is sufficient proof that Christ taught us humility, if we but see that God became a man. This is the humility that the pagans cannot accept, and for which they attack us: "What kind of a God is this that you worship? A God who was born! A God who was crucified!" The humility of Christ displeases the proud; if it pleases you who are a Christian, then imitate it! (*Expositions of the Psalms* 94, 15).

Why does iniquity abound? Because of pride. Cure pride, and there will be no iniquity. Precisely to cure pride, the source of all evils, the Son of God came down and became a lowly man. You might be ashamed to imitate a humble man; at least imitate a humble God! (*Homilies on the Gospel of John* 25, 26).

Christ is a teacher of humility, for *he humbled himself, obediently accepting even death, death on a cross!* (Phil 2:8). He did not lose his divinity by teaching us humility; in the one he is equal to the Father, in the other he is like us. Through the divinity in which he is equal to the Father, he created us and made us be; through the humanity in which he is like us, he redeemed us lest we be lost (*Homilies on the Gospel of John* 51, 3).

So useful is humility to human beings that the divine majesty itself recommended it to us by example. Proud humanity was on the way to being forever lost, if a humble God had not sought it out. For *the Son of Man has come to search out and save what was lost* (Lk 19:10). Humankind have gone astray by following the proud deceiver; now that they are found, let them follow the humble redeemer (*Homilies on the Gospel of John* 55, 7).

Are you longing to be happy? Come to him who cries out, *I will refresh you.* The only thing is, you must learn what he says: *Learn of me, because I am meek and humble of heart.* You're looking at that rich neighbor of yours, a man of property and of pride. By looking at him and trying to compete with him, you will grow proud too. You won't become humble unless you look at the one who became humble for your sake. Learn from Christ what you won't learn from man; in him is to be found the standard of humility. Those who measure up to him are first formed in humility, in order to be eventually honored with high nobility. I mean, what, I ask you, did he look like? *Who, though he was in the form of God, did not think it robbery for him to be equal to God, but he emptied himself, accepting the form of a slave, made in the likeness of men; and being found in condition as a man, he humbled himself, becoming obedient to the point of death, death too on a cross* (Phil 2:6-8).

He said all that, and he wouldn't have defined the full measure of his humility yet, if he hadn't added, *death too on a cross.* You see, this kind of death was regarded by the Jews as peculiarly disgraceful. And that's what he took upon himself, something peculiarly disgraceful, in order to provide a reward for those who are not ashamed of this thing, humility. How far was he prepared to go in cutting out your swelling tumor of pride? As far as the indignities of the cross (Sermon 68, 11).

The humility of the Word of God is a profound mystery which only the Word himself can reveal to some extent to those who open their inner ears to him.

I am speaking, brothers and sisters, of the humility of Christ. Yet who can speak either of the majesty of Christ or of his humility? When we seek to explain even in small degree the humility of Christ, we do not succeed; indeed we fail badly. Therefore we entrust the whole subject to your reflection and make no attempt to satisfy your desire to hear of it from us. Meditate, then, on the humility of Christ. But, you may say, "Who will explain it to us, if you do not speak?" Christ himself speaks, interiorly. He who dwells within will speak better of the mystery than he who raises his voice outside you. May he show you the grace of his humility, now that he has begun to dwell in your hearts (*Homilies on the Gospel of John* 3, 15).

Humility is the great lesson the divine Teacher gives to humanity.

The master of the angels cries out, the Word of God cries out on which all rational minds are nourished unfailingly, the food that restores and remains entire cries out, and says, *Learn from me*. Let the people listen carefully to the one who says, *Learn from me*. Let them answer, "What are we to learn from you?" It is, after all, a great architect and craftsman from whom we are going to hear I don't know that, when he says, *Learn from me*. Who is it, saying *Learn from me*? The one who shaped the earth, who divided the sea and the dry land, who created flying creatures, who created land animals, who created all swimming creatures, who placed the constellations in the sky, who distinguished the day and the night, who fixed the very firmament; that's who says, *Learn from me*. Is this perhaps what he is going to tell us, that we are to make these things with him? Who could do that? Only God can make them. "Don't be afraid," he says, "I'm not laying a burden on you. What you must learn from me is what I became because of you. . . . My dearest brothers and sisters, that is the sum total of the medicine required to cure us: *Learn from me, because I am gentle and humble of heart*. What good does it do you if you can perform miracles, and are proud, are not gentle and humble of heart? (Sermon 142, 11).

Augustine likes to hark back to Christ's example of humility especially during Lent when the Church is preparing for the commemoration of the passion. In a sermon during this season he says:

> Life in this world is the time of our humility, and is signified by these days, when Christ the Lord, who suffered once by dying, is so to say going to suffer again for us as this solemnity comes round again every year. What happened once in the whole of time, that our life might be renewed, is celebrated every year, in order to be kept fresh in our memories. So if we ought to be humble of heart out of the sincerest devotion during the whole time of this wandering exile, in which we are living in the midst of trials and temptations, how much more should we be so during these days, when as well as spending this time of humility by living it, we are also signifying it by our liturgical celebration of it? The lowliness of Christ has taught us to be lowly, because by dying he yielded to the godless; Christ's highness makes us exalted, because by rising again he has led the way for the godly (Sermon 206, 1).

Augustine sees another example of humility in the fact that Christ followed the passover observances prescribed in the law. "You see, it was all part of his giving us an example of humility and devotion, that when he came he should condescend to receive even those sacraments which symbolically foretold that he would come, thus showing us with what religious devotion we should receive these sacraments which proclaim that he has come" (Sermon 210, 3).

If Christ likes to call himself "Son of Man," the reason is, according to Augustine, that he wants to teach us humility.

> He didn't wish merely to be man, which he could have been had he wished, but he preferred to be the son of man. And how vehemently, how assiduously he insists that he is the son of man! Just notice, and you'll agree, when the holy gospels are chanted, how incomparably more frequently he calls himself the son of man than the Son of God. This means that the majesty that is befitting to God needed only brief commendation, while on the other hand the humility of the Most High had to be more constantly drummed into us (Sermon 306D, 3).

Every stage in Christ's life furnishes a proof and example of humility.

> The divine arrangement, as far as any human being can investigate it, better minds in a better way, lesser minds less effectively — this divine arrangement is giving us hints of a great and significant mystery. Christ, you see, was going to come in the flesh, not anyone at all, not an angel, not an ambassador; but *he himself*

will come and save you (Is 35:4). It wasn't anyone who was going to come; and yet how was he going to come? He was going to be born in mortal flesh, to be a tiny infant, to be laid in a manger, wrapped in cradle clothes, nourished on milk, going to grow up, and finally even to be done to death. So in all these indications of humility there is indeed a pattern of an extreme humility. Who is showing this humility? Someone very exalted (Sermon 293, 5).

So let us understand how Christians ought to follow Christ, short of the shedding of blood, short of the danger of suffering death. The apostle says, speaking of the Lord Christ, *Who, though he was in the form of God, did not think it robbery to be equal to God.* What incomparable greatness! *But he emptied himself, taking the form of a servant, and being made in the likeness of men, and found in condition as a man.* What unequalled humility! Christ humbled himself; you have something, Christian, to latch on to. Christ *became obedient.* Why do you behave proudly? To what point did Christ become obedient? To the point of the Word becoming flesh, of sharing our human mortality, of a triple temptation by the devil, of being mocked by the people of the Jews, of spittle and chains, of being knocked about and scourged; if that's still too little, *to the point of death*; and if something still has to be added about the kind of death, *even the death of the cross* (Phil 2:6-8). Such is the example we have of humility, such the remedy for pride (Sermon 304, 3).

Christ's humility brings strength and courage to the believer. But the demon, through the mouths of unbelievers, points to the ineffable majesty of the risen Christ in order to shake the Christian's faith in his own resurrection.

He exaggerates the sovereign majesty of Christ in order to make him out quite unique, to stop you hoping for anything like what was demonstrated in his rising again. And he seems, apparently, to be all the more religiously respectful of Christ, when he says, "Look at the person who dares to compare himself with Christ, so that just because Christ rose again, he can imagine he's going to rise again too!" Don't let his perverse praise of your emperor disturb you. The insidious tricks of the enemy may disturb you, but the humility and humanity of Christ should console you. This man emphasizes how high above you Christ is lifted up; Christ, though, says how low he came down to you (Sermon 361, 15).

Christ has become little and humble in order to take us under his protection.

> Let us flee under the wings of Wisdom, our mother, for Wisdom itself has become weak for our sake, inasmuch as *the Word became flesh* (Jn 1:14). As the hen accepts weakness with her chicks in order to protect them with her wings (Mt 23:37), so our Lord Jesus Christ, *though he was in the form of God, . . . did not deem equality with God something to be grasped at,* but, in order to share our weakness and protect us with his wings, *emptied himself and took the form of a slave, being born in the likeness of human beings* and being *known to be of human estate* (Phil 2:6-8) (*Expositions of the Psalms* 91, II, 2).

Motives for Humility

Once we have fully grasped the principle that the Christian's duty to be humble is grounded essentially in the mystery of the redemptive incarnation, we can follow Augustine in the various considerations in which he finds the reason for exhorting us to humility.

The lowly human condition

In God's sight all human beings are beggars and have nothing to boast of; only if they recognize this fact can they win God's favor.

> Learn, then, [from Abraham] to be needy and poor; this applies to those who possess worldly goods as well as to those who do not. You can, after all, find a beggar who is proud, and a rich man who recognizes his own lowliness. *God resists the proud* whether they go in silks or rags *but bestows his favor on the lowly* (Jas 4:6) whether or not they have this world's goods. God looks at us from within; there is where he examines and weighs us. You do not see the scales of God, but your thoughts are weighed in them. You can see that the reason why God hears prayers is because the person says to God: *I am afflicted and poor* (Ps 86:1). Be sure that you are indeed afflicted and poor; otherwise you will not be heard. If you find any basis within you or around you for being presumptuous, rid yourself of it; let your whole trust be in God. Be in need of him, and he will fill you (*Expositions of the Psalms* 86, 3)

In commenting on Psalm 39:12, Augustine observes that a human being is as fragile as a spider's web.

> What is weaker than a spider? And what weaker than the spider's web? Look at the spider itself: press your finger down lightly on it and it is destroyed. What could be weaker? From

this example we should learn how weak we are and not lay claim to illusory strength. "That kind of strength makes us displeasing [to God], for it is from our weakness that we should learn. Proud people always claim to be strong. That is why many from the East and the West will overcome and sit down with Abraham and Isaac and Jacob in the kingdom of heaven (see Mt 8:11). Why will they overcome? It means they fear being presumptuous; they do not seek to establish their own justice but subject themselves to the justice of God (see Rom 10:3). . . . Remember, you are mortal and clothed in decaying flesh; *like human beings you shall die, and fall like any prince* (Ps 82:7), like the devil shall you fall. How shall the medicine of mortality help you? The devil is proud, being an angel without mortal flesh. You are clad in mortal flesh, and if such an infirmity does not help you to humble yourself, you shall *fall like any prince.* The first grace God bestows on us, then, is to force us to admit our weakness and to confess that if we can do any good, if we have any ability, it is because of him. Then, *whoever boasts will boast in the Lord* (1 Cor 1: 31) (*Expositions of the Psalms* 39).

Elsewhere too the preacher invites his hearers to come to a sense of sincere humility by reflection on their mortal condition.

But to the reprobate, who were called to be sons of God, but preferred rather to be merely men, that is, to live according to merely human standards, *But you,* it says, *shall die like men, and fall like one of the princes* (Ps 82:6-7). Surely the fact that we human beings are mortal should serve to teach us our place not to make us boastful. What's a worm got to boast about, due to die tomorrow? Let me tell your graces something, brothers and sisters; proud mortals ought to be ashamed in the presence of the devil. After all, he may be proud, but at least he's immortal; he's pure spirit, even if he is evil and malicious. The last day is reserved for his punishment at the end; still, he doesn't undergo the death that we do. Man, on the other hand, heard the words, *You shall die the death* (Gn 2:17). That's our punishment, let us make good use of it. What do I mean by making good use of our punishment? Don't let us proceed from it to the pride for which we received the punishment; let us recognize our mortality, and break in pieces our self-esteem. Let us listen to what we are told: *Why is dust and ashes proud?* (Sir 10:9). Even if the devil is proud, he isn't dust, he isn't ashes. That's why it was said, *But you shall die like men, and fall like one of the princes.* You don't notice that you are mortal, and yet you are as proud as the devil (*Sermon* 97, 2).

If our ontological situation of limitation and mortality gives us good reason to be humble, we find even greater reason in our sinfulness which adds to our connatural wretchedness the burden of an enslaved will. The *Confessions* offer a strong and sincere expression of humility by a man who recognizes that he is a sinner and praises the Lord from the depths of his poverty.

What Augustine says of himself in the *Confessions* is also, as he knows, the state of every sinful man and woman.

> We too must come to realize the depths from which we cry out to the Lord. For this mortal life of ours is a deep abyss. All who realize they are cast down in an abyss cry and groan and sigh until they are rescued from it. . . . Whence do they cry out? From the depths. And who are they that cry? Sinners. What hope inspires their cry? The fact that he who came to forgive sins gave hope even to sinners in the depths. Therefore, what do we read after the words about crying out? *If you, O Lord, mark iniquities, who can stand?* (Ps 130:2). See, they show us the depths from which they are crying. They are crying from under the weight and overwhelming flood of their own sins. They look about them, they look around at their own life; they see it filled at every point with shameful deeds. Wherever they turn, they find no good in themselves, no bit of justice to give them joy (*Expositions of the Psalms* 130, 1-2).

Even if they are not conscious of any grave sin, Christians will always have reason for humility when they seriously compare their imperfections and weakness with the holiness their calling requires of them.

Augustine comments as follows on Psalm 39:5:

> *Let me know, O Lord . . . what is the number of my days, that I may learn what is still lacking in me.* It is lacking to me because I am toiling here on earth. As long as it continues to be lacking, I cannot say I am perfect. As long as I have not received it, I must say: *I have not reached it yet, I have not finished the race; but I pursue the palm God calls me to receive in heaven* (Phil 3:12.14). I shall receive it as the reward for the race I shall have run. At the end of the race a dwelling waits for me, and this dwelling shall be a country in which there is no more exile or dissension or temptation. Therefore, *let me know the number of my days, that I may learn what is still lacking in me.* For I am not yet at the finishing line. Let me not grow proud of what I have achieved, that *I may be in him, not having any justice of my own* (Phil 3:9). Faced with my present state, awaiting what is not yet given, and more aware of what I lack than what I have, I will be humble because

of what is still lacking, rather than be puffed up at what I have. Those who think they already possess while here on earth proudly refuse what they do not have, for they think their possessions important. But *if anyone thinks he amounts to something, when in fact he is nothing, he is only deceiving himself* (Gal 6:3) (*Expositions of the Psalms* 39, 8).

After all, what you should rather be thinking about is what you lack, instead of what advantages you have. As for what you have, be careful you don't lose it; as for what you haven't got yet, pray hard that you may get it. It's on all the ways in which you fall behind others that your thoughts should dwell, not on all the ways in which you excel them. I mean, if you're thinking how much better you have done than the other person, beware of getting a swollen head. But if you're thinking how much you're still falling short, you start groaning; and when you groan, you are worrying about yourself, you will be humble, you will walk more securely, you won't tumble over a cliff, you won't be puffed up like a balloon (Sermon 354, 5).

The need of God's grace

Crushed beneath the weight of their unhappiness and sinfulness, human beings know that they cannot raise themselves up unless helped by the Lord's grace and that they have nothing they can rely on but the Lord's mercy.

This, then, is what Christianity teaches: that no one does any good act except by the grace of Christ. The evil we do comes from ourselves; the good we do we do by God's gift. If we begin to do good deeds, let us not attribute this to ourselves; if we do not attribute it to ourselves, we should thank him from whom we received the power. When we do do good deeds, let us not look down on those who do not or rank ourselves higher than them; for the grace of God is not so limited to us that it cannot be given to others as well (*Expositions of the Psalms* 94, 15).

Show us, O Lord, your kindness, and grant us your salvation (Ps 85:8), that is, your Christ. Happy they to whom God shows his kindness. It is to those who do not know how to be proud that God thus shows mercy. For by showing them mercy, God convinces them that any good in them comes only from him who is our whole good. And when they see that any good in them does not come from themselves but from their God, they realize that everything praiseworthy in them is due not to their own merits but to God's mercy. Realizing this, they cannot be proud; not being proud, they do not exalt themselves; not exalting themselves, they do not fall; not falling, they stand firm; standing firm, they abide; abiding, they rejoice and are glad in the Lord their God (*Expositions of the Psalms* 85, 9).

This, then, is the important knowledge [that must inspire true zeal; see Rom 10:2], the whole knowledge a man and woman should have: to know that of themselves they are nothing and that whatever they are is from God and for the sake of God. *Name something you have that you have not received. If, then, you have received it, why are you boasting as if it were your own?* (1 Cor 4:7). . . . What does this mean? That all our hope should be put in God and that we ought not to trust in ourselves, that is, in our own strength, lest in attributing to ourselves what comes from him we lose what we have already received. . . . *In your justice rescue me and deliver me* (Ps 71:2). Not in my justice but in yours. For if in my own, I will be numbered among those of whom it is said that *unaware of God's justice and seeking to estab-lish their own, they did not subject themselves to the justice of God* (Rom 10:3). Therefore *in your justice*, not in mine. After all, in what does my justice consist? It was preceded by injustice, and, if I am just at all, it will be your justice in me, for I am just only by reason of a justice given me by you, and it will be mine in such a way as to remain yours, that is, something given me by you. For I believe in him who justifies the wicked, so that my faith is credited to me as justice (see Rom 4:5). Thus my justice will not really be my own, that is, will not be given me by myself, as they think who boast of the letter and reject grace (*Expositions of the Psalms* 71, I, 1 and 4).

The texts which provide the basis for Augustine's reasoning are those to which Augustine the polemicist and the theologian is con-stantly appealing as he demonstrates against the Pelagians the native incapacity of the human person for achieving justice and the conse-quent necessity of grace. But, as a master of the spiritual life, he is seeking among these texts documents of value in educating the faithful to humility.

He comments as follows on the words of Elijah (1 Kgs 19:18), later quoted by Paul: *I have left for myself seven thousand men who have not bowed the knee to Baal* (Rom 11:3):

What's the meaning of *I have left of me?* "It's I who chose them, because I could see their minds relying on me, not on them-selves, not on Baal. They haven't changed, they are as I made them. And you, doing all this talking, where would you be unless you relied on me? Unless you were full of my grace, wouldn't you too be bowing your knee before Baal? But you are full of my grace, because you haven't relied in the least on your own strength, but entirely on my grace." . . . Beware, O Christian, beware of pride. You may well be an imitator of the saints, but always put it all down to grace, because that you should be something left over is the work of God's grace in you, not of your own merits (Sermon 100, 3-4).

I shall enter into the power of the Lord (Ps 71:16), not mine, but the Lord's. *Lord, I will tell of your singular justice.* I acknowledge no justice of my own; of yours alone shall I be mindful. Whatever good is in me is from you; whatever evil is in me is from myself. You have not punished me as I deserve, but have given your grace freely; therefore *I will tell of your singular justice.*

O God, you have taught me from my youth (verse 17). What have you taught me? That I must be mindful of your singular justice. For when I reflect on my past life I see what I really deserved and what I received instead. I deserved punishment; I received grace. I deserved hell; I received eternal life. *O God, you have taught me from my youth.* From the very first moment of the faith by which you made me a new man, you have taught me that nothing preceded faith by reason of which I could say your gifts were owed to me. . . . *O God,* he says, *you have taught me from my youth.* From the time I turned to you, having been made new by you after first having been made by you, having been re-created after first having been created, re-formed after being formed — from the time I turned to you, I learned that no merits of mine had preceded your gifts, and that your grace came to me as a free gift, so that I might be mindful of your justice alone.

And after my youth? The psalmist says, *You have taught me from my youth.* What, then, of the time following youth? In your first conversion you learned that before that conversion you had not been just and that iniquity had been your earlier state. Iniquity was cast out and love took its place. Having been made a new person, though in hope only and not yet in reality, you learned that there had been no good in you and that it was by God's grace you were converted to God. Well, now, since that time of conversion, do you perhaps have something that is really your own? Can you now trust in your own strength? After all, men say to a helpful fellowman: "You can leave me now. I needed you to show me the way, but I do not need any more help; I can travel on by myself." The other, who showed you the way, may answer: "Do you perhaps want me to go along with you?" If you are proud, you will say: "No! You have done enough, I will travel on by myself." He lets you go, and then because of your weakness you lose the way again. It would have been better had he who first set you on your path continued to accompany you; otherwise, unless he continues to lead you, you will go astray.

Tell the Lord: *Teach me, O Lord, your way that I may walk in your truth* (Ps 86:11). Your entering upon the way was your youth, when you were made new and first believed. Before that, you had gone straying along your own paths, lost amid thorny woods and wounded in every limb. You were looking for your native land, that is, for a resting place for your spirit, where you could say, "It is well with me," and say it with peace and in freedom from every anxiety and temptation and enslavement. But you could not find that native land.

At this point did someone come to show you the way? No, the very way itself came to you, and you were set upon the right way through no prior merit of your own, since you had been going astray. Since the time when you entered upon the right way, have you been leading yourself? Has he who taught you the way let you go? No! says the psalmist, but: *O God, you have taught me from my youth, and till the present I proclaim your wondrous deeds* (Ps 71:17). For it is indeed a wondrous thing that having set me on the path you still lead me. These are your wondrous deeds (*Expositions of the Psalms* 71, II, 1-3).

The Effects of Humility

Purification

By inspiring heartfelt gratitude and the sorrowful confession of our sins and unhappiness humility purifies us and disposes the heart for God's coming.

So he gave us the way of humility. If we keep to it we shall confess to the Lord, and not without reason shall we sing *We will confess to you, O God, we will confess and call upon your name* (Ps 75:1). It is rather shameless to call upon his name if you don't confess to him. First confess, in order to prepare a dwelling place for the one you are calling on, that is to say, calling in. After all, your heart is full of wickedness. But confession sweeps out the uncleanness you are cluttered up with inside, and cleans the house into which the one you are calling in is coming. But anyone who calls him in before confessing is deliberately insulting him by asking him in. If you wouldn't dare invite some holy person into your house unless you had first cleaned it out, in case something should offend their eyes, will you have the nerve to call the name of God into your heart full of wickedness, unless you have first swept out all the iniquity inside by confession? So confession, my brothers, humbles us, humbled it justifies us, justified it lifts us up on high. Because if we are proud, God opposes us; if we are humble, God exalts us; for *he opposes the proud, but gives grace to the humble* (Jas 4:6), and *Whoever exalts himself shall be humbled, and whoever humbles himself shall be exalted* (Lk 14:11) (Sermon 23A, 4).

Way of Return to God

The history of salvation repeats, but in inverse order, the history of sin and humanity's loss. Pride led us far from God; humility will be the way by which we shall return to God. For this reason, Christ, being the teacher and model of humility, is called "the way."

In commenting on the words of Jesus, *I am the way, and the truth, and the life* (Jn 14:6), Augustine sees Christ's "way" as consisting essentially in humility, through which we attain to truth and life.

Christ the way is the humble Christ; Christ the truth and the life is Christ exalted and God. If you walk along the humble Christ, you will arrive at the exalted Christ; if in your sickly health and debility you do not spurn the humble one, you will abide in perfect health and strength with the exalted one. What else, after all, was the reason for Christ's humility, but your debility? You were, you see, completely and irremediably in the grip of your debility; and this was the fact that made so great a doctor come to you. After all, if your sickness had even been such that you were able to go to the doctor, your debility could have seemed to be tolerable. But because you were not able to go to him, he came to you. He came teaching humility. Why? Let us see. It was because pride would not allow us to return to life, and had itself made the human heart exalt itself against God and turn away from life; and the soul, being neglectful in its healthy condition of the rules of health and salvation, fell into this state of debility. Let it listen in its enfeebled state to the one whom it ignored when it was in the best of health (Sermon 142, 2).

David represented Christ as Goliath did the devil. As David slew Goliath, so Christ slew the devil. What am I saying when I say Christ slew the devil? I am saying that humility slew pride. In the person of Christ, then, brothers and sisters, it is chiefly humility that is being urged upon us. For Christ made a way for us through humility; since we had abandoned God through pride, it was impossible for us to return to him except through humility, and there was no one we could take as a model in this effort. Pride had corrupted the whole human race. And even if there were some people to be found who were humble in spirit, such as the prophets and patriarchs, humankind could not bring itself to imitate mere human beings, however humble. In order then that human beings might not disdain to imitate a humble man, God himself became humble; even human pride could not refuse to follow in the steps of God! (*Expositions of the Psalms* 34, I, 4).

Let not the foot of pride overtake me (Ps 36:12). The psalmist had said earlier: *The children of men take refuge in the shadow of your wings. They have their fill of the prime gifts of your house* (verses 8-9). When we begin to be filled more abundantly from this fountain, we must be on guard against pride. Even Adam, the first man, was not free of this temptation; in fact, *the foot of pride* did overtake him and *the hand of the wicked* (verse 12b), that is, the hand of the proud devil, did disquiet him. The seducer claimed: *I will set up my throne in the North* (Is 14:13), and in truth he persuaded Adam: *The moment you eat of it you will be like gods* (Gn 3:5). It was through pride, then, that we fell into our present mortality. And because pride has wounded us, humility brought healing. Our humble God came to heal humanity's dreadful wound of pride. He came, because *the Word became flesh and made his dwelling among us* (Jn 1:14). He was taken prisoner by the Jews and insulted. . . . Christ ignored what he heard, as though he had not heard it. For he was a physician and had come to cure a madman. A physician pays no attention to what a madman says to him, but is concerned only that he return to health and become sane. Even if he is struck by the madman, he does not care. The madman inflicts new wounds, the physician cures the original illness. So too the Lord came to a sick man, a madman; he paid no attention to the insults he received and the wounds inflicted on him, thereby teaching us humility so that having been taught by humility we might be cured of pride (*Expositions of the Psalms* 36, 17).

Augustine tells us that the subject of humility is especially close to his heart, and he frequently returns to it in his sermons.

You know, brothers and sisters—I mean as believers in Christ you have learned it, and I in my ministry have been conscientious in urging it upon you regularly—you know that the medicine for the human swelling of pride is the humility of Christ. After all, man would not have perished if he had not swollen up with pride. *The beginning of all sin*, as the scripture says, *is pride*

(Sir 10:11). What was needed against the beginning of sin was the beginning of justice. So if the beginning of all sin is pride, how else could the swollen tumor of pride be cured, but by God agreeing to become humble? Let man be ashamed of being proud, seeing that God became humble. In fact, when people are told to humble themselves, they are not prepared to do so; and what makes people want to get their own back when they are injured is pride. When they are not prepared to be humble, they are intent on getting their own back; as though anybody could profit from someone else's pain and punishment. He has been injured and suffered an insult, and he wants to get his own back; he seeks a remedy for himself in the other person's pain, and all he gets is a terrible shock himself. That's why the Lord Christ was prepared in all circumstances to humble himself; he was showing us the way—provided, of course, we are prepared to proceed along it. . . . So the one who had such enormous power was hungry, was thirsty, went to sleep, was arrested, beaten, crucified, killed. That's the way; proceed along humility, in order to come to eternity. Christ as God is the home country we are going to; Christ as man is the way we are going by (Sermon 123, 1.3).

The Foundation of Christian Life

If, then, we wish to return to God from whom pride has separated us, we must walk the way of humility. Augustine expresses the same idea in a text that has become a classic in the ascetical tradition; in it he pictures humility as the foundation upon which the structure of Christian life and holiness is built.

Take my yoke upon you, and learn from me (Mt 11:29), not how to construct the world, not how to create all things, visible and invisible, not how to perform miracles in this world, and raise the dead, but because I am meek and humble of heart (Mt 11:29). Do you want to be great? Start from the bottom. Are you thinking of constructing a great skyscraper of a building? First give thought to the foundation of humility. And however much anybody may wish to spend on piling story upon story in his building, the bigger the building is meant to be, the deeper he digs the foundation. As the building is being constructed, of course, it rises higher and higher, but the one who is digging the foundations is pushed down lower and lower. So the building has to be humbled before it reaches its loftiest height, and its topmost pinnacle can only be erected after it has been humbled to the depths. What is the topmost pinnacle of the building we are striving to construct? How far does the top of our skyscraper reach? I'll tell you straightaway: as far as the sight of God himself. You can see how high that is, what a great thing is it, to see God (Sermon 69, 2-3).

Means of spiritual progress

The image of the foundation shows that humility is the means of rising up and that the deeper our humility the higher we will rise toward him who exalts the humble.

Till the pit be dug for the wicked (Ps 94:13). God by his hidden justice spares those he knows to be sinners and wicked; yet the very fact that they are spared by God makes them proud and gives them a feeling of impunity. They think themselves set on high and they fall; they fall by the very fact that they think themselves set on high! They think they walk along a high road, and God calls that very thought a pit. A pit opens downward, not heavenward; proud sinners think they are moving heavenward and they are being drawn downward into the earth. The humble, on the contrary, bury themselves in the earth, as it were, but in fact they are scaling the heights. All you, then, who believe, be meek and your heart will be in the heights of heaven — or have you really not learned the lesson of God's law after all? . . .

The proud rebel against God, and God casts them down; they are cast down precisely because they rose up against God. For, as another psalm says: *While they were rising up, you hurled them down* (Ps 73:18). It does not say: "Because they rose up, you hurled them down," nor: "After they had risen up, you hurled them down," as though the rising up and the hurling down were successive; it says that in the very act of rising up they were hurled down. For, the prouder the heart, the further it moves away from God, and to move away from God is to descend into the depths. A humble heart, on the contrary, brings God down from heaven to come near to the person. God is the Most High God, of course; he is above all the heavens and greater than all the angels. How high must you rise to reach the Most High? Do not destroy yourself in the effort to reach him. I give you different advice so that you may not ruin yourself through such a proud effort. God is the Most High indeed, but humble yourself and he will come down to you (*Expositions of the Psalms* 94, 16).

The Christian must experience what Christ experienced and find in humiliation the beginning of the road to glorification.

In order to rise from the dead, you [Christ] died; in order to ascend, you rose; in order to sit at the Father's right hand, you ascended; therefore, in order to sit at the Father's right hand, you died. For from death comes resurrection, from resurrection ascension, from ascension the sitting at the Father's right hand; therefore the whole process began in death, and the glorious splendor had its source in humility (*Expositions of the Psalms* 110, 11).

Just now the psalm was being sung, just now the alleluia was being recited: *Who is like the Lord our God, who dwells on high and observes humble things?* (Ps 113:5-6). When he observes you, may he find you humble, and not condemn you. He's the one who said it, his was the keynote address, he was the one inviting the human race to this salvation: *Learn from me*, he says, not how to create the creation; learn *that I am meek and humble of heart*. He was in the beginning; what could be more sublime? *The Word was made flesh* (Jn 1:1, 14); what could be more lowly? He rules the world; what could be more sublime? He hangs on the cross; what could be more lowly? When he did all this for you, why do you still rear up, still swell up, you inflated balloon? God is humble, and are you proud? Perhaps because it said *The Lord is sublime and observes lowly things* (Ps 128:6), you say to yourself, "Then he doesn't observe me." What could be more unfortunate than you, if he doesn't observe you, but ignores you? Observing indicates compassion, ignoring indicates contempt. But no doubt, because the Lord observes lowly things, you imagine you escape his notice, because you are not humble or lowly, you are high and mighty, you are proud. That's not the way to be missed by the eyes of God. I mean, just see what it says there: *The Lord is sublime.* Sublime indeed. How are you going to get to him? Will you look for a ladder? Look for the wood of humility, and you have already got to him (Sermon 70A, 2).

The Lord is close to the broken-hearted, and those who are crushed in spirit he saves (Ps 34:19). The Lord is exalted; Christians must be humble. If Christians want the exalted God to draw near them, let them be humble. Here, brothers and sisters, is a great mystery indeed! God is above all things: rise aloft and you will not touch him; humble yourself and he will come down to you (*Expositions of the Psalms* 34, II, 23).

A heart contrite and humbled, O God, you will not spurn (Ps 51:19). You know that God is the Most High; if you try to rise on high, he will move away from you; if you humble yourself, he will draw near to you (*Expositions of the Psalms* 51, 21).

You well deserve, you see, to be glorified in the one who reigns, if you have learned to glory in the one who was crucified. That's why the apostle himself, who could see not only where he should cross over to but also how he should cross over—many people, after all, have seen where, and haven't seen how; they have loved the stately home on high, but have been ignorant of the humble way there—so the apostle, who knew about and thought about and reflected in good time on how as well as on where, *Far be it from me*, he said, *to glory in anything but the cross of the Lord Jesus Christ* (Gal 6:14). He could have said "in the wisdom of our Lord Jesus Christ," and he would have said something true; he could have said "in the sovereign majesty," and it would have been the truth; he could have said "in the power," and it would have been the truth. But in fact he said *in the cross*. Where the philosopher of the world was just embarrassed, there the apostle found a treasure; by not spurning the cheap wrapping, he came to the valuable thing wrapped up in it. *Far be it from me*, he says, *to glory in anything but in the cross of the Lord Jesus Christ*. You have picked up a fine load, everything is there you have been looking for; and you have shown what great thing was concealed in it. How did it help? *Through whom*, he says, *the world was crucified to me and I to the world* (Gal 6:14). When would the world have been crucified to you, if the one through whom the world was made hadn't been crucified for you? So, *whoever boasts should boast in the lord* (1 Cor 1:31). What Lord? Christ crucified. Where there's humility, there's majesty; where there's weakness, there's might; where there's death, there's life. If you want to get to these things, don't disdain those (Sermon 160, 4).

Augustine then goes on to comment, in the same vein, on the request made to Jesus by the sons of Zebedee.

We are striving for great things; let us lay hold of little things, and we shall be great. Do you wish to lay hold of the loftiness of God? First catch hold of God's lowliness. Deign to be lowly, to be humble, because God has deigned to be lowly and humble on the same account, yours, not his own. So catch hold of Christ's humility, learn to be humble, don't be proud. Confess your infirmity, lie there patiently in the presence of the doctor. When you have caught hold of his humility, you start rising up with him. Not as though he has to rise, insofar as he is the

Word; but it's you, rather, who do so, so that he may be grasped by you more and more (Sermon 117, 17).

Human beings rise through humility, either because humility draws upon them the grace of God that gives them power to rise, or because the awareness of what they lack is a source of strength for continuous progress.

You can see that we are travelers. You ask, "What does walking mean?" I'll tell you very briefly; it means forging ahead, in case you should possibly not understand, and start walking sluggishly. Forge ahead, my brothers and sisters; always examine yourselves without self-deception, without flattery, without buttering yourselves up. After all, there's nobody inside you before whom you need feel ashamed, or whom you need to impress. There is someone there, but one who is pleased with humility; let him test you. And you, too, test yourself. Always be dissatisfied with what you are, if you want to arrive at what you are not yet. Because wherever you are satisfied with yourself, there you have stuck. If, though, you say, "That's enough, that's the lot," then you've even perished. Always add some more, always keep on walking, always forge ahead. Don't stop on the road, don't turn round and go back, don't wander off the road. You stop, if you don't forge ahead; you go back, if you turn back to what you have already left behind; you wander off the road, if you apostatize. The lame man on the road goes better than the sprinter off the road (Sermon 169, 18).

Humility, then, is the ladder by which we mount up to God. The reason for this is to be found in the dispensation proper to the redemptive incarnation, in which, as I pointed out at the beginning of the chapter, the whole Augustinian doctrine of humility is grounded. In practicing humility with God's grace we travel, in the opposite direction, the road traveled by the Son of God when he humbled himself by becoming a human being and dying on the cross.

For human nature in the person of Christ there was reserved an elevation so great and sublime that there are no greater heights it could reach. So too, God himself could not have lowered himself any more than he did when he took human nature to himself with all the weakness of the flesh, even to the point of dying on a cross (*The Predestination of the Saints* XV, 31).

Preparation for divine illumination

But they faded away in their thoughts. What made them fade away? It can only have been because they were proud. Smoke too fades away, as it surges upward; and the fire shines more brightly and gains in strength, as it catches hold at humble ground level. *They faded away in their thoughts, and their foolish heart was darkened.* Smoke too, while it is higher than the fire, is dark. Finally, notice what follows, and see what the whole matter springs from: *For calling themselves wise, they became foolish* (Rom 1:20-22). By arrogating to themselves what God had bestowed on them, they forfeited what God had given. So he hid himself from the proud, God who through his creation had given those diligently seeking the creator hints of himself alone. So it was well said by the Lord, *You have hidden these things from the wise and the knowing,* whether from those who with their complex calculations and skillful researches made such thorough investigations into created nature, but failed totally to recognize the creator, or from those who recognized God but did not glorify him as God or give thanks, and were unable to see things straight and as they are, because they were proud. So, *You have hidden these things from the wise and the knowing, and have revealed them to the little ones.* What little ones? The humble. He says, *Upon whom shall my Spirit rest? Upon one who is humble and quiet and trembles at my words* (Is 66:2). At these words Peter trembled, Plato didn't; let the fisherman keep what the great and famous philosopher lost. *You have hidden these things from the wise and the knowing, and have revealed them to the little ones.* You have hidden them from the proud and revealed them to the humble. So what are we, however important we are? If we are humble, we shall deserve to be given the bliss of seeing God fully face to face provided we deserve to be counted among the little ones (Sermon 68, 7).

I confess to you, Father, Lord of heaven and earth, that you have hidden these things from the wise and the knowing, from those who thought they were light, and they were in fact darkness; and because they were darkness and thought they were light, they weren't even able to be lit up. But those who were darkness and confessed that they were darkness were little ones, not big ones; they were humble, not proud. So they were rightly able to say, *You will light up my lamp, O Lord.* They recognized themselves, they praised the Lord, they did not turn aside from the way of salvation. Praising they called upon the Lord, and they were saved from their enemies (Sermon 67, 9).

If we want to be protected by him who accepted humiliation for our sake and was exalted in order to protect us, we must be humble. Let us make no claims for ourselves. We have no good in us, except what we have received from him who alone is good. If we claim wisdom for ourselves, we are stupid. Let us be humble and wisdom will come and enlighten us. But if we think ourselves already wise before wisdom thus comes to us, we are people who rise before dawn and walk about in darkness. What are such people told in the psalm? *It is vain for you to rise up before the light* (Ps 127:2). What does that mean: *It is vain for you to rise up before the light*? If you rise before the light breaks, you must remain in emptiness because you will be in darkness. Christ our light has risen; the right thing for you is to rise after Christ, not before him. Who are the ones who rise before Christ? Those who wish to set themselves above Christ. And who are these? Those who want to be exalted here on earth, whereas he was lowly. Instead, let them be lowly here, if they want to be exalted there where he is now exalted (*Expositions of the Psalms* 127, 4).

God gives grace to the humble

Amen I tell you, I have not found such great faith in Israel. What do you suppose he praised in this man's faith? Humility. *I am not worthy that you should enter under my roof.* That's what he praised; and because he praised that, he did enter there. The centurion's humility was the door for the Lord to enter by, so that he might possess more fully one whom he possessed already (Sermon 62A, 2).

The image of water which runs down from a height and comes to rest in the valley below is used by Augustine to illustrate the way in which the humble receive God's grace. Mary "was sitting at the feet of our head; the more lowly her position, the more ample her gains. Water, after all, flows down into the lowliness of the valley" (Sermon 104, 3).

For it is God who is at work in you both to will and to work, for his good pleasure (Phil 2:12-13). *It is God who is at work in you*; therefore, *with fear and trembling* make a hollow, receive the shower. Depressions get filled, high places dry up. Grace is rain. So why be surprised if God withstands the proud but gives grace to the humble (Prv 3:34)? That's the reason for *with fear and trembling*, which means "with humility." *Do not be high minded, but fear* (Rom 11:20). *Fear*, in order to get filled; *do not be high minded*, in order not to dry up (Sermon 131, 3).

The Canaanite woman, the centurion, and the image of water are all brought together in the following passage.

It was such humility this [Canaanite] woman showed when she said, "*Yes, Lord*; I am a dog, I'm eager for the crumbs." It was the same sort of humility that made the centurion acceptable, the one who wanted his servant cured by the Lord, and when the Lord said, *I will come and cure him*, answered, *Lord, I am not worthy that you should come under my roof; but only say the word, and my servant will be healed* (Mt 8:7-9). *I am not worthy that you should come under my roof.* He wasn't receiving him under his roof, he had already received him in his heart. The more humble he was, the greater his capacity, the fuller he became. Hills, after all, shed water, valleys are filled (Sermon 77, 12).

Humility induces us to presume on our own strength but to trust in God; thus we win grace and strength from God.

The saints and the humble of heart trust in you and do not fall away when persecution comes. But those who trust in themselves have fallen away, although they continue to belong to the body of the Church. For they have later come to recognize their true selves and, in losing their pride, have become more solidly established in your grace (*Expositions of the Psalms* 119, XIII, 3).

Humility is what protects us in all temptations, for we ascend out of the valley of tears singing a song of ascent [a "gradual" psalm] and the Lord guards our *going* (Ps 121:8), so that we may enter safely. Let our faith be firm when temptation comes, and he will guard our *coming . . . both now and forever. . . .* Guard yourselves, then, but not by yourselves, for the Lord is your shield who guards and does not *slumber or sleep*. He slept once for our sake and then rose up; he will not sleep again. Rely not on yourself. . . . For if you rely on yourself, your foot will be rendered uncertain; and if your foot becomes uncertain, you will think you are on a slope; then you will fall if you are proud, while the humble in the valley of tears can say: *May he not suffer [my] foot to slip* (Ps 121:3) (*Expositions of the Psalms* 121, 14).

Here we should recall the divine plan singling out humility as the path of humanity's return to the heights from which pride cast it down. "It is chiefly humility that restores us to the place from which pride cast us down. Humility is also the disposition that best fits us to receive the grace of Christ, who is the outstanding model of humility" (*Commentary on the Letter to the Galatians* 25).

Humility protects love

In the commentary just now quoted Augustine indicates another beneficial effect of humility.

It is easier to see something in another that needs correction and to correct it in a censorious way, than to recognize what needs correction in yourself and to correct it willingly on your own, to say nothing of letting it be corrected by someone else, much less *in the presence of all* — as was the case of Peter at the hands of Paul — (Gal 2:11). Yet such conduct is a great example of humility, which is the most important part of Christian disciplines, for humility protects love (*Commentary on the Letter to the Galatians* 15).

Later on, Augustine gives the reason for this last statement.

Lest people think they are really instructing others even when they rage pitilessly at them or ridicule them for their faults or arrogantly treat them as incorrigible, Paul tells us that we are to *gently set him right, each of you trying to avoid falling into temptation himself* (Gal 6:1). Nothing makes us more inclined to mercy than the thought of our own danger. Therefore Paul wanted us neither to avoid correcting our brother or sister nor to do it in a contentious way. Many persons are no sooner awake than they are ready for an argument, and if they cannot find one prefer to go back to sleep. Let the thought of the danger lurking all around us keep peace and love alive in our hearts (*Commentary on the Letter to the Galatians* 56).

Humility teaches me to see my neighbors — even those who are in some respects inferior to me — as equals, inasmuch as they are fellow servants of God and in need of God.

I say to the Lord: You are my God. Why? *Because you have no need of my possessions* (Ps 16:2). He has no need of us, but we need him; therefore he is truly the Lord. You are not to any great extent truly the lord of your slave, for both of you are men and both need God. Your slave needs you to give him food? But you need him to help in your work. Each of you needs the other. Therefore none of you is unqualifiedly a lord, and none unqualifiedly a servant. I will show you the true Lord, to whom you are truly a servant: *I say to the Lord: You are my God.* Why is he the Lord? *Because you have no need of my possessions.* And what are you? *I am poor and needy.* Behold, then, human beings who are poor and needy! May God feed and help and raise them up. As the psalmist says: *O God, hasten to me* (Ps 70:6) (*Expositions of the Psalms* 70, 7).

None of us, then, may look down on our brother or sister, as the Pharisee looked down on the tax collector. "It is not enough simply to acknowledge that any good in you comes from God. You must also not consider yourself superior to those who do not yet have the same good. Perhaps, when they do receive it, they will surpass you!" (*Expositions of the Psalms* 71, I, 4).

Augustine himself provides us with a good example of a fraternal love that is nourished by a simple and sincere humility. It comes from a sermon given in the early years of his episcopate; its tone is half serious, half humorous. After explaining that his role is to be a "steward" who dispenses to those in the house possessions that belong not to him but to the father of the family, he goes on to say:

> So you ought to listen to what also concerns the stewards, so that you may rejoice with us, if you find us to be up to the mark, or even so that you may be instructed in this matter yourselves. How many future stewards, after all, are present in this congregation? We too were once where you are now. We are to be seen now distributing their rations to our fellow servants from a higher place; but not so many years ago we were receiving our rations with our fellow servants in the lower place. I'm speaking as a bishop to lay people; but how can I tell how many future bishops I'm talking to? (Sermon 101, 4)

Humility assures interior peace and stillness.

> *Come to me, all you who are weary* (Mt 11:28). You cry out, you argue, you insult each other. But he says: *Come to me, all you who are weary* in your pride, and you shall find rest in my humility. *Learn from me*, he says, *for I am gentle and humble of heart. Your souls will find rest* (Mt 11:29). For what other reason are they weary, except that they are not gentle and humble of heart? God became humble; let us be ashamed to be proud (*Expositions of the Psalms* 55, 13).

Elsewhere Augustine comments along the same lines on these same words of Jesus.

> *I am gentle*, Jesus said, *and humble of heart*. Jesus is suggesting love, and the more genuine sort of love for one's fellows, love without mixed motives, without conceit, without arrogance, without deceit. That's what is being suggested, ingrafted, by the one who says, *Learn from me, because I am gentle and humble of heart*. When can proud and self-important people ever have real, honest-to-God love or charity? They are bound, indeed, to be envious. Or perhaps we've all got it wrong, and to be envious is to love? Perish the thought that anyone could get it so wrong as to say that the envious person has charity! (Sermon 142, 12)

Pride is the mother of envy as humility is the protector of love.

Humble yourself the more, the greater you are, and you will find favor with God (Sir 3:18). The humility of human beings must be in proportion to their greatness, for pride is all the more dangerous the higher they stand. And envy lurks behind pride, like a daughter following it about; indeed pride continually begets envy and is never to be found without this offspring. It is by means of these two evils — pride and envy — that the devil exercises his domination. Therefore the whole of Christian morality is directed chiefly against pride, the mother of envy. For this morality stresses humility, which is both the way to and the guardian of love (*Holy Virginity* 31, 31).

Further on in the same work Augustine turns the virgin's attention to the supreme model, Jesus Christ, in whom humility is the striking fruit of love.

I do not send you to the publicans and sinners for a lesson in humility, even though they go before the proud into the kingdom of heaven. . . . I send you to the king of heaven, through whom human beings were created and who himself became a man among human beings for their sake; to the fairest *of the sons of men* (Ps 45:3), who was scorned by the sons of men for the sake of the sons of men; to him who, though his is lord of the undying angels, did not refuse to be the servant of mortals. It was not sin, but love, that made him humble (*Holy Virginity* 37, 38).

Augustine, therefore, can speak, in richly meaningful language, of a "humble love," as when he seeks to excuse the conduct of Saint Cyprian to whom the Donatists were unjustifiably appealing. "At times therefore some truth is not revealed to the learned in its entirety so that their patient and humble love may be tested, for it is this last that produces the greatest fruit" (*Baptism: Against the Donatists* II, 5, 6).

Humility in Practice

In the texts of Saint Augustine which we have thus far read we have been hearing more than the voice of the exegete and theologian who is bent on examining the meaning of the divine message and illustrating the truth it contains. We have also been listening to the zealous pastor of souls and the skilled spiritual director, who has been showing how to translate into daily practice the teaching and example of the divine Master. We shall now bring to the reader some other passages on these more practical aspects of humility.

"Recognize that you are human"

The Son of God came as a human being and became humble. You too are bidden to be humble, but you are not bidden to become a beast of the field. God indeed became a human being, but you, a human being, are to recognize that you are indeed human. Your whole humility consists in knowing what you are (*Homilies on the Gospel of John* 25, 16).

Since all human beings are sinners, humility will lead them to confess their sins with sincere repentance. The publican or tax collector gives us an example.

When he was beating his breast, he was punishing his sins; when he was punishing his sins, he was associating himself with God as judge. God, you see, hates sins; if you too hate them, you are beginning to join God, so that you can say to him, *Turn your face away from my sins* (Ps 51:9). Turn your face away — but what from? From my sins. *Do not turn your face away from me* (Ps 27:9). What's the meaning of *your face from my sins?* Don't see them, don't look at them; overlook them instead, so that you can pardon me. So there is hope, even for the sinner. Pray to God, don't despair, beat your breast, take it out on yourself by repentance, so that he won't take it out on you in judgment. Whoever humbles himself and lowers himself draws near to the Most High (Sermon 136A, 2).

Humility requires that we not only admit our own unhappiness and our sins, but also that we acknowledge the good which is in us, although this must be referred to God, its true and only source.

And they will proclaim your might (Ps 145:4). In praising your works, they will proclaim your power. These praisers — holy and pious believers, true praisers who are not ungrateful for grace — as they praise the varied works of God, great and small, heavenly and earthly, find themselves to be among the works of God they are praising, for, after all, they too are indeed works of God. He who made all things made us a part of this all. Therefore if you praise the works of God you will have to praise yourself, for you too are a work of God. But what about the warning: *Let another praise you — not your own mouth* (Prv 27:2)? Well, now you have a way of praising yourself without being arrogant! Praise not yourself but God in you; not because you are this or that kind of fellow, but because he made you; not because you possess a certain power, but because he shows his power in you and through you. In this way they will

praise you [God] and *proclaim your might* — not their own
power, but yours. Learn, then, to praise. Contemplate the work
and admire the maker — thankfully, not arrogantly. Praise him
because he made you and established you thus and gave you
such gifts (*Expositions of the Psalms* 145, 7).

These passages are enough to show that in Augustine's view humility, far from degrading us, brings out our true values, throws the
proper light on us as the work and gift of God, and, in the last analysis,
exalts us by discovering, beyond the limits and imperfections which
mark all created persons, the pure and authentic meaning of person-
ality. The important thing is that we should honestly accept our situation and claim nothing as our own but attribute everything to God
alone.

It follows that humility does not require us to repress ourselves and
mistakenly renounce the fulfillment of our potentialities of good. On
the contrary, it is a religious duty for us to develop our God-given
capacities. Augustine puts us on guard against any dangerous equivo-
cations.

There are some people who, on hearing that they are to be
humble, put themselves down; they are unwilling to learn anything, thinking that if they do they will become proud; as a result
they remain milk-drinkers. Scripture chides such people: *You
have fallen back to needing milk instead of solid food* (Heb 5:12).
God indeed wants us to be nourished with milk, but not so as
to stay at that stage; we are to grow with the help of the milk
and come to the stage where we eat solid food. We should,
therefore, not exalt our hearts into pride, but should raise them
up to the teaching given by God's word. For, if the heart were
not to be raised up at all, the psalmist would not say: *To you I lift
up my soul, O Lord* (Ps 25:1). And if the soul does not reach above
itself, it will never reach the vision of God and the knowledge of
his unchangeable being (*Expositions of the Psalms* 131, 12).

"Humility does the will of God"

Humility is translated into action when, aware of our own nothing-
ness before God, we endeavor with a good spirit to do God's will.

No one who comes will I ever reject (Jn 6:37). And, as though you
had asked for the reason, he adds: *Because it is not to do my own
will that I have come down from heaven, but to do the will of him who
sent me* (verse 38). I suspect that the reason why the soul had
separated from God was because it was proud; in fact, I have no
doubt about it. For it is written: *Pride is the reservoir of sin* and
The beginning of pride is man's stubbornness in withdrawing his heart

from his Maker (Sir 10: 13.12). It is written, it is sure, it is true. . . . Therefore, because God is teaching humility, he says: *It is not to do my own will that I have come down from heaven, but to do the will of him who sent me.* This is certainly a recommendation for humility! Pride does its own will; humility does the will of God. Consequently, *No one who comes will I reject.* Why? *Because it is not to do my own will that I have come down from heaven, but to do the will of him who sent me!* (*Homilies on the Gospel of John* 25, 15-16).

"Let us drink from the cup of his humility"

Christ is the most perfect model of humility. Because he humbled himself to do the Father's will and accepted contempt, suffering, and death, Christians in their turn cannot practice humility unless they overcome themselves and accept suffering and the cross.

A teacher of humility both by word and dead. By word, in fact, from the beginning of creation he never kept quiet about it, teaching the human race humility by angels, by prophets. He also deigned to teach it by his own example. Our creator came humbly, to be created among us; the one who made us, who was himself made for our sakes; God before all time, man in time, in order to set man free from time. The great doctor came to heal our swollen condition. From the east as far as the west the human race was lying there like one great big invalid, and was requiring a great physician. This physician first sent his lads, and came himself later on, when some were despaired of. Just as a doctor too sends his lads, when there's something simple to be done; when there's great danger, he comes himself. In the same sort of way the human race was very dangerously ill, caught up in all sorts of vices, especially the one flowing from the source of pride; and that's why he came to cure this pride by his own example. Be ashamed, man, of still continuing to be proud, you on whose account God humbled himself. God would have humbled himself very considerably if he had only been born for your sake; he was prepared even to die for you. So there he was on the cross, as a man, when his Jewish persecutors were wagging their heads in front of the cross, and saying, *If he is the Son of God, let him come down from the cross, and we can believe in him* (Mk 15:29-32). But he was keeping hold of his humility; that's why he didn't come down. He hadn't lost his power, but he was giving a demonstration of patience. I mean, just think about his effectiveness and his might, and see how easily he could have come down from the cross, seeing that he was able to rise from the grave. But if you were not to be given a demonstration of humility, of patience, then you should not be given a command about them; if, however, you were to be given a command about them in words, then they were also to be demonstrated and commended to you by example. This then is what we should pay attention to in the Lord; let us mark his humility, let us drink the cup of his humiliation, let us constrict ourselves to his limits, let us meditate on him. It's easy enough to think about grandeur, easy enough to enjoy honors, easy enough to give our ears to yes-men and flatterers. To put up with abuse, to listen patiently to reproaches, to pray for the insolent, that is the Lord's cup, that is sharing the Lord's table (Sermon 340A, 5).

I mean, who wouldn't want to advance to the heights? Everyone delights in being at the top. But the step up to it is humility. Why stretch your foot out to what is beyond you? That way, you want to fall, not climb higher. Begin with the step, and you have already climbed higher. Those two disciples didn't want to bother with this step of humility when they said, *Lord, give orders that one of us in your kingdom should sit on your right, the other on your left.* They were after a place at the top, they didn't see the step. The Lord, however, pointed out the step. How did he reply? *Can you drink the cup which I am going to drink?* (Mk 10:37-38). You are after a place of supremacy, can you drain to the dregs the cup of humility? That's why he didn't simply say, *Let him deny himself and follow me,* but added, *Let him take up his cross and follow me* (Mk 8:34) (Sermon 96, 3).

Conclusion

A fervent exhortation by Augustine reminds us once again of the example of Christ who became humble for our sake and recalls the great promises given to the Christian who follows Christ on the path of humility. The passage is a fragment of a sermon preached during the Easter vigil.

In this life we celebrate his death, because after this death we hope to share his life. So by our own humility let us call back to remembrance the humility of our Lord Jesus Christ. Let us watch in humility, pray in humility, and with the most devoted faith, the firmest hope, the most fervent charity, reflecting what sort of day will be ours in glory, if we turn night into day by our humility. And so may God, *who commanded the light to shine out of the darkness, shine in our hearts* (2 Cor 4:6), so that within ourselves we may do something similar to what we have done in this house of prayer by lighting all these lamps. Let us adorn

God's true dwelling place, our consciences, with the lights of justice. Or rather not us, but God's grace with us, of which we have the promise in the words of the prophet: *He will bring forth your justice like the light* (Ps 37:6) (Sermon 223I).

CHAPTER 3

CONQUEST OF THE SENSES

The two wills fought it out — the old and the new, the one carnal, the other spiritual — and in their struggle tore my soul apart.

I thus came to understand from my own experience what I had read, how the flesh lusts against the spirit and the spirit strives against the spirit and the spirit strives against the flesh. I was aligned with both, but more with the desires I approved in myself than with those I frowned upon, for in these latter I was not really the agent, since for the most part I was enduring them against my will rather than acting freely. All the same, the force of habit that fought against me had grown fiercer by my own ding, because I had come willingly to this point where I now wished not to be. And who has any right to object, when just punishment catches up with a sinner?

I had grown used to pretending that the only reason why I had not yet turned my back on the world to serve you was that my perception of the truth was uncertain, but that excuse was no longer available to me, for by now it was certain. But I was still entangled by the earth and refused to enlist in your service, for the prospect of being freed from all these encumbrances frightened me as much as the encumbrances themselves ought to have done (*Confessions* VIII, 5, 10-11).

A few lines later, Augustine says: "Now I will relate how you set me free from a craving for sexual gratification which fettered me like a tight-drawn chain, and from my enslavement to worldly affairs: *I will confess to your name, O Lord, my helper and redeemer* (Ps 54:8)" (*Confessions* VIII, 6, 13).

Augustine thus realizes from hard personal experience that a person cannot enter the army of God and serve him if the grace-supported will has not conquered the rebellious senses. In the passages quoted he is alluding to his personal vocation which required the renunciation of marriage and a career in the acceptance of the ascetical life. But the underlying principle, which I shall illustrate by numerous other passages, clearly applies to the Christian calling as such, apart from particular vocations.

Necessity of the Conquest

The necessity emerges, first of all, from *psychological analysis*, of which Augustine is a master without peer, as illuminated by the work of God. In his introspective efforts, Augustine often returns, as in the passages just quoted, to the conflict between the higher and lower elements in human beings: between flesh and spirit, senses and will.

Two loves

Everyone has heard of the Augustinian thesis that "two loves" are struggling for the heart of the human person, and that this struggle provides the key for understanding history as a struggle between "two cities."

> In this life there are two loves wrestling with each other in every trial and temptation: love of the world, and love of God. And whichever of these two wins, that's where it pulls the lover as by the force of gravity. It isn't, you see, on wings or on foot that we come to God, but on the power of our desires. And again, it isn't with knots and chains that we find ourselves stuck to the earth, but with contrary desires. Christ came to change our love, and to make lovers of the heavenly life out of earthly lovers; he was made man on our account, having made us men in the first place; he was God taking on a human being, in order to make human beings into gods.

> This is the combat we are challenged to, this the struggle with the flesh, this the struggle with the devil, this the struggle with the world. But let us have confidence, because the one who instituted this contest does not watch his own champions without helping them, nor does he encourage us to rely on our own strength (Sermon 344, 1).

Elsewhere Augustine speaks of "two delights or pleasures."

> In the mortal body sin dwells. But what does the Apostle say? *Do not let sin rule your mortal body and make you obey its lusts* (Rom 6:12). When shall this freedom begin? When we reach the fulfillment of what Paul says elsewhere: *This corruptible body must be clothed with incorruptibility, and this mortal body with immortality*

(1 Cor 15:53). Before that happens, the pleasure of sinfulness stays in the body; but the pleasure to be found in the word of wisdom, God's commandment, is even greater. Conquer sin and its pleasure. Hate sin and evil-doing, so that you may be united to God who will hate it with you. You are already united in your mind to the law of God; with your mind you serve the law of God. And if you are still subject in your flesh to the law of sin,[1] inasmuch as some fleshly pleasures still dwell there, they shall vanish when the time of struggle is over. It is one thing not to struggle but to enjoy true and permanent peace; it is another to struggle and overcome; it is still another not to struggle but let yourself be drawn.

There are indeed those who do not struggle, like the man of whom it is said that he has *no repugnance for evil* (Ps 36:5). If he has no repugnance for it, how can he struggle against it? He is drawn by evil and fails to fight it. There are others who begin to fight, but they trust in their own strength. Therefore God lets them see that he is the one who conquers, provided we subject ourselves to God. Consequently these people are overcome by their very struggle, for when they think they have begun to be holy they grow proud and are crushed. They fight, then, but are conquered. Is there anyone who struggles and is not overcome? Yes, the one who says: *I see in my body's members another law at war with the law of my mind* (Rom 7:23). There are those who struggle, but do not trust in their own strength, and therefore they overcome. For what does the text go on to say? *What a wretched man I am! Who can free me from this body under the power of death? The grace of God through Jesus Christ our Lord* (Rom 7:24-25). He puts his trust in the one who bids him struggle, and, helped by this commander, overcomes (*Expositions of the Psalms* 36, 6).

The love of sensible things carries us away so that we forget eternal realities. Augustine comments thus on Psalm 137:3:

Sing your songs for us, sing a hymn, sing for us the songs of Zion! What shall we reply? Babylon sustains you, Babylon contains you, Babylon nourishes you, Babylon speaks through you. And you can understand only what shines in the light of time; you cannot contemplate eternal things; therefore you do not know what you are speaking. . . . [The Lord] has taught us how to answer someone who asks for such a song: How could we sing a song of the Lord in a foreign land? He says to the rich young man: If you seek perfection, go, sell your possessions, and give to the poor. You will then have treasure in heaven. Afterward, come back and follow me (Mt 19:21). If he is to learn many of the songs of Zion, he must first rid himself of all that holds him back, so that he can walk as a free person, unhindered by any burdens. Then he will learn something of the songs of Zion (*Expositions of the Psalms* 137, 11-13).

Testing, and therefore the necessity of struggling, arises from two contrary sources, namely, the good and evil things we meet with in this life.

> In both the good things and the bad things of this world, in all of them temptation is to be met. The good things are liable to deceive us with their blandishments, the bad things to break us with their menace. So because temptation is to be met in both sorts, that is in the good things and bad things of this present age, the Christian is never wholly safe (Sermon 20A).

Inner conflict is not reserved to those who are taking their first steps as a Christian; it is also the lot of those who are well advanced along the way.

> Whatever progress you make, you are going to be battling with desires, battling with lusts. However much progress you make, even if you have peace at home and abroad, in yourself you will have war, in yourself you are going to be engaged in combat, and you won't stop engaging in combat, watched by him who is ready to help you in the struggle and give you the prize when you win (Sermon 61A, 7).

The conquest of the senses is necessary if we are to *cleanse the eye of the heart* and enable it to see God. Since I have already dealt with this point in Chapter 1 when I showed that the purification of the heart is necessary for an interior life, I shall limit myself here to adding one more text.

> What calls for all our efforts in this life is the healing of the eyes of our hearts, with which God is to be seen. It is for this that the holy mysteries are celebrated, for this that the word of God is preached, to this that the Church's moral exhortations are directed, those, that is, that are concerned with the correction of our carnal desires, the improvement of our habits, the renunciation of this world, not only in words but in a change of life. Whatever points are made by God's holy scriptures, this is their ultimate point, to help us purge that inner faculty of ours from that thing that prevents us beholding God (Sermon 88, 5).

Source of interior conflict

The word of God teaches us the source of interior conflict and thereby asserts the necessity of struggling for victory.

The *prince of this world* (Jn 12:31)

> is the true master of those who love the temporal goods of our visible world. It is not that he is really master of the world itself. He is, however, master of the desires of human beings for passing things, and they become his subjects who pay no heed to the external God but love what is changing and impermanent. *The love of money is the root of all evil. Some people in their passion for it have strayed from the faith, and have come to grief amid great pain* (1 Tm 6:10). Through such greed the devil rules in human beings and possesses their hearts. All who love this world are in the same situation. But we cast the devil out when he wholeheartedly renounces this world. For you renounce the devil, prince of this world, when you renounce his seductions, pomps, and messengers (*The Christian Combat* I).

Elsewhere Augustine quotes Peter's words: Do you not know that *your opponent, the devil, is prowling like a roaring lion looking for someone to devour?* (1 Pt 5:8), and comments thus:

> He described the devil as a roaring lion prowling round, and trying to grab and harm something from the sheepfold. He never stops; never, till the very end, does he refrain from stalking his prey. So if our adversary never sleeps, it means we are fighting every day. And we can't see this adversary of ours, and we can defeat him. Why can't we see him? Because it is inside us that we experience and check what he wishes to defeat us with. You can't see your enemy the devil, but you experience your avarice in yourself. You can't see your enemy the devil, but you experience your lust in yourself. You can't see your enemy the devil, but you experience your anger in yourself. Defeat what you experience inside you, and those who are stalking you outside are already defeated (Sermon 328).

Original sin is responsible for the state of conflict in which all the children of Adam find themselves.

> Concerning this [concupiscence] the Apostle says: *For I take delight in the law of God according to the inner self. But I see another law in my members fighting against the law of my mind, and taking me prisoner to the law of sin which is in my members* (Rom 7:22-23). This law was born when the first law was broken. Then, I repeat, was this law born when the first law was ignored and

broken. What is the first law? The one the man was given in paradise? Why were they naked, and unashamed, if not because there was as yet no law in their members fighting against the law of the mind? Man committed a deed which deserved to be punished, and discovered in himself a motion of which he must blush. . . . There you have what original sin is derived from, there you have the reason why nobody is born without sin (Sermon 151, 5).

The interior struggle continues even after baptism. Explaining the sixth petition of the Lord's Prayer to the *competentes* (people in the final stage of the catechumenate and enrolled for baptism at the next Easter vigil), Augustine comments:

Bring us not into temptation. For each one, says the same apostle James, is tempted when he is pulled awry and enticed by his covetousness; then *after covetousness has conceived, it brings forth sin, and sin, when it is completed, generates death* (Jas 1:14-15). What was he teaching us? To fight against our covetous desires. It's true that in holy baptism you are going to shed your sins; desires will remain, which you've got to fight against when you are reborn. The conflict continues, you see, in your own selves. You needn't dread any foe outside; conquer yourself, and you've conquered the world. What is an external tempter going to do, whether it's the devil or the devil's agent? Suppose someone wants to corrupt you by making a profitable proposal; let him only find no avarice in you, and what can the proposer of profit do to you? But if avarice is found in you, you are excited by the prospect of profit, you are caught by the lure of the cruel bait. But if he doesn't find any avarice in you, the mousetrap is set for you in vain. The tempter presents you with a very beautiful woman; chastity is present inside, and iniquity is conquered outside. So to stop him catching you with the offered chance of enjoying the beauty of another man's wife, fight inside with your own lust. You are not aware of this foe of yours, but you are aware of your desires. You can't see the devil, but you can see what gives you pleasure. Conquer what you are aware of inside you. Fight, fight, because the one to whom you owe your rebirth is the judge. He has instituted the contest, he is preparing the prize (Sermon 57, 9).

In another passage, Augustine explains that while baptism does away with sin, there remain the habits against which a man must struggle.

He has been baptized, all his sins of drunkenness have been forgiven him; there remains as his adversary the habit. So he has something to fight with once he has been born again. His past vicious behavior has all been forgiven him; he must be alert, keep awake, fight, in order not to get drunk again sometime. So the lust for a tipple wells up in him, tickles his fancy, parches his throat, lays siege to his senses; it would like, if it possibly could, to penetrate the very walls, to get at him sheltering behind them, to drag him away prisoner. It's fighting, fight back. So we always have a fight on our hands, because the very covetousness we are born with can never be finished off as long as we live; it can be lessened day by day, it can't be finished off completely (Sermon 151, 4-5).

Among the motives which urge Christians to struggle for the conquest of their senses, Augustine likes to emphasize the transiency and inadequacy of temporal things. These qualities are symbolized by the rivers of Babylon.

If we are the citizens of Jerusalem, that is, of Zion, and while we are on earth must live not as citizens but as prisoners amid the confusion of this world, this Babylon, then we must not only sing these words[2] but also put them into practice in the pious desires of our hearts and our religious longing for the eternal city. This present city, called Babylon, also has its lovers who seek to provide for temporal peace but hope for nothing beyond it; they find all their joy in that peace and limit themselves to it; we see them labor greatly for the earthly commonwealth . . .

But, dear friends, take note of what the rivers of Babylon are. They are all things human beings love on earth and which pass away. They may, for example, love to engage in farming, to grow rich thereby, to concentrate their souls on it and find their pleasure in it. Let them wait for the outcome and learn that what they have loved is not the basis for Jerusalem but a river of Babylon. Another person says: "The soldier's life is the thing! Farmers fear soldiers, kowtow to them, and tremble before them. If I were a farmer, I would fear the soldier; if I were a soldier, the farmers would fear me." Fool! You are throwing yourself into another river of Babylon, and one that is even more raging and hungry for victims. You want to be feared by someone lesser than you. Fear, rather, him who is greater. The very person who fears you may suddenly become your superior, but he whom you should fear will never become inferior to you.

Still another says: "To be a lawyer is a splendid thing! And what is mightier than eloquence? To have clients wholly dependent on their shrewd patron's tongue and hoping to win through his condemnation or gain, death or life, destruction or safety!" You do not know what you are getting into, for this is but another river of Babylon, and its great noise is but the water dashing on the rocks. See how the waves speed by as they rush downstream, and, if you do see, be on guard, for they will sweep you away.

Another: Going to sea on business is my ambition. I want to become acquainted with many lands, earn money everywhere, and not be the subject of a powerful fellow in some city or other; I plan to be always on the move, find ever new interest in the affairs of varied peoples, and come home rich! But this too is a river of Babylon. Where shall you call a halt to your gains? When will you feel safe through your possessions? The richer you become, the more fearful will you be! It will take but a single shipwreck to strip you naked, and then you will wail in a river of Babylon, because you had not been willing to sit and weep beside the streams of Babylon (*Expositions of the Psalms* 137, 2-3).

Do you want to grasp the Word that abides? Don't follow the river of the flesh. This flesh is indeed a stream, because it does not abide. Human beings are born, as from some hidden spring of nature, they live, they die; we do not know where they come from, and we do not know where they are going. The water is hidden until it issues from the spring; it flows openly in the river; but again it hides itself in the sea. Let us not think highly of this stream that bubbles up, flows, ceases; let us not think very highly of it. *All flesh is grass, and all the honor of the flesh like the flowers in the grass. The grass withers, the flowers fall away.* Do you want to remain? *But the word of the Lord remains for ever* (Is 40:6-8) (Sermon 119, 3).

All the seeming happiness of this world is but a sleeper's dream. Those who see a treasure in their dreams are rich only when they sleep; when they wake they are poor again. So too, all the vanities people enjoy in this world, they enjoy only in a dream. They will awake at last against their will if they do not awake now when the waking can be helpful to them; when it is too late, they will find it was all a dream and has passed away (*Expositions of the Psalms* 132, 8).

Yesterday will not return again. After yesterday, today; after today, tomorrow. All times and all things temporal pass away (*The Excellence of Widowhood* XX, 25).

How much the world has to say to you, how much it chatters away behind your back, to make you look round behind you, to make you, that is, place your hope in things present (and not even present; I mean, things that never stay put can't be said to be present), and turn your mind away from what Christ has promised and not yet given, but will give because he is faithful, and so make you willing to take your rest in a world that is perishing (Sermon 105, 7).

Human beings fall victim to a deadly illusion when they think they have a sure hold on what by its very nature passes away and vanishes.

You know, dearly beloved, on what advice people greedy for money act, when they see they have accumulated an amount of coins. What do they say? "The thing's round, it rolls, it vanishes; it must be tied up with some purchase of real estate." And they want to tie their money up by buying a country house. And hey presto, they've bought a house in the country, they will have a house in the country. Will the country house, though, always have them? But neither will they have it always, seeing that after a short while they will move on without any deferment. You can't tie up your soul to the place where you've tied up your money. They time will come, you see, when your soul will be required of you; what you have bought, whose will it be then? So you won't have the country house, and the house in the country won't have you, except perhaps as regards your body, if you're buried there when you're dead. Why, then indeed something wonderful happens; it will have you, you won't have it (Sermon 335C, 9).

What is happiness? Not lacking anything.

"Well there you are; these people don't lack anything. They have plenty of everything, and are looking for nothing more."

I've still got a question to ask: Don't they want to have more?

Answer: "They don't."

Aren't they afraid of losing what they have?

Answer: "They are."

So how can you say they lack nothing? Even if they are not lacking in means, they are lacking in security. And is there any-one who can provide them with such security in this world, that what they possess cannot be lost? From whom can they receive any assurance about things that of their nature totter and stagger so unsteadily, slither and slide about in such uncertainty? Many people have gone to sleep rich and woken up poor. So nobody can give them this assurance. And they themselves know this, and that's why they are afraid (Sermon 359A).

Augustine knew from experience the inability of earthly things to satisfy the human heart. Even while he was pursuing so intensely his dream of a brilliant career and constantly hungering for sensual pleasure, he knew that he was not happier than the beggar he met in an alley in Milan, who was carefree and merry because he had had a bit to drink.[3]

Meaning and Extent of the Conquest

The three types of disordered tendencies which Saint John lists — fleshly desire, the avarice of the eyes, and worldly ambition[4] (1 Jn 2.16) — provide Augustine with a key for the analysis of his own temptations,[5] and show the direction to be taken by the effort to conquer the senses. Here we shall take account of what Augustine has to say in regard to our present limited theme.

Lust

In this area, in which Augustine had to accuse himself of having sinned seriously since his adolescent years, the great battles are now over for him. God has called him to perfect continence and helped him be faithful to his resolve. But the bishop is still tested by temptations rising out of memory, and he humbly confesses that though they have no power over him in his waking hours they do create illusions and cause pleasure in his dreaming state.[6]

Gluttony

It is not always easy to distinguish between the desire for food and drink that arises from the body's need of sustenance and the desire that springs from gluttony. By taking food and drink we replace the body's daily losses, while we wait for you [God] to do away with both stomach and food (see 1 Cor 6:13). Then through a marvelous repletion you will put an end to our feeling of need, and you will clothe this corruptible body in an eternal incorruptibility (see 1 Cor 15:53). At present, however, I find eating a sweet necessity, and I struggle against the sweetness lest I become its captive, and I wage daily war on it through fasting; often I turn the tables and reduce my body, instead, to servitude (see 1 Cor 9:26). In eating, pain is put to flight by pleasure; hunger and thirst, after all, are a kind of suffering that burns and kills like a fever, unless the remedy of food and drink is taken. And since the remedy is one of your consoling gifts, in which earth and water and sky aid us in our weakness, we call such an unfortunate necessity a pleasure.

> You have taught me to take food at mealtimes as though it were medicine. But when I pass from uncomfortable need to tranquil satisfaction, the snare of concupiscence lies waiting for me in the very passage from one to the other; for this transition itself is pleasurable, yet there is no other route for us to take if we are to arrive where necessity forces us to go. Preservation of health is our justification for eating and drinking, but perilous partiality comes hot on its heels, and indeed often tries to run ahead, and so becomes the real motive for what I profess to do (and hope I am doing) in the interests of health. The same stand-ard does not apply to both, for what suffices to maintain health appears meagre to appetite, and it is frequently hard to tell whether proper care for the body indicates that further support is needed, or deceitful, pleasure-seeking greed is demanding what will gratify it. At this uncertainty the wretched soul cheers up and marshals excuses in its own defence, glad to take advan-tage of the ambiguity about what temperate preservation of health requires, and cloaks its self-indulgence under the pre-tence that health is being prudently provided for (*Confessions* X, 31, 44).

Avarice

In reviewing his temptations Augustine makes no mention of ava-rice. He admitted, while at Cassiciacum, that at the age of nineteen he had learned from reading *Hortensius* not to desire riches and to make good use of riches if they should come his way.[7] He puts more stress, however, on the necessity of repressing this disordered desire than he does on the mastery of the other passions. Clearly, it was his pastoral experience that bade him return so often to this point.

He defines the *nature* of avarice. "What does it mean to be avari-cious? To seek more than one needs" (*Homilies on the First Letter of John* 8, 6) What is condemnable, then, is neither riches as such nor the moderate and ordered use of riches, but the avidity of those who are not satisfied with what they need. "Avarice," Augustine explains else-where, "means wanting to be rich, not already being rich" (Sermon 85, 6).

Augustine speaks of avarice explicitly and at length in a sermon in which he comments on I Timothy 6:7-19: "We brought nothing into this world, nor have we the power to take anything out. If we have food and clothing, we have all that we need." I shall follow the thread of this sermon, while introducing at various points passages from other sermons and writings.

After noting that Paul's words contain a clear-cut indictment and condemnation of avarice. Augustine calls attention to the prevailing inconsistency, in this matter, between speech and action.

> I don't know how it is, but avarice manages to act on people's hearts in such a way that everybody — or to speak more accurately and carefully, nearly everybody — pronounces it guilty in talk, and in behavior wants to have it protected. Many things, many fine and weighty and true things, have been said against it by both poets and historians and orators and philosophers; and every kind of literature and public pronouncement has had much to say against avarice. It's a great thing to be without the lady, and it's much more important to be without her than not to keep silent about what's wrong with her (Sermon 177, 1).

The speaker goes on to say that there is an essential difference between the invectives of the philosophers against avarice and those of the apostles. The former have been negative in their approach; only the indictments of the apostles have been able to ground their charges in our essential duties toward God and to put eternal goods in the place of transient ones.

> If we pay attention, we can learn about something which is peculiar to the school of Christ. Here's what I have just reminded you of: *We brought nothing into this world, and what is more we cannot take anything out of it; having board and lodging, with these let us be content.* Many people have said that. Also this: *The root of all evil is avarice*; there have been people who would say that. What follows, none of them has said: *You though, man of God, flee from these things; rather, pursue justice, faith, charity, with those who call upon the Lord from a pure heart* (1 Tm 6:11). Things like that none of them has ever said. Far from their pompously pontificating cheeks is such solid piety. So, dearly beloved, since there are people outside our company who have both found fault with and despised avarice, it was in order to save us, or men of God, from thinking too highly of them, that he began, *You though, man of God* (Sermon 177, 2).

To forestall any real comparison, what we must first and foremost discern and hold onto is that it is for God's sake that we do whatever we do. I mean, if you leave aside the worship of the true God, the lovers of avarice are still disapproved of. Nonetheless, our truer rule of religion ought to instill in us a greater

watchfulness in the matter. It's disgraceful, after all, and altogether too shameful and lamentable, if the worshippers of idols
are found to be tamers of avarice, and the worshipper of the
one God is put in harness by avarice, and becomes avarice's
slave, when the blood of Christ was the price of his freedom
(Sermon 177, 2).

After reading verses 13-16, Augustine continues:

It is of this God that we have become the family, into his family
that we have been adopted; we are his children, not by our own
merits but by his grace. It's simply too unbearable, too horrible,
that avarice should hold us in her grip on earth, when we are
saying to him, *Our Father, who art in heaven* (Mt 6:9). In our desire
for him all other things should grow cheap in our eyes; the
things among which we were born are not meant to be our
destiny, because it is on his account that we have been reborn.
Let them be for our use as we need them, not for our affections
to cling to them. Treat them like a tavern for a traveler, not like
a mansion for a landowner. Stop for refreshment, and then go
on your way. You're on a journey; think about whom you're
going to, because great indeed is the one who came to you. By
departing from this life you make way for someone else coming
along; that's the rule with taverns; you go, so that someone else
may take your place. But if you want to reach the safest of all
places, don't let God depart from you, seeing that we say to
him, *You have led me along the paths of your justice, for the sake of
your name* (Ps 23:3), not for the sake of my merits (Sermon 177,
2).

We must, then, be content to have what we need as we pass along
the road all mortals must travel.

To the first belongs being born, growing up, growing old, dying.
It's for all this that we need board and lodging. Let our expenses
be simply what is enough for this journey. Why weigh yourself
down? Why carry so much on a short road, stuff that doesn't
help you reach the end of it, but that becomes in fact an even
heavier burden for you at the road's end? It's a wretched
enough matter, what you apparently want to happen to you;
you load yourself up, you carry a vast amount of baggage, money
weighs you down along this road, and after this road ends, you
are weighed down by avarice. Avarice, you see, is an uncleanness of the heart. You can take nothing that you've loved from
this world; what you do take is the vice of having loved it. If you
persist in loving the world, the one who made the world won't

find you clean. So keep a moderate amount of money for temporal uses, treat it as journey money, with the end in view stated in the text: *A measure of money without love is sufficient for present needs* (Heb 13:5) (Sermon 177, 3).

Notice above all what he put first: *Without love*, he says; put your hand in the purse in such a way that you release your heart from it. Because if you are prepared to have your heart tied up with love of money, you're involving yourself in many pains; and then where are the words, *You though, man of God, flee from these things* (1 Tim 6:11)? You see, he didn't say, "Leave and forsake," but *Flee from*, as from an enemy. You were trying to flee with gold; flee from gold instead. Let your heart flee from it, and your use of it need have no worries. Do without greed, don't do without concern for others. There's something you can do with gold, if you're its master, not its slave. If you're the master of gold, you can do good with it; if you're its slave, it can do evil with you. If you're the master of gold, the person clothed by you praises the Lord. If you're the slave of gold, the person despoiled and stripped by you blasphemes God. Now it's cupidity that enslaves you, charity that sets you free (Sermon 177, 3).

Augustine then exhorts his hearers to love true riches, those which are interior, that is, God himself, and refutes the pretenses of those who want to lay up possessions, by showing that avarice can never be satisfied. He bids rich and poor alike be on guard against avarice and urges them not to place their hopes in wealth, since God alone can satisfy us. The proof that one does not love money is one's generosity to the poor; by such generosity, moreover, one wins eternal riches.[8]

Augustine is not unaware that there is another extreme which is just as blameworthy: that of prodigality, which is bent on satisfying its own whims by whatever means are available. Prodigality must be offset by a "holy avarice," which teaches us to use our possessions in order to help our brothers and thereby win eternal life.

Sometimes two opposing mistresses take possession of a person: avarice and extravagance. Avarice says, "Save"; extravagance says, "Spend." Under two such mistresses, giving contradictory orders, making contradictory demands, what are you going to do? They each have their own little speeches. And when you start showing unwillingness to comply with them, and entering into the inheritance of your proper freedom, they start coaxing, because they can no longer command. And we should be more on our guard against their coaxings than against their commands.

What does avarice say? Save up for yourself, save up for your children. If ever you are in need, no one is going to give you anything. Don't just live for the moment; take thought for yourself in the future. Extravagance takes the opposite line: Live while you are alive; treat yourself well. You are going to die, and you don't know when; nor do you know whether the one you plan to leave your estate to is going to gain possession of it. You are severely rationing your gullet; but perhaps when you are dead, he will neglect to set a cup over you; or if he does, perhaps he himself will get drunk on it, and not a drop will trickle down to you. So treat yourself well, when you can, while you can (Sermon 86, 6).

Program and Means

In pointing to the dangers arising from sensible things and the need of neutralizing them with the help of the Spirit and his grace. Augustine has already been suggesting what we must do to win the victory. Let us turn now to some further passages on this matter.

"Acknowledge true order, seek true peace" ("Agnosce ordinem, quaere pacem")

There is an order intrinsic to creation which must be respected: if human beings, who are creatures of God, freely subject themselves to their creator, the lower part of themselves will be subject to the higher.

The soul obeys God who dwells within it, and in turn commands its members. For your soul commands your foot and hand to move, your eye to see and your ear to hear; it commands your members as its servants. But in turn it serves its Lord who dwells within it. Now it cannot in fact properly rule what is subject to it, unless it first serves its own Lord worthily (*Expositions of the Psalms* 47, 10).

It is proper that the inferior be subject to the superior. . . . Acknowledge true order, seek true peace. You are to be subject to God, your flesh to you. What could be more just, what more beautiful? You are subject to what is greater than you, and what is lower than you is subject to you; serve the one who made you, so that what was made for you may serve you. The order I acknowledge and urge upon you is not one of subjecting your flesh to you and you to God, but rather one of subjecting you to God and your flesh to you. If you refuse to obey God, you will never make your flesh obey you. If you do not serve your

Lord, you will be tormented by your own servant (*Exposistions of the Psalms* 144, 6).

Augustine does not doubt at all that temporal goods are genuine values, but he sees as far more valuable the eternal blessings to which the temporal are ordered.

So this temporal salvation or health, common to men and brutes, was made light of by the martyrs, the health they had with Adam the man, not with the son of man. But the sons of men who belong to the son of man, in order to make light of the health common to men and brutes, *were hoping under the cover of your wings* (Ps 36:7). So what's the case, dearly beloved? For the martyrs to make light of this health, is this health not something good? If it wasn't good, who would be proud of making light of what is no good? They make light of the good, in order to come to the better. We are speaking about this kind of health here which nobody is to be blamed for seeking. We see people busying themselves with nothing else, as far as the support of this life is concerned, but with restoring this health if it has failed, or obtaining it if it has been lacking. But how long — it's going to come to an end, whether you like it or not — how long will you be able to hold on to this health, seeing that you can't cancel your last day? (Sermon 306D, 4).

The purpose of mortification is precisely to reestablish order within the person and to subject the body to the spirit.

As for their apparently harrying their bodies with self-restraint and hard toil, if they are doing this in the right manner, they are not doing it in order not to have bodies at all, but in order to have them broken in and ready for any necessary work. They are aiming, you see, by subjecting the body to a kind of arduous drill, at extinguishing the lusts that make bad use of the body, that is to say the habits and tendencies of the soul to seek enjoyment in inferior things. They are not, after all, doing away with themselves, but taking care of their true health of mind and body. As for those who do this in the wrong manner, they are waging war against their bodies as if they were their natural enemies. Here they are being misled by their reading of the text, *The flesh lusts against the spirit, and the spirit against the flesh; for these are opposed to each other* (Gal 5:17). Now this was said with an eye to the undisciplined habits of the flesh, against which the spirit is lusting, not in order to do away with the body, but in order to break in its lusts, that is its bad habits, and thereby make it subject to the spirit, as the natural order of things requires (*Teaching Christianity* I, 24-25).

Once the proper order has been restored, a proper use of sensible goods, in conformity with reason and the Christian law, will be possible.

Augustine therefore does not deny that some little peace can be achieved in the present life. "We are called happy when we have peace in the measure, minimal indeed, that it can be had here on earth by means of a good life. But this happiness, when compared with the happiness we call final, seems to be merely a form of unhappiness" (*The City of God* XIX, 10).

Furthermore, Augustine does not even condemn those who seek a little rest and satisfaction in the legitimate joys life brings.

> Every soul, because of the weakness proper to this life, looks for something earthly in which it may find rest, for it is difficult to labor without ceasing and to keep the mind constantly bent upon God. The mind seeks, then, to find some source of repose on earth, some refreshing rest, in such things as even good people love. I am not speaking here of the passions to which evil persons give rein, as when many find rest in the theater or the circus or the amphitheater or the gaming-house, in the revelry of the tavern, the lust of adultery, the violence of robbery, or the deceits and snares of fraud. Many seek their rest in such things too. But should I say "rest" or rather simply pleasure? But, again, I am not concerned with these but with people of innocent life. These find rest in their home, family, wife, and children, in a modest way of life, in a little plot of land, in a vine they have planted themselves or a home built with their own hands; in such things as these do people of innocent life find rest. God, however, wants us to have no love save for eternal life and therefore with even these innocent pleasures he mingles bitterness (*Expositions of the Psalms* 41, 5).

Admittedly, there are passages in Augustine's writings which seem to call for total renunciation and to banish all joy from our present life. "We are Christians only for the sake of the world to come. Let no one then hope for blessings now or promise themselves happiness in this world on the grounds that they are Christians." The immediately following exhortation reasserts an order of earthly values, however, by declaring the legitimacy of earthly joys that are accepted or sought in faith or in love for the heavenly Father. "But let people make us [*utatur*, not 'enjoy': *fruatur*] present happiness if they can, in what way they can, when they can, as much as they can. If they have it, let them thank God for his consolation; if they do not, let them thank God for his justice. In all situations let them be grateful, not ungrateful: grateful to the Father who consoles and caresses; grateful to the Father who corrects and chastises and subjects them to discipline. For God always loves us, whether he caresses or threatens (*Expositions of the Psalms* 92, 1).

The problem of using and even loving sensible creatures is explicitly faced in the commentary on the First Letter of Saint John: *Have no love for the word, nor the things that the world affords* (2:15).

Let us not love the world, nor the things that the world affords. For the things that the world affords are *carnal allurements, enticements for the eye, the life of empty show* (2:16). These three things are mentioned explicitly, so that no one may object: *But God made what is in the world — heaven and earth and sea, sun and moon and stars, and all that adorns the heavens. What are the adornments of the sea? All the aquatic animals. What are the adornments of the earth? Animals, trees, and birds. These are the things that are in the world, and God made them! Am I not to love what God has made?* If the Spirit of God abides in you, you will see that all the things you have named are indeed good. Yet, woe to you if you love created things and abandon their creator! They are beautiful in your sight; but how much more beautiful is he who made them! . . . God does not forbid you to have affection for them; he does forbid you so to love them that you seek your happiness in them, and he tells you to find them good and to praise them so that your love is drawn to their creator.

Augustine goes on to illustrate his thought with a comparison. A person who loves creatures in place of God is like a wife who receives a ring from her husband and then, conceiving a greater love for his gift than for him, says: All I want is the ring; I do not care to see his face again. Created things are a pledge of love from God who wants to give us something far greater — his very self — and asks us to love him above all else. Augustine continues:

When God tells you: *Do not love these things*, is he telling you not to eat or drink or beget children? Of course not! He is telling you to observe moderation for the sake of the creator, lest you make yourself a prisoner by your love of creatures. You should not love creatures so as to find your joy in them (*ad fruendum*), but possess them so as to make use of them (*ad utendum*) (*Homilies on the First Letter of John* 2, 11-12).

In such a right and ordered vision of reality, even things that often lead people away from God can become a ladder for mounting up to him.

Let me turn now to that man. You're greedy and grasping, you love money. Do you want to know bliss? Love your God. Money doesn't bring you bliss; you make it into handsome coins, it doesn't make you into a blissful person. But because you love money so much, and I can see that you go in whatever direction greed or cupidity bids you, go instead, idle fellow, in the direction love or charity bids you. Look up, and observe what a difference there is between your money and your God. This sun in the sky is more beautiful than your money, and yet this sun is not your God. Accordingly, if this sunlight is more beautiful than your money, how much more beautiful must he be who made this sunlight? (Sermon 399, 10).

"Fight a hard battle, and you need not despair of victory" (Struggle and mortification)

Order cannot be restored and peace attained in the present life except at the cost of a diligent and persevering struggle.

But if you lust indeed, which the law forbids when it says *You shall not lust* (Rom 7:7), but all the same keep the other commandment of the same law, *Do not go after your lusts* (Sir 18:30), then you are spiritual in the mind, flesh-bound in the flesh. It's one thing, after all, not to lust, another not to go after one's lusts. Not to lust is the mark of the altogether perfect person; not to go after one's lusts marks the person who is fighting, struggling, toiling. While the battle rages, why despair of victory? When will victory come? When death is swallowed up in victory. Then will be the time for the victor's triumphant shout, now is the time for the fighter's sweat (Sermon 154, 8).

Those who do not experience the struggle as a bitter one should ask themselves whether they have not given up the struggle and been already overcome.

Do you really live in this corruptible body, which weighs down the soul, in such a way that the flesh does not lust against the spirit, and the spirit against the flesh? Is this kind of brawling unknown in you? Is there no lust of the flesh in you, resisting the law of your mind? Well, if there is nothing in you resisting something else, consider where you as a whole must be. If your spirit has no disagreement with the flesh lusting against it, consider that perhaps your whole mind may be in agreement with the flesh, consider that the reason why there is no war may perhaps be that there is an unwholesome sort of peace. Perhaps you are in total agreement with the flesh, and so there is no brawling going on. What hope have you got of being able to win eventually, if you haven't yet even started to fight? (Sermon 30, 4).

This does not mean, Augustine points out, that we should want to feel concupiscence so that we may fight against it. On the contrary.

> For my part, I tell you, anything in me that rebels against my mind, and argues with me in favor of a contrary kind of pleasure, anything in me of that sort I would like to slay completely. And if by chance it happens with the Lord's help that I defeat it, I would still much rather not have anything to argue with. For me, not having an enemy is infinitely preferable to defeating one (Sermon 30, 4).

> And yet your desire ought to be so totally directed toward God, that there isn't even any lust for you to resist. Notice what I've said: Your desire, I repeat, ought to be so totally directed toward God, that there is absolutely no lust at all which you have to resist. Yes, you are resisting, and by not agreeing to it, you are overcoming it; but it's better not to have an enemy than to overcome one. *Do not go after your lusts* (Sir 18:30). It would be better not to have any; but because they are there, do not go after them. They aren't keen to go after you; don't you be keen to go after them. If they did want to go after you, they would cease to be, because they would not be rebelling against your mind. They are rebels, be a rebel yourself against them; they are fighting, fight them back; they are fighting to the finish, fight to the finish yourself; make sure of one thing alone: don't let them win (Sermon 151, 3).

In this struggle the apostle Paul is our teacher and model.

> The Apostle tells us: *I do not fight as if I were shadowboxing. What I do is discipline my own body and master it, for fear that after having preached to others, I myself should be rejected* (1 Cor 9:26). He also says: *Imitate me as I imitate Christ* (1 Cor 11:1). . . . Let us, too, imitate him therefore, as he exhorts us to do, and discipline our body and make it our servant, if we want to overcome the world. For, through its illicit pleasures, its ostentation, and its destructive curiosity that world can become our master — I mean those things of the world which bind lovers of temporal things in the bonds of destructive pleasure and force them to become servants of the devil and his angels — if we renounce all these things, we are seeking to make our body our servant (*The Christian Combat* 6).

Augustine does not hesitate to confess that he must struggle daily against temptations to gluttony.

Beset by these temptations I struggle every day against gluttony, for eating and drinking are not something I can decide to cut away once and for all, and never touch again, as I have been able to do with sexual indulgence. The reins that control the throat must therefore be relaxed or tightened judiciously; and is there anyone, Lord, who is not sometimes dragged a little beyond the bounds of what is needful? If there is such a person, he is a great man, so let him tell out the greatness of your name. I am not he, for I am a sinful man (*Confessions* X, 31, 47).

Meditate on the word of God

Now I regarded Ambrose as a fortunate man as far as worldly standing went, since he enjoyed the respect of powerful people; it was only his celibacy which seemed to me a burdensome undertaking. I had not begun to guess, still less experience in my own case, what hope he bore within him, or what a struggle he waged against the temptations to which his eminent position exposed him, or the encouragement he received in times of difficulty, or what exquisite delights he savoured in his secret mouth, the mouth of his heart, as he chewed the bread of your word (*Confessions* VI, 3, 3).

By the time he came to write these lines, Augustine had indeed had the happy experience and had learned that a person who "tastes the bread of God," that is, meditates on God's word, finds in it the strength to put up with the daily struggle. Hence he exhorts us: "*Do not let sin reign in your mortal body, so that you obey its desires.* That's what I don't want you to do; evil desires arise, but don't obey them. Arm yourself, take up the weapons of war. God's commandments are your weapons" (Sermon 128, 12).

Faith in God's word cleanses the heart and makes it worthy to see God.

So if we long to see God, how is this eye going to be purified? Who wouldn't take pains, who wouldn't look for ways of purifying the instrument with which he can see the one he is longing for with all his heart? Divine authority has given us this clear answer to our question: *Purifying their hearts,* it says, *by faith* (Acts 15:9). Faith in God purifies the heart, the pure heart sees God. *Faith which works through love* (Gal 5:6).

By making the soul submissive to God, faith enables it to subject the body to itself in turn, in accordance with that natural order of which we spoke earlier.

Someone may ask how we can make our body our servant. The thing is easy to understand and effect, provided we first submit to God with a good will and in heartfelt love. Every creature, of course, is willy-nilly subject to its one God and Lord. But we humans are bidden to serve God with our entire will. The just person serves freely; sinners serve because they are forced. All therefore serve divine providence; but some obey as children and, with the help of providence, do what is good; others are bound as slaves, and God does with them what is just (*The Christian Combat* 7).

And later in the same work: "Let us therefore subject our soul to God, if we want to subject our body to ourselves and thus triumph over the devil. Faith is the basic thing that subjects the soul to God; then come the moral commandments, the observance of which strengthens our hope and nourishes our love and makes what initially was an object of faith alone become transparent to our gaze" (*ibid.*, 14).

"Follow the Lord" (Imitate Christ)

Is love of the flesh crucifying you? Pick up your cross and follow the Lord. He too, your saviour, though God in the flesh, though God with flesh, still gave you a demonstration of purely human feelings, when he said, *Father, if it is possible, let this cup pass from me* (Mt 26:39). He knew that this cup could not pass from him, that it had come to him in order to be drunk. That cup was to be drunk willingly, not out of necessity. He was almighty; if he wished, it would most certainly pass from him, because he was God with the Father, and he and God the Father were one God. But in the form of a servant, in the form he took from you for you, he uttered those words in the voice of a man, in the voice of the flesh. He stooped to transposing you into himself, so that you in him might utter words of weakness, so that you in him might take a grip on decisive strength. He showed you the will through which you could be tempted; and straightaway he taught you which will you should prefer to which. *Father,* he said, *if it can be so, let this cup pass from me.* This is a human wish; I am wearing a man, I am speaking from the form of a servant. *Father, if it can be so, let this cup pass.* It's the voice of the flesh, not of the spirit, the voice of infirmity, not of divinity (Sermon 344, 3).

Look to the goal

The sermon just quoted continues:

Why, then, did the martyrs overcome? Because they set the spiritual will over the fleshly will. They loved this present life, but they gave it its true value; they thought how greatly eternal life should be loved if our present passing life can be so lovable. Those who are to die do not want to die; yet die they must, even though they continue to wish not to die. You accomplish nothing by wishing not to die, you wrest no longer life for yourself; in short, you have no power at all of doing away with the necessity of dying. What you fear will come, whether you like it or not; what you put off will come despite your resistance. You exert yourself to put death off; but do you think you can abolish it? Well, if those who love this present life take so much trouble to delay death, what would they have to do to do away with it completely? Of course, you do not want to die! Change your love, and you will learn of a death of a different kind: not the death that comes against your will, but a death that will not come if you will it not to. . . .

Take heed and set these two deaths before you. If possible, of course, you would prefer to suffer neither death. Naturally, you want to live, not die, and to pass from this life to the other without having to die and rise again, by simply being changed to a more perfect state. That is what you would like and what human instinct prefers; such a transition is what the human soul naively wills and desires. . . .

Certainly, you don't want to die. Change your kind of love, and you will be shown, not a death that will present itself to you against your will, but a death which will, if you so will, absent itself altogether. Listen, don't hesitate to lose your life for Christ's sake. You are in fact entrusting to a trustworthy creator what you are said to be losing. You, indeed, will lose it; but he will receive it, and for him nothing perishes and is lost. If you love life, lose it in order to find it; because when you find it, it won't any longer be the sort of thing you can lose, there won't be any reason why you should lose it. The life in fact that will be found is one that will be found to be such that it cannot ever perish or be lost at all, because Christ too, who by his birth, death and resurrection has given himself to you as a model, rising from the dead dies no more, and death will no longer lord it over him (Rom 6:9) (Sermon 344, 3-4 and 7).

"Give what you command, and command what you will" ("Da quod iubes, et iube quod vis") (Pray)

Human efforts and cleverness, however, are not enough to assure the mastery of spirit over flesh. As he begins the description of his own temptations, Augustine says:

> On your exceedingly great mercy rests all my hope. Give what you command, and then command whatever you will. You order us to practise continence. A certain writer tells us how I know that no one can be continent except by God's gift, and that it is already a mark of wisdom to recognize whose gift this is. By continence the scattered elements of the self are collected and brought back into the unity from which we have slid away into dispersion; for anyone who loves something else along with you, but does not love it for your sake, loves you less. O Love, ever burning, never extinguished, O Charity, my God, set me on fire! You command continence: give what you command, and then command whatever you will (*Confessions* X, 29, 40).

What human weakness cannot accomplish, divine omnipotence can.

> Is your hand not powerful enough to heal all my soul's ills, all-powerful God, and by a still more generous grace to extinguish unruly stirrings even in my sleep? Yes, Lord, you will heap gift after gift upon me, that my soul may shake itself free from the sticky morass of concupiscence and follow me to you (*Confessions* X, 30, 42).

> *For no one can be continent except by your gift* (Wis 8:21). When we pray you grant us many things; whatever good we had before we prayed was ours because we received it from you; and even the grace to recognize this afterward is received from you as gift. . . . But dust we are, Lord, and remember *that from this dust you made us* (Ps 103, 4), and that our race, *once lost, was found again* (Lk 15, 24). I love Paul for saying what he did in response to the breath of your Spirit, but not even he could have spoken so by his own powers, for he was made of the same dust; but, he declared, *I am capable of anything in him who strengthens me* (Phil 4:13). Strengthen me too, that I may be capable, give what you command, and then command whatever you will (*Confessions* X, 31, 45).

The devil, our invisible enemy, cannot be overcome except with the help of God, our invisible protector.

> So here we have a combat on our hands; this life is an amphitheatre for God, who has a ringside seat. Here it's a fight, here

a conflict with all the vices, and supremely with the prince of vices, as with Goliath. The devil, you see, is so to say challenging the soul to single combat. He can be defeated, it's agreed, but in the name of the Lord, not in the might of the warrior. So whatever evil or unlawful thing may be suggested to your thoughts, whatever dark, unwholesome desire wells up from your flesh against your mind, these are the weapons of the enemy, who is challenging you to single combat. Remember, you're fighting. The foe is invisible, but your protector also is invisible. You can't see the one you are locked in combat with, but you do believe in the one you are protected by. And if you have the eyes of faith, you can even see the former; every believer, after all, can see with the eyes of faith the opponent challenging him every day (Sermon 335K, 3).

So when you begin to find the going hard in your fight against the lusts of the flesh, walk by the Spirit, call upon the Spirit, start seeking the gift of God. And if the law for your members is fighting back against the law of your mind from the lower part, that is from the flesh, is holding you captive under the law of sin, even that will be corrected, even that will be changed into the rights of victory. All you have to do is cry out, all you have to do is call upon him. *It is necessary to pray always and not grow slack* (Lk 18:1). Just go on calling on him constantly, calling on him for help (Sermon 163, 12).

The sixth petition of the Lord's Prayer had shown Augustine the necessity of struggling; from it he also proves the necessity of praying.

Bring us not into temptation, but deliver us from evil (Mt 6:13). Will this too be necessary in that life? You don't say *Bring us not into temptation* except where it is possible to be tempted. In the book of holy Job we read, *Is not human life on earth a temptation?* (Job 7:1). So what are we pleading for? Listen, I'll tell you what. The apostle James says, *No one when he is tempted should say that he is tempted by God* (Jas 1:13). By temptation here he meant the bad sort by which one is deceived and subjugated to the devil; that's what he called temptation. There is another kind of temptation, which is called testing; about this kind of temptation it is written, *The Lord your God is tempting you, to know whether you love him* (Dt 13:3). What does it mean, "to know"? To make you know; he himself knows already. With the sort of temptation by which people are deceived and led astray, God tempts nobody, but he does, certainly, according to his deep and inscrutable judgment, forsake some. When he has forsaken a person, the tempter discovers what he can do. He doesn't find anyone struggling against him, you see, but immediately presents himself to the person as his owner-occupier—if God forsakes him. So it's in order that God may not forsake us that we say, *Bring us not into temptation* (Sermon 57, 9).

You see, when he says *The flesh lusts against the spirit, and the spirit against the flesh*, you mustn't imagine it only refers to the human spirit. The Spirit of God is the one who fights in you against you, against that in you which is really against you. . . . I mean it was this redeemer, after all, who gave you the Spirit by which to put to death the deeds of the flesh. *As many as are influenced by the Spirit of God, these are children of God.* They are not children of God if they are not influenced by the Spirit of God. But if they are influenced by the Spirit of God, they fight, because they have a powerful champion. God, you see, doesn't watch us fighting in the way the people watch the hunters in the arena. The people can back a hunter; they can't help him when he's in danger (Sermon 128, 9).

A passage toward the end of *True Religion* can fittingly sum up the teachings and exhortations of Augustine which I have been presenting in this chapter. "I urge you, therefore, dear friends and neighbors, and I urge myself along with you, that we run as swiftly as we can to the goal to which God in his wisdom calls us. Let us not love the world, for the things that the world affords are *carnal allurements, enticements for the eye, the life of empty show* (1 Jn 2:16). Let us not love to corrupt and be corrupted by the pleasures of the flesh, lest we fall into a far worse corruption of pain and torment" (*True Religion* 55, 107).

NOTES

1. See Rom 7:25.
2. Psalm 137.
3. See *Confessions* VI, 6, 9.
4. See 1 Jn 2:16.
5. See *Confessions* X, 30, 41 — 39, 64.
6. See *Confessions* X, 30, 41-42.
7. See Soliloquies I, 17.
8. For the entire text see Sermon 177.

CHAPTER 4

GOD

"Unhappy is anyone who knows it all but does not know you, whereas one who knows you is blessed, even if ignorant of all these. Nor is anyone who knows both you and them more blessed for knowing them, but blessed on your account alone, provided that such a person recognizes you as you are, and glorifies you and gives you thanks, and does not drift off into unsound reasoning" (*Confessions* V, 4, 7).

Therefore this impassioned prayer: "Give me yourself, O my God, give yourself back to me. Lo, I love you, but if my love is too mean, let me love more passionately. I cannot gauge my love, nor know how far it fails, how much more love I need for my life to set its course straight into your arms, never swerving until hidden in the *covert of your face* (Ps 31:21). This alone I know, that without you all to me is misery, woe outside myself and woe within, and all wealth but penury, if it is not my God" (*Confessions* XIII, 8, 9).

The Desire for God

People thus tend toward God by a necessity of their nature and with a desire that penetrates their whole being. "You arouse us so that praising you may bring us joy, because you have made us and drawn us to yourself, and our heart is unquiet until it rests in you" (*Confessions* I, 1, 1). "In this gift of yourself [the Holy Spirit] we find our rest, in it our joy. Our rest is our true place. Love lifts us up to that place, and *your good spirit* (Ps 143:10) raises our lowly selves *from the gates of death* (Ps 9:14). In good will lies our peace" (*Confessions* XIII, 9, 10).

God himself inspires in us the desire for him. "I call upon you, *my God, my mercy* (Ps 59:18), you who created me and have not forgotten me though I have forgotten you. I call you into my soul which you prepare to receive you through the desire you inspire. Do not abandon me now that I am calling to you, *for you came to my aid* (Ps 59:11) before I called to you, and you importuned me through frequent calls of every kind to hear you from far off and to be converted and to call within me the one who was calling me" (*Confessions* XIII, I, I).

The long prayer that opens Book I of the *Soliloquies* expresses this desire for God. I shall be quoting passages from it in the course of this chapter.

The statement that every being loves God, whether or not it be aware of loving him, can be illustrated from Augustine's account of an experience he had while a student at Carthage. "In love with loving, I was casting about for something to love; the security of a way of life free from pitfalls seemed abhorrent to me, because I was inwardly starved of that food which is yourself, O my God. Yet this inner famine created no pangs of hunger in me. I had no desire for the food that does not perish, not because I had my fill of it, but because the more empty I was, the more I turned from it in revulsion" (*Confessions* III, I, I).

People tend toward God — as does every rational creature — because of the very structure of their being, which aspires to the changeless good. "The rational reaction, be it an angelic spirit or a human soul, is such that it cannot itself be the good that makes it happy. If the changeable self cleaves to the changeless good, it becomes happy; if it departs from that good, it is unhappy" (*Letter* 140, 56).

People must become aware of this need and therefore experience the hunger which Jesus calls a beatitude and which God is ready to allay.

God *gives food to the hungry* (Ps 146:7). To which of those who hunger? To all. What do you mean by "all"? He gives food to all the animals and to all. "Does he then reserve no food for those he loves?" If they have another kind of hunger, they will also have another kind of food. Let us look for the hunger proper to his beloved, and we will discover their special food. *Blest are they who hunger and thirst for holiness; they shall have their fill* (Mt 5:6). We must be hungry for God! Let us sit at the door of his gaze and play beggar in our prayers; he *gives food to the hungry* (*Expositions of the Psalms* 146, 17).

Augustine was one of those who hungered for God.

Who will grant me to find peace in you? Who will grant me this grace, that you would come into my heart and inebriate it, enabling me to forget the evils that beset me and embrace you, my only good? What are you to me? Have mercy on me, so that I may tell. What indeed am I to you, that you should command me to love you, and grow angry with me if I do not, and threaten me with enormous woes? Is not the failure to love you woe enough in itself? Alas for me! Through your own merciful dealings with me, O Lord my God, tell me what you are to me. Say to my soul, *I am your salvation*. Say it so that I can hear it. My heart is listening, Lord; open the ears of my heart and say to my soul, *I am your salvation*, Let me run toward this voice and seize hold of you. Do not hide your face from me: let me die so that I may see it, for not to see it would be death to me indeed (*Confessions* I, 5, 5).

O Truth, illumination of my heart, let not my own darkness speak to me! I slid away to material things, sank into shadow, yet even there, even from there, I loved you. Away I wandered, yet I remembered you. I heard your voice behind me, calling me back, yet scarcely heard it for the tumult of the unquiet. See now, I come back to you, fevered and panting for your fountain. Let no one bar my way, let me drink it and draw life from it. Let me not be my own life: evil was the life I lived of myself; I was death to me; but in you I begin to live again. Speak to me yourself, converse with me. (*Confessions* XII, 10, 10).

The desire of the soul for God is hidden, as God himself is hidden. In a sermon preached during the octave of Easter Augustine thus explains God's work on the third day.

What, in the Church, is the dry land? Every soul thirsting for God is called dry land. How can we prove that this land is dry, which signifies people desiring good things? The psalm says to God, *My soul is like land without water to you* (Ps 143:6). My soul has thirsted for you; it's thirsty, it's dry, it's been segregated from the waters of the sea. It mustn't bother about not yet being segregated in the body; its desire has already made the separation. Some desire God, others desire the world. So what does the dry land thirst for? Showers from heaven, showers from the clouds, showers from the scriptures, showers from the firmament. But when it desires showers, it is desiring fresh water, separated from salt water. Only God, though, knows what the dry land desires; it's hidden, you see, it's secret (Sermon 229S).

No creature can satisfy the desire of those who yearn for God.

Let all of us then, my brothers and sisters, take a look at ourselves inside, weigh ourselves up, test ourselves in all our deeds, our good works, to see which ones we do with love and for love, not expecting any temporal reward, but only God's promise, the sight of God's face. After all, whatever God promises

you, none of it is worth anything apart from God himself. Most
certainly, God would never satisfy me, unless he promised me
God himself. What's the whole earth, what's the whole sea,
what's the whole sky worth? What are all the stars, the sun, the
moon? What's the host of angels worth? It's the Creator of all
these that I am thirsting for; I'm hungry for him, thirsty for him,
it's to him I say, Since with you is the fountain of life (Ps 36:9). And
he says to me, I am the bread who came down from heaven (Jn
6:41). May I hunger and thirst for this in my exile, on my journey,
so that I may take my fill of it when I arrive in his presence. The
world smiles on us with many things, things of beauty, power,
variety; more beautiful is the one who made them, mightier and
more brilliant the one who made them, more delightful, more
delicious the one who made them. I will be satisfied, when your
glory is revealed (Ps 17:15) (Sermon 158, 7).

The inability of any creature to fill the human heart is proof of the
human being's greatness.

The very heaven above our heaven would have been a dark
abyss in itself, whereas now it is light in the Lord. When spirits
slide away from you they are stripped of their vesutre of light
and exposed in their native darkness, and then their unhappy
restlessness amply proves to us how noble is each rational creature you have made, for nothing less than yourself can suffice to
give it any measure of blessed rest, nor indeed can it be its own
satisfaction. For it is you, Lord, who will ight up our darkness.[1]
From you derives our garment of light, and in you our darkness
will be bright as noon[2] (Confessions XIII, 8, 9).

Even when we have found God through faith, we continue to seek
him through hope and with a love that knows no limitation.

What is meant by the words, Seek his face always (Ps 105:4)? I
know indeed that it is good for me to cleave to God (Ps 73:28), but
if he is always being sought, when will he ever be found? Does
the Psalmist mean by always the whole of our life on earth, from
the time when we realize that we ought to seek God, from the
time when, having found him, we must go on seeking him? For
it is a fact that faith has indeed found him; but hope seeks him
still. Love has found him through faith but seeks to possess him
through vision. At that point he shall be found in a way that
satisfies us, and there shall be no further seeking. . . . Or shall it
perhaps be that even when we see him face to face (1 Cor 13:12)
as he is (1 Jn 3:2), we shall still have to seek him, and seek him
unendingly, since we shall be loving him unendingly? We may say

to someone in his presence, "I do not seek you," that is, "I do not love you." On the contrary, if we love someone, we seek him, even though he be present, for we aim in our endless love to prevent his absence. . . . . Therefore, *Seek his face always* means that the finding does not put an end to the search which love implies and that the growth of love, on the contrary, brings a more intense search for him who is already found (*Expositions of the Psalms* 105, 3).

In his work, *The Trinity*, Augustine takes up the same problem but puts the emphasis on the intellectual significance of the search.

So if he can be found when he is sought, why does it say *Seek his face always*? Does he perhaps have to be sought even when he has been found? That is indeed how incomprehensible things have to be searched for, in case the man who has been able to find out how incomprehensible what he is looking for is should reckon that he has found nothing. Why then look for something when you have comprehended the incomprehensibility of what you are looking for, if not because you should not give up the search as long as you are making progress in your inquiry into things incomprehensible, and because you become better and better by looking for so great a good which is both sought in order to be found all the more delightfully, and it is found in order to be sought all the more avidly (*The Trinity* XV, 2).

How To Reach God

I touch on this problem, in keeping with the scope of the book, not from the philosophical or apologetic standpoint (evidently this is pre-supposed), but as a problem of religious life which is topical both for the person far from God and for the person who believes in God but wants to be united to him in a more fully conscious way and in a manner more in keeping with our calling as human beings and Christians.

Through creatures

For his invisible things can be observed, being understood through the things that were made (Rom 1:19). Question the world, the furniture of the heavens, the brightness and arrangement of the stars, the sun providing for the day, the moon which comforts the night; question the earth bearing its yield of herbs and trees, full of animals, completely furnished in every respect; question the sea, full of so many and such a variety of swimming creatures; question the air, pulsing with so many flying things; question them all, and see if they don't answer you, after a fashion in their own way, "God made us." Serious and great-minded philosophers have inquired into these things, and have come to a knowledge of the artist through the works of art (Sermon 141, 2).

This whole creation with its ordered beauty that rises by degrees from lowest to highest and descends from highest to lowest, without any break in the chain of varied beings — this whole creation praises God. In what sense does the whole praise God? In the sense that when you look out upon creation and find it beautiful, you praise God on its account. The beauty of the earth is, as it were, the earth's silent voice. You take note and see its beauty, its fruitfulness, its powers: how it conceives through seed and how, so very often, it brings forth fruit though no seed has been sown. You see and, by your reflection, you ask it questions, as it were; your very reflection is a questioning. Thus, when you have questioned it with admiring mind and examined it and found its great energies and beauty and splendid power, you realize it could not have such power as its own and out of its own being. Then it suddenly dawns on you that the earth could not exist by its own power but only by the creator's power. Your discovery is the voice by which the earth utters its confession, stimulating you to praise the creator. When you reflect on all the beauty of the universe, does not that beauty answer you: "I did not make myself; God did"? (*Expositions of the Psalms* 145, 13).

Let your soul travel about the whole of creation. On every side creation will cry out to you: "God made me." Whatever delights you in the work of art turns your mind to the artist. The more you move about in creation, the more your contemplation will arouse your praise of the creator. Look at the heavens; they are God's mighty work. Look at the earth; it was God who gave it the vast variety of seeds, the different kinds of growth, the multitude of animals. Move from heaven to earth and omit nothing from your consideration; all things echo the creator's name. The very beauty of creatures is the voice with which they praise their maker (*Expositions of the Psalms* 27, II, 12).

Reason thus ascends from visible things to invisible and brings us to the discovery of God.

Let us see how far reason can go as it rises from the visible to the invisible, the temporal to the eternal. We should not gaze in an idle and profitless way upon the beauty of the heavens, the ordered stars, the brilliant light, the succession of days and nights, the monthly cycle of the moon, the four seasons of the year, that match the fourfold division of the elements, the immense power contained in the seeds that produce so many species and individual plants, and indeed visible reality as a whole wherein each thing manifests the nature and manner of action proper to its type. In contemplating all this we should not be indulging in an idle, passing curiosity, but using it as a ladder to what is deathless and abides forever (*True Religion* 29, 52).

However, we hear this "voice" of creation only if we are attentive to confront it with the truth that speaks within us.

I, who was that inmost self, I, who was mind, knew them through the senses of my body; and so I questioned the vast frame of the world concerning my God, and it answered, "I am not he, but he made me."

Surely this beauty is apparent to all whose faculties are sound? Why, then, does it not speak the same message to all? Animals, both small and large, see the beauty, but they are not able to question it, for in them reason does not hold sway as judge over the reports of the senses. Human beings have the power to question, so that by understanding the things he has made they may glimpse the unseen things of God;[3] but by base love they subject themselves to these creatures, and once subject can no longer judge. Creatures do not respond to those who question unless the questioners are also judges: not that they change their voice — that is, their beauty — if one person merely sees it, while another sees and enquires, as though they would appear in one guise to the former, and differently to the latter; no, the beauty appears in the same way to both beholders, but to one it is dumb, and to the other it speaks. Or rather, it speaks to all, but only they understand who test the voice heard outwardly against the truth within (*Confessions* X, 6, 9-10).

It is a great thing, and very rare, for an individual to contemplate the whole of creation, material and immaterial, and grasp its mutability, and then to pass beyond it by an effort of the mind and reach the changeless substance of God, there to learn from God himself that whatever is not identical with him has been created by him. This is how God speaks to us through material creatures . . . but he speaks through the mouth of truth itself, provided we are able to hear the truth with our minds, not with our bodily ears (*The City of God* XI, 2, 1).

If we leave aside the voices of the prophets, the world itself with its ordered change and freedom and with the beauty possessed by all visible things proclaims, mutely as it were, that it has been created and could have been created only by God who is invisibly and indescribably great and beautiful (*The City of God* XI, 4, 22).

> And so it was a very good thing and absolutely right to blame those who were able to investigate the mathematical relations of the constellations, their time cycles, to tell the eclipses of the great lights and predict them; it was right to blame them, because they didn't find the one by whom these things were made and set in order because they didn't take the trouble to look for him. You, however, shouldn't care very much if you are ignorant of the circuits of the constellations and of heavenly, or earthly, bodies. Observe the beauty of the world, and praise the plan of the creator. Observe what he made, love the one who made it. Hold on to this maxim above all; love the one who made it, because he also made you, his lover, in his own image (Sermon 68, 5).

They, too, are guilty who love beautiful creatures more than their far more beautiful creator.

> Love, if you can, something that God has not made! Look about the whole of creation and see whether anything that enslaves through desire, and keeps you from loving the creator, has not itself been made by him whom you neglect. You love such created things because they are beautiful, do you not? But can they be as beautiful as their maker? You admire created things because you do not see the maker, but through the things you admire, you should come to love him whom you do not see (*Expositions of the Psalms* 80, 14).

Through Human Beings

Men and women are called to rise up to the creator through created things and through their own being. The answer they seek from creatures they seek from themselves as well.

> Then toward myself I turned, and asked myself, "Who are you?" And I answered my own question: "A man." See, here are the body and soul that make up myself, the one outward and the other within. Through which of these should I seek my God? With my body's senses I had already sought him from earth to heaven, to the farthest place whither I could send the darting rays of my eyes; but what lay within me was better, and to this all those bodily messengers reported back, for it controlled and

judged the replies of sky and earth, and of all the creatures dwelling in them, all those who had proclaimed, "We are not God," and "He made us." My inner self recognized them all through the service of the outer. I, who was that inmost self, I, who was mind, knew them through the senses of my body (*Confessions* X, 6, 9).

So there you are. I too will show you my God from his works. And I won't go off far away, I won't send your unbelief to remote things you cannot, perhaps, grasp. I won't run through the works of my God in this sort of way: "He made things invisible, he made things visible, that is, *heaven and earth, the sea and all the things that are in them* (Ps 146:6)." I'm not dispatching you through many things; I'm going back to you yourself. You're certainly alive; you have a body, you have a spirit. The body's visible, the spirit's invisible. The body's the habitation, the spirit the inhabitant; the body's the vehicle, the spirit the user of the vehicle; the body's like a vehicle which has to be driven, the spirit the driver of your body. Look at the senses of your body; they're plainly like doors in your body, through which messages may be brought to your spirit living inside; eyes, ears, sense of smell, taste, touch, the arrangement of limbs. What's that inside, that you think with, that you give life to all these other things with? The whole of that, which you marvel at in yourself — the one who made that, that's who my God is (Sermon 223A, 4).

From the human person, as image of God, we can rise up to the divine Trinity, although we must bear in mind the degradation of human beings that has been caused by sin.

Although it is a great nature, it could be spoiled because it is not the greatest; and although it could be spoiled because it is not the greatest, yet because it is capable of the greatest nature and can share in it, it is a great nature still. Let us search then in this image of God for some special trinity that is *sui generis*, with the help of him who made us to his own image (*The Trinity* XIV, 6)

"For although the human mind is not of the same nature as God, still the image of that nature than which no nature is better is to be sought and found in that part of us than which our nature also has nothing better" (*The Trinity* XIV, 11). "Let it then remember its God to whose image it was made, and understand and love him. To put it in a word, let it worship the uncreated God, by whom it was created with a capacity for him and able to share in him. In this way it will reign in happiness where it reigns eternal. For this is called man's wisdom in such a way that it is also God's" (*The Trinity* XIV, 15).

As far as we could, we have also used the creation which God made to remind those who ask for reasons in such matters that as far as they can they should descry his invisible things by understanding them through the things that are made, and especially through the rational or intellectual creature which is made to the image of God, so that through this, as a kind of mirror, as far as they can and if they can, they might perceive in our memory, understanding and will that God is a Trinity. Anyone who has a lively intuition of these three (as divinely established in the nature of his mind) and of how great a thing it is that his mind has that by which even the eternal and unchanging nature can be recalled, beheld and desired — it is recalled by memory, beheld by intelligence, embraced by love — has thereby found the image of that supreme Trinity (*The Trinity* XV, 39).

Through Revelation

Human beings can — always, of course, with the help of God — move from the consideration of created reality to God the creator; through the image of God that makes his own spiritual being they can achieve a certain knowledge of the Trinity. Revelation will show this same God mercifully acting in history.

And so God took pity, and the one who *is*, and the one who said, *This is what you shall say to the children of Israel: He who is has sent me to you* (Ex 3:14), having spoken the name of his substance, goes on next to speak the name of his mercy. What is the name of his substance? *I am who am; you shall say to the children of Israel: He who is has sent me to you.* But Moses was a man, and was up to his neck in things that in comparison with that other one are not; he was on earth, he was in the flesh; and in that flesh he was a soul, he was a changeable nature, he was carrying the load of human frailty. I mean, when was he ever going to grasp what was said to him, *I am who am?* After all, the one who could not be seen was speaking to him by means of what his eyes could see, and the hidden God was using what could be seen as his instrument. (I mean, none of what Moses could see was God, because even the sound that proceeds from me, a mere human being, isn't the whole of my word; I've a word in my mind which makes no sound; the sound passes, the word remains.)

So when God said, *I am who am*, and *You shall say to the children of Israel: He who is has sent me to you, as though he was incapable of understanding what I am who am could mean, not to mention He who is has sent me to you* (or perhaps, if he himself could understand it, it would still have to be read to us, who wouldn't be able to understand it), immediately after the name of substance, he told him his name of mercy. It's as though he said to Moses, "You can't grasp what I said, *I am who am.* Your mind doesn't stand still, you are not unchangeable together with me, nor is your mind unchangeable. You have heard what I am; now hear what you can grasp, hear what you can hope in." *God said again to Moses, I am the God of Abraham, and the God of Isaac, and the God of Jacob* (Ex 3:15). "You cannot grasp the name of my substance; grasp the name of my mercy. *I am the God of Abraham and the God of Isaac and the God of Jacob.*" But what I am is eternal; Abraham, Isaac and Jacob, indeed, are eternal; or rather I shouldn't say eternal, but made eternal by him (Sermon 223A, 5).

Who Is God?

The Mystery of God

God is beyond description, so that we may more easily say what he is not than what he is. Think of the earth: God is not the earth. Think of the sea: God is not the sea. Think of all the beings — men and animals — on the land: God is not these. The beings of sea and air: God is not these. The sun and stars and moon that light the heavens: God is not these. Think of the Angels, Virtues, Powers, Archangels, Thrones, Seats, and Dominations: God is not these. But what is he? I can only say what he is not. Do you want to know what he is? I can only say what he is not. Do you want to know what he is? He is *what eye has not seen, ear has not heard, nor has it so much as dawned on the human heart* (1 Cor 2:9) (*Expositions of the Psalms* 86, 12).

Since we cannot say anything about God that really captures the reality of his being, we cannot even say that he is "ineffable," if this term is intended in any sense to define him! After having stated in its essential terms the mystery of the Trinity, Augustine asks:

Have I said anything, in my audible words, that is worthy of God? No: I realize that I simply wanted to speak; yet whatever I said is not what I wanted to say. How do I know that? Because God is ineffable, whereas if anything I said was ineffable, it could not have been said! Therefore, we cannot even claim that God is ineffable, because in saying that we are saying something. Thus there arises a contradiction in terms, and it is better to avoid that by silence than to try to get around it in words. Nonetheless, though we can say nothing worthy of him, God accepts the homage of the human voice, and wants us to find joy in praising him vocally. This is why we call him "God." It is not that he is made known by the sound of the word, but that anyone who knows the language will, on hearing the word, be moved to think of a perfect and immortal being (*Teaching Christianity* I, 6).

We deceive ourselves, therefore, if we think we have understood God.

> You are far, far above, I am far, far below. So what are we to say, brothers, about God? For if you have fully grasped what you want to say, it isn't God. If you have been able to comprehend it, you have comprehended something else instead of God. If you think you have been able to comprehend, your thoughts have deceived you. So he isn't this, if this is what you have understood; but if he is this, then you haven't understood it. So what is it you want to say, seeing you haven't been able to understand it? (Sermon 52, 16).

On the other hand, even this negative idea of God is no little achievement. "For it is no small part of knowledge, when we emerge from these depths to breathe in that sublime atmosphere, if before we can know what God is, we are at least able to know what he is not" (*The Trinity* VIII, 3).

If it is true that we can say nothing of God, it is also true that we can predicate of God every good found in creatures, provided we take the predication in a sense that leaves behind the materiality and limitations of creatures. Thus, for humans God is bread, water, light, and robe of immortality. "Everything can be said of God, but nothing can be said of him worthily. No penury could be greater. Seek an appropriate name, and you will find none. Try to speak in some little way of God, and you will find endless things to say" (*Homilies on the Gospel of John* 13, 5).

The conclusion to be drawn is that we ought humbly to confess our ignorance and to value as a tremendous gift the little knowledge given us of God.

> And such ignorance is more religious and devout than any presumption of knowledge. After all, we are talking about God; so why be surprised if you cannot grasp it? I mean, if you can grasp it, it isn't God. Let us rather make a devout confession of ignorance, instead of a brash profession of knowledge, Certainly it is great bliss to have a little touch or taste of God with the mind; but completely to grasp him, to comprehend him, is altogether impossible (Sermon 117, 5).

God is light and truth

O Light, Tobit saw you when despite the blindness of his carnal eyes he pointed out the path of life to his son, and strode unerringly ahead, borne by the feet of charity. Isaac saw you, though his bodily eyes were dimmed and closed by age, when true insight was granted him in blessing his sons, notwithstanding his inability to tell one from the other as he uttered his blessing. Jacob saw you when, likewise blinded by advanced age, he beheld by the radiant vision of his heart the tribes of the people that was to be, prefigured in his sons; and when, stretching out crossed hands in a gesture full of mystery, he laid them on his grandsons, Joseph's children, not in the way indicated by their father, who saw only the externals, but as he himself judged to be right by the vision that guided him within. All these enjoyed the same Light, the Light that is one in itself and unites all who see and love it (*Confessions* X, 34, 52).

Augustine invokes God as light and truth,[4] because light and truth are one and the same thing in the Bible. "Come, see if you can, O *soul weighed down with the body that decays*[5] and burdened with many and variable earthy thoughts, come see it if you can — God is truth. For it is written *that God is light* (I Jn 1:5) not such as these eyes see, but such as the mind sees when it hears *he is truth*" (*The Trinity* VIII, 3).

"The brightness of God is indescribable light, a changeless fountain of light, perfect truth, wisdom ever abiding in itself yet renewing all things.[6] Such is the very substance of God" (*Expositions of the Psalms* 110).

But we are victims of our passions, and should not delude ourselves into thinking we understand God when we say that God is truth. The passage I have just quoted from *The Trinity* goes on to say:

Do not ask what truth is; immediately a fog of bodily images and a cloud of fancies will get in your way and disturb the bright fair weather that burst on you the first instant when I said "truth." Come, hold it in that first moment in which so to speak you caught a flash from the corner of your eye when the word "truth" was spoken, stay there if you can. But you cannot; you slide back into these familiar and earthly things. And what weight is it, I ask, that drags you back but the birdlime of greed for the filthy junk you have picked up on your wayward wanderings? (*The Trinity* VIII, 3).

God enlightens us first of all by giving us intelligence, as Augustine argues from Psalm 119:73: *Give me discernment*.

God, being *light* (Jn 1:4, 9), directly enlightens devout minds, so that they may understand the divine things said to them or shown to them. . . . God it is who has made our minds rational and intellectual, so that it may be able to receive his light. . . . He himself so illumines that mind that it can not only perceive what the truth shows it but even advance and perceive the truth itself (*Expositions of the Psalms* 119, XVIII, 4). "No creature, however rational and intellectual, is enlightened by itself, but only by participation in eternal truth" (*Expositions of the Psalms* 119, XXIII, 1).

God is "the Father of intelligible light, Father of our awakening and enlightenment." He is "the truth, in whom and by whom and through whom all true things are true." He is "the intelligible light in whom and by whom and through whom all intelligible things are intelligible" (*Soliloquies* I, 2-3).

The statement that God is light for us is to be taken in an even deeper sense. Out of goodness, God communicates his light and truth to us, so that it may be a source of happiness within us.

Following God means desiring happiness; the attainment of God is this happiness itself. We follow him, however, by loving him, and we attain him, not in the sense that we become identical with him but in the sense that we draw close to him in a wonderful, intelligible contact, being enlightened by and enfolded in his truth and holiness. for he is the very light, and we may be enlightened by him (*The Catholic Way of Life* I, 18).

After all, is it is a great thing to see the light of the heavens; how much greater is it to see the light of God. Because that is what the eyes of the heart are cured for, for that they are opened, for that purified, to see the light which is God. *God is light*, says scripture, *and there is no darkness in him at all* (1 Jn 1:5); and the Lord says in the gospel, *Blessed are the heart-pure, because they shall see God* (Mt 5:8) (Sermon 136C, 1).

We are therefore invited to draw near to God the light so that he may be enlightened.

Brothers and sisters, consider the condition of the human soul. It has no light or strength from itself. The beauty to be found in the soul is virtue and wisdom; but the soul is not wise of itself nor strong of itself; light and virtue are not native to it. There is a source and fountain of virtue; there is a root of wisdom; there is, if I may so put it, a region of changeless truth. If the soul moves away from this, it is darkened; if it draws near, it is en-

lightened. Approach it then and be enlightened (see Ps 34:6), for
if you move away you grow dark (*Expositions of the Psalms* 59, 1,
18).

Only if we are united to God do we live in light; when separated
from him, we fall back into darkness.

Such a creature's good is to hold fast to you always,[7] lest by
turning away it lose the light it acquired by its conversion, and
slip back into the old life, dark and abysmal. We ourselves, who
in respect of our souls are also your spiritual creatures, were
once turned away from you who are our Light; in that earlier
life we were darkness, and even now we labour in our residual
gloom, until in your only Son we become your righteousness;
for that righteousness is like God's high and holy mountains,
while your judgments, which were all the being we then had, are
like the deep (*Confessions* XIII, 2, 3).

God is the supreme truth and gives answer to all who harken to him
with good will.

O Truth, you hold sovereign sway over all who turn to you for
counsel, and to all of them you respond at the same time, however diverse their pleas. Clear is your response, but not all hear
it clearly. They all appeal to you about what they want, but do
not always hear what they want to hear. Your best servant is
the one who is less intent on hearing from you what accords
with his own will, and more on embracing with his will what he
has heard from you (*Confessions* X, 26, 37).

Augustine blames himself for not having listened with good will.

So now under the three headings of temptation I have taken
stock of the sickly state to which my sins have reduced me, and
I have called upon your right hand for saving help. I have seen
your blazing splendour, but with a wounded heart; I was beaten
back, and I asked, "Can anyone reach that?" I was flung far out
of your sight. You are the Truth, sovereign over all. I did not
want to lose you, but in my greed I thought to possess falsehood
along with you, just as no one wants to tell lies in such a way
that he loses his own sense of what is true. That was why I lost
you, for you did not consent to be possessed in consort with a
lie (*Confessions* X, 41, 66).

Let religion bind us, then, to the one and all-powerful God. For
no creature stands between this mind of ours with which we
understand him as Father, and the truth, that is, the interior light
by which we understand him. Let us therefore venerate also the

truth itself which is in him and with him without any dissimilarity and is the form of all things which were made by one creator and tend toward one end (*True Religion* 55, 113).

God is beauty

God is "beauty ever old and ever new!" (*Confessions* X, 27, 38); "very beautiful and very powerful" (*Confessions* I, 4, 4); "most beautiful of all things" (*Confessions* II, 6, 12); and "the beauty in which all beauty shares" (*Confessions* III, 6, 10).

It is because he is truth that God is also beauty. Cicero was right when he saw that "truth has an incorporeal form and beauty which dwell within the soul and enable us to ascribe beauty to all the deeds of the wise. Therefore God must be supremely beautiful, since nothing can be more beautiful than changeless, intelligible truth" (*Letter* 118, 23).

Because he is justice, God is, once again, beauty as well.

If we must avoid thinking of God's justice as being like ours (for the light which enlightens is incomparably superior to that which is enlightened by it), how much more must we avoid thinking of it as something inferior to and, in a way, colorless by comparison with ours! Now, for those who live rightly and wisely, what is justice, or any other virtue, in us but a beauty of the interior self? Moreover, it is undoubtedly by reason of this beauty that we are made in the image of God, rather than by reason of our bodies. . . . It is through a spiritual gift, such as justice, that we say or know or desire the mind to be beautiful; and it is through such beauty that we are remade in the image of God. Therefore, the beauty which formed us and now re-forms us in his image must not be thought of as having a bodily measure; and we must think that God is incomparably more beautiful than the souls of holy persons because he is incomparably more holy than they (*Letter* 120, 20).

God is the creator and source of all beauty. He "created from nothing this world which all see to be very beautiful"; he is "the father of what is good and beautiful"; he is himself "the good and the beautiful in whom and by whom and through whom all else is good and beautiful" (*Soliloquies* I, 2-3).

"Heaven and earth exist; they cry out that they were made, for they change and vary. . . . You made them, Lord, and you must be beautiful, since they are beautiful; you must be good, since they are good; you must exist, since they exist. But they are not beautiful or good as you are, nor do they exist as you exist, for, compared to you, their creator, they are not beautiful or good nor do they exist" (*Confessions* XI, 4, 6).

"All things are beautiful because you made them, but you who made them all are indescribably more beautiful than they" (*Confessions* XIII, 20, 28).

> Just cast your minds, dearly beloved, over the whole of creation, heaven, earth, sea, everything in heaven, everything on earth, everything in the sea; how beautiful they are, how wonderful, how properly and harmoniously arranged! Do these things move you at all? Of course they do. Why? Because they are beautiful. So what about the one who made them? I imagine you would be absolutely stunned if you could see the beauty of the angels. So what about the creator of the angels? (Sermon 19, 5)

God's beauty, though essentially spiritual, is thus reflected and revealed to some extent in material realities. Even the body

> is endowed with a certain harmony between its parts, for otherwise it would not exist at all. Therefore the body too was made by him who is the source of all harmony. The body enjoys a peace deriving from its form, and without that peace it would not exist at all. Therefore the body was created by him from whom all peace comes and who is the uncreated form, superior in beauty to all other forms. The body has a certain beauty, without which it would not be a body. If, then, you ask who made the body, you are asking about him who is the most beautiful being of all. For all beauty derives from him. And who can that being be, except the one God, the one truth, the one salvation of all, the first and supreme essence from whom everything that is derives its existence such as it is, for to the extent that any being exists, it is good (*True Religion* II, 21).

> Brothers and sisters, reflect on his beauty. He made the things you see and love. If they are beautiful, what must he be? If they are great, how great is he? From the things we love here on earth, let us arouse in ourselves a greater desire for him. Let us scorn earthly things and love him, so that by that very love we may cleanse our hearts, and our hearts, once cleansed, may see his face (*Expositions of the Psalms* 85, 9).

"If splendid scenes and beauty delight us, let us yearn to see Wisdom itself that *reaches from end to end mightily and governs all things well* (Wis 8:1). For what could be more wonderful than the incorporeal power that creates and governs the corporeal world? What more beautiful than he who orders and adorns it?" (*True Religion* 51, 100).

The contemplation of supreme beauty makes us forget lesser realities. "When I set before the eyes of my heart, such as they are, the intelligible beauty of him from whose mouth no falsehood can come, then, although the growing radiance of truth leaves me weak and trembling, I am so fired with love of such great beauty that I can only scorn the human things that distract me from its contemplation" (*Against Lying* 36).

It was the happy lot of the Eastern monks to devote themselves to that experience. "Completely separated from the sight of other men and content with water and the bread that is brought to them from time to time, they dwell in utterly deserted areas. Here they enjoy converse with God to whom they are united by purity of heart, and they are blessed with contemplation of his beauty which cannot be perceived except by saintly minds" (*The Catholic Way of Life* I, 66).

But "woe to you and your love, if you even entertain the notion that there may be something more beautiful than he from whom all beauty comes, and it prevents you from thinking of him!" (*Expositions of the Psalms* 44, 16).

God is power

When your saints bless you, what do you say? *Let them discourse of the glory of your kingdom and speak of your might* (Ps 145:11). How powerful the God who made the earth and filled it with good things! How powerful the God who gave each living thing its own kind of life and sowed the earth with varied seeds that they might produce such different fruits and beautiful trees! How powerful God is, and how great! Ask, and creation answers. And hearing creation's answer, its confession, as it were, do you, saint of God, bless him and speak of his might (*Expositions of the Psalms* 145, 14).

Need we be surprised if God produces visible and sensible effects as he pleases in sky and earth, sea and air, to signify and show himself as he knows best, without the very substance of his being ever appearing immediately manifest, since it is altogether changeless. . . . It is by the power of God administering the whole spiritual and corporeal universe that on certain days every year the waters of the sea are summoned and poured out as rain on the face of the earth. . . . So too the recurrent phenomena of thunder and lightning are the work of God. . . . Again, who but God draws up the sap from the roots of the vine into the grape clusters and makes wine, *God who gives the increase*, though man *plants and waters* (1 Cor 3:7)? . . . And certainly all vegetation and all animal bodies are produced and fashioned from one common material element of earth, and who makes them if not the one who commanded the earth to

bring them forth, who also controls and activates what he created by the same word of command (*The Trinity* III, 10-11).

God is goodness

This statement is true first of all in the metaphysical sense, according
to which "everything that exists, insofar as it exists, is good" (*True
Religion* 21), or "any degree of existence, however small, is good, since
the supreme good is to exist in the best possible way" (*ibid.*, 35).

From "goodness" in the metaphysical sense to "goodness" in the
moral sense is an easy step.

> The Lord is good! (Ps 135:3). But he is not good in the way the
> things he made are good. God indeed made all things *very good*
> (Gn 1:31) — not just good, but very good. Heaven and earth
> and all that they contain he created good; he made them very
> good. If he made all these things good, then what is he like who
> made them? . . . All good things he made; he himself is good, but
> no one made him. He is good by his own native goodness, not
> by a share in someone else's goodness. . . . I experience an in-
> describable sweetness when I hear the words: 'The Lord is
> good!' I contemplate all the things I see outside and I consider
> that all come from him; then, even though they please, I go be-
> yond them to him from whom they come, in order that I may
> realize that *the Lord is good.*
>
> As I approach him to the extent that I can, I find him within me
> and above me, for his goodness is such that he does not need
> all these things in order to be good. Consequently, I do not
> praise all these things without praising him as well, but I find that
> even without these things he is perfect and lacks nothing, that
> he is changeless, not seeking good from anyone that he may be
> increased nor fearing evil from anyone lest he be diminished.
> What more can I say? In creation I find the heavens, the sun,
> moon, and stars, to be good; I find the earth and what is born
> within and rises from its roots to be good; I find all that walks
> and moves, or flies in the air or swims in the waters to be good.
> I proclaim human beings good, for *good persons produce good
> from their store of goodness* (Mt 12:35). And I call the angels good
> who did not fall through pride and become devils, but cleaved
> in obedience to him who made them.
>
> All these things, then, I proclaim good, but each in its limited
> way: good heavens, good angels, good human beings. But when
> I come to God, I think it better to say simply *good.* The Lord
> Jesus Christ himself said: *No one is good but God alone* (Mk
> 10:18). Was he not perhaps urging us to reflect and distinguish

between the good which is good by reason of another good, and the good which is good by itself? (*Expositions of the Psalms* 135, 3-4).

God reveals his goodness in the gifts he lavishes on us, to the point of giving his very self.

He who has given you everything — he who made you be and has provided you, along with your fellows even though they be evil, sun, and rain, fruits and fountains, life, health, and so many consolations — has something in reserve for you which he will give to you alone. What can he have in store for you but his very self? . . . God is ours! But is there anyone whose God he is not? True enough, but he does not belong to all in the same way! He belongs most of all to us who live upon him as our bread. Let him be our inheritance and possession! (*Expositions of the Psalms* 33, *Exposition* 2, II, 16-17).

God is good and merciful to all, be they virtuous or evil and this is true even when he sends us suffering.

Good is the Lord (Lam 3:25) and his mercy is poured out everywhere. Here is a very evident proof of his great love for those who believe and trust in him and love him and one another, as well as of the future gifts he has in store for them: to those who have neither faith nor hope nor love and persevere to the end in bad will he threatens eternal fire along with the devil, yet in this world he bestows rich blessings upon them, for *his sun rises on the bad and the good, he rains on the just and the unjust* (Mt 5:45). A brief reference is made to these gifts of nature in order to remind us of many others. Who, in fact, can number the many benefits and freely given blessings which the wicked receive in this life from him whom they scorn? One of the greatest gifts is the trials which he mixes, like a good physician, with the pleasures of this world. These trials are examples by which God warns the wicked to flee from the wrath to come[8] while they can, that is, during this life, and to bring their lives into accord with the word of God of which they have made an enemy by their evil ways.[9] Hence, there are good things which the Lord God in his mercy does not give to human beings, while even trials coming from him are a blessing. Prosperity is a gift of God as consoler, while adversity is the gift of God as admonisher. If he consoles even the wicked, as I have said, then what must he be preparing for those who patiently await him[10] (Letter 210, 1).

The goodness of God to us is shown most of all in the work of redemption. "To begin with, I was nothing, and he made me; I had got lost, and he looked for me; looked for me and found me; I was a captive and he redeemed me; having bought me, he set me free; from a slave he made me into a brother. *What shall I render to the Lord?*" (Sermon 254, 6).

God is good because he is a father; he is so good in fact that he wants to become our father by the gift of adoption.

> *I said: You are gods, all of you sons of the Most High; yet like human beings you shall die, and fall like any prince* (Ps 82:7). It is evident, then, that he is calling human beings gods, not because they are born of his substance but because his grace deifies them. For he who makes holy is the one who is holy by his own nature, not because of someone else; and he who deifies is the one who is God by his own nature and not because he shares in someone else's. Now, he who makes holy is he who deifies, for in justifying human beings he also makes them sons of God. *He empowered them to become children of God* (Jn 1:12). If we have become the children of God, then we have become gods; but this is due to the grace of God who adopts us, not to the nature of God as when he begets his own Son (*Expositions of the Psalms* 50, 2).

Adoption as children of God came to us through the incarnation, when the Son of God became a son of man. "I have given human beings the power to do good; that power they have from me, not from themselves, for of themselves they are wicked. They are the children of men when they do evil, but my children when they do good. — This, then, is what God does: he makes children of God out of children of men, because he first made the Son of God a man" (*Expositions of the Psalms* 53, 6).

The Christian should find great joy in the divine fatherhood, Augustine observes in a sermon in which he is explaining the Creed to catechumens. "*I believe in God the Father almighty*. Notice how quickly it's said, and how much it's worth. He's God, and he's Father; God in power, Father in goodness. How lucky we are, to have discovered that our God is our Father! So let us believe in him, and promise ourselves everything from his kindness and mercy, because he is almighty. That's why we believe in God the Father almighty" (Sermon 213, 2).

God is life

> There is no life that is not from God, for God is supreme life and the source of life; nor is any life evil insofar as it is life, but only insofar as it tends toward death" (*True Religion* 21). In God "is supreme and primordial life, such that it is not one thing to live and another to be, but being and living are the same; and where there is supreme and primordial understanding is identi-

cal with living, identical with all things, being as it were one perfect Word to which nothing is lacking, which is like the art of
the almighty and wise God, full of all the living and unchanging
ideas, which are all one in it, as it is one from the one with
whom it is one" (*The Trinity* VI, 11). God is "the true and supreme life, in whom and by whom and through whom all things
live which truly and supremely live. . . . To depart from him is
to die; to return to him is to come back to life; to dwell in him
is to live (*Soliloquies* I, 3).

"You are the life of souls, the life of lives; you live your very being
and do not change, O life of my soul" (*Confessions* III, 6, 10). At the
dawn of creation, "your incorruptible and changeless will, that was
sufficient unto itself, reached out to the life you had made. For this life,
to live is not the same as to live happily, for it lives even when it is
tossed about in its own darkness. It must turn to its creator and live
ever closer to the fountain of life and see light in his light,[11] if it is to
be perfect, enlightened, and happy" (*Confessions* XIII, 4, 5). Augustine
speaks thus to the soul: "You energize the mass of your body by giving
it life — something no body can do for another body. But God is even
for you, O soul, the life of life itself" (*Confessions* X, 6, 10). "Let me seek
you, that my soul may life. For my body lives by my soul, and my soul
lives by you" (*Confessions* X, 20, 29).

"Death for your body means losing its life, and death for your soul
means losing its life. The life of your body is your soul, the life of your
soul is your God. As the body dies because it loses its soul, so the soul
dies because it loses God who is its life" (*Homilies on the Gospel of John*
47, 8). "The soul is nothing by itself, and whatever being it has is from
God. If it remains in its own proper order, it is vivified in mind and
conscience by the presence of God" (*Music* VI, 40).

> When the soul reaches up to something not itself but superior
> to itself, to that from which it derives its own being, then it
> receives wisdom, holiness, and piety. As long as it lacked these,
> it was dead, and did not possess the life by which it itself would
> be alive, but only the life by which it could enliven the body. For
> there is one power in the soul by which it enlivens the body, and
> another by which it is itself made alive. The soul is superior to
> the body, but God is superior to the soul. The soul therefore
> continues to be the life of the body even when it is itself foolish,
> unholy, and wicked. The soul's own life is God; just as the soul,
> when in the body, communicates energy, beauty, mobility, and
> functions to the body, so God, when in the soul, communicates
> wisdom, piety, holiness, and love to it (*Homilies on the Gospel of
> John* 19, 12).

God is joy and blessedness

God is "the blessedness in which and by which and through which all blessed beings have blessedness" (*Soliloquies* I, 3).

"And we human beings are made blessed by our hearts just brushing against that which abides always blessed; and that is itself eternal blessedness; and that by which we are made alive is eternal life; that by which we are made wise is perfect wisdom; that by which we are enlightened is eternal light" (Sermon 117, 5).

"Far be from my heart, Lord, far from the heart of your servant who is confessing to you, the thought that any joy whatsoever could make me happy! For there is a joy not given to the wicked but only to those who serve you without looking for reward; you yourself are their joy. And the happy life is to rejoice in you, because of you, and for your sake" (*Confessions* X, 22, 32).

Rise up to him! (Erige te ad illum)

It is evidently impossible, in a brief conclusion to this chapter, to treat fully the theme of one's duties toward God. Augustine spoke of these, explicitly or implicitly, every time he spoke of God. Later on in this book, in my discussion of love, I will have to deal with the first and most important duty we have toward God. For the rest, one's duty to God is concertized, for Augustine, in the program of Christian life which he is proposing to us in the selections being presented in this book. At this point, I shall simply gather together a few of his thoughts and exhortations in which he is concerned with the decisive orientation of the Christian's heart toward God.

Submission to God

"So God puts everything under man, man under himself. You want everything God has made to be under you, see to it you yourself are under God. It's the last word in impudence for you to require the lower creation to be beneath you, when you won't even acknowledge him who created you to be your superior. God, then, so arranged what he created that he placed his image beneath himself and everything else under that. Accept him, and you will trample on man. Don't despise him, and then let anyone who likes to despise you" (Sermon 20A, 3).

If the rational soul serves the creator by and through whom it was made and for whom it is destined, everything else will serve it: our ultimate life, which is so close to the soul and is the instrument by which it rules the body; the body itself, which is the lowest nature and essence in us and which the soul will rule entirely as it wishes, holding it in total submission and receiving no opposition from it, since the soul will not be looking for its happiness from the body nor by means of the body, but directly from God (*True Religion* 44, 82).

Rising up to God

"Above you there is only the creator. Rise up to him! Do not despair and say: 'He is too far above me!' The gold you may be seeking is far more difficult to obtain, for even though you want it badly, you may not obtain it, whereas if you want God, you have him!" (*Expositions of the Psalms* 33, Exposition 2, II, 16).

"If God is good because he has given you all these gifts, how much happier you will be when he shall have given you his very self! You have asked him for so many gifts; I beg you, ask him for himself! For his gifts are not more filled with delights than he himself is, nor are they at all comparable to him" (*Expositions of the Psalms* 145, 22).

The soul is called to enter into union with God.

> There is such potency in this image of God in it that it is capable of cleaving to him whose image it is. It is so arranged in the order of natures — not an order of place — that there is nothing above it except him. And then when it totally cleaves to him it will be one spirit, as the apostle testifies when he says, *Whoever cleaves to the Lord is one spirit* (1 Cor 6:17). This will come about with the mind attaining to a share of his nature, truth, and happiness, not with him growing in his own nature, truth, and happiness. So when it blissfully cleaves to that nature, it will see as unchangeable in it everything that it sees. Then as divine scripture promises, its desire will be filled with good things, with unchangeable good things, with the Trinity its God whose image it is, and to save it from ever again being violated anywhere it will be in the hidden place of his countenance, so filled with his plenty that sinning can never delight it again (*The Trinity* XIV, 20).

"*Show us the Father and it suffices us;* but *Am I with you all this time,* came the answer, *and you do not know me? Whoever has seen me has also seen the Father* (Jn 14:8-9). God, Father, Son and Holy Spirit, is all things. Quite rightly does he alone suffice. If we must be avaricious, let us love him. If we desire wealth, let us desire him. He alone will be able to satisfy us, about whom it says, *Who satisfies your desire with good things* (Ps 103:5)" (Sermon 177, 9).

"Listen to me, you that are poor; what haven't you got, if you've got God? Listen to me, you that are rich; what have you got, if you haven't got God?" (Sermon 311, 15). "If a rich man hasn't got God, what has he got? Don't look for anything else from God, except God. Love him for nothing, desire from him only himself. Don't be afraid of going without; he gives himself to us, and that is enough for us. May he give himself to us, and let that be enough for us. Listen to the apostle Philip in the gospel: *Lord, show us the Father, and that is enough for us* (Jn 14:8)" (Sermon 331, 4).

NOTES

1. See Ps 18:29.
2. See Is 58:10.
3. See Rom 1:20.
4. See *Confessions* X, 21, 30.
5. See Wis 9:15.
6. See Wis 7:27.
7. See Ps 73:28.
8. See Mt 3:7.
9. See Mt 5:25.
10. See Is 64:4.
11. See Ps 36:10.

CHAPTER 5

JESUS CHRIST

Without attempting to be complete or to follow a strictly logical sequence, I shall review some of the "names" (in the patristic tradition of *epinoiai* or "conceptions") which recur in Augustine when he would describe the mission and work of our Lord Jesus Christ. Then, by way of conclusion, I shall offer a few passages in which the bishop speaks of the various duties of the Christian toward Christ which correspond to the various aspects under which Christ encounters us.

Christ Is the Way

"We must run, then, and run in the way. If we run but not on the path, we run in vain and win nothing but woe; the farther we are from the path, the further we go astray. What is the way on which we are to run? Christ tells us: *I am the way!* And what is the country to which we run? Christ tells us again: *I am the truth.* You run by way of him, you run to him, you rest in him. So that we might run by way of him, he reached out to us, for we were far off in exile" (*Homilies on the First Letter of John* 10, 1).

Augustine had himself experienced this upon his reading of the neo-Platonists.

> Being instructed to seek incorporeal truth, I saw your invisible realities, *recognized through the things* you *made* (Rom 1:20), but I was checked by my failures to ascend to you and realized what the darkness in my soul would not allow me to contemplate. I was certain that you exist and are infinite, even though not extended in finite or infinite space; that you are always identical with yourself, without becoming different or changing in any part or by any movement, whereas all other beings derive from you, as is proved by the undeniable fact that they exist. Of all this I was certain, but I was still too weak to enjoy you. I talked,

of course, like an expert, but if I had not sought your way in Christ our Savior I would not have been an expert (*peritus*) but a man on the road to ruin (*periturus*) (*Confessions* VII, 20, 26).

Since, then, we are entered upon a way which does not pass through places but through interior dispositions and which was blocked by the wickedness of past sin as by a thorny hedge, what greater act of generosity and mercy could he have done who made himself the way of our return, than to forgive all the sins of those who turn to him? When set upon the cross, he removed for our sake all the serious barriers set upon the road of our homecoming (*Teaching Christianity* I, 16).

"That's why the Lord Christ was prepared in all circumstances to humble himself; he was showing us the way — provided, of course, we are prepared to proceed along it. . . . Christ as God is the home country we are going to; Christ as man is the way we are going by. It's to him we are going, by him we are going; why are we afraid of going wrong?" (Sermon 123, 1-3).

"Christ became the way for us, and do we despair of arriving? This way cannot be closed down, cannot be cut, cannot be broken up by rain or floods, nor blocked by bandits. Walk securely in Christ without anxiety; walk. Don't stumble, don't fall, don't look back, don't stick on the road, don't wander away from the road. Only beware of all these things, and you have arrived" (Sermon 170, 11).

Christ Is the Savior
The basic truth of the Christian life

"Consider closely, brothers, the two births: that of Adam and that of Christ. Both of these figures are men; but one of them is a man-human, the other is a man-God. Because of the man-man we are sinners; because of the man-God we are justified. The one birth cast us down into death; the other birth raised us up into life. The one brought sin in its wake; the other frees us from sin. For Christ came as a human being to do away with the sins of humanity" (*Homilies on the First Letter of John* 4, 11).

"*For the Son of man came to seek and to save what had got lost* (Lk 19:10). If man had not got lost, the Son of man would not have come. So man had got lost, God did come as man, and man was found. Man had got lost through free will; God came as man through the grace that sets free" (Sermon 174, 2).

How did Christ save us?

The "wonderful exchange"

Because he did not refuse to take *the form of a slave* (Phil 2:7), he who did not disdain to take us into himself also did not disdain to transform us into himself and to speak in our language [in the Psalm in which Augustine is preaching] so that we in turn might be able to speak in his language. And in fact this wonderful exchange took place, a divine trade as it were, an exchange of goods effected in this world by the divine merchant. He came to receive contempt and bestow honors, to drink the cup of suffering and give salvation, to undergo death and give life. Therefore, as he was about to die in the human nature he had received from us, he experienced dread, not in himself but in us; for, as he had said, his soul was sad to the point of dying (see Mt 26:38), and all of us with him. For, without him we are nothing; but in him we are both Christ and ourselves (*Expositions of the Psalms* 31, *Exposition* 2, I, 3).

"Our fellow-citizen"

So where are we moving to? To our home country. What is our home country? Jerusalem, mother of the faithful, mother of the living. That is where we are going. That is our end. And because we didn't know the way, the chief citizen of this city made himself into the way. We didn't know which way to go. The road had heaven knows how many twists and turns, thorny and stony and extremely difficult. The leader himself, who is the prince there, came down here; he came down to seek out the citizens of that city. We had all gone astray, you see, and though we are citizens of Jerusalem we have become citizens of Babylon, we have become sons of confusion: Babylon means confusion. He came down here looking for his citizens, and he became our fellow-citizen. We didn't know this city, we didn't know this province. But because we were not coming to it, he came down here to his citizens, and became a citizen himself, not to conspire with us but to take our part. He came down here. How did he come down? In the form of a servant. God walked here among us as a man. You see, if he had been only a man, he would not have led us through to God. If he had only been God, he would not have been joined to men (*Sermon* 16A, 9).

Suffering and dying

"What is a human wretch to do? Who will free him from this death-laden body, if not your grace, given through Jesus Christ our Lord,[1] whom you have begotten coeternal with yourself and created at the beginning of all your works? In him the ruler of this world found nothing that deserved death, yet slew him all the same; and so the record of debt that stood against us was annulled" (*Confessions* VII, 21, 27).

"Do not scorn Christ who for your sake was born in the flesh and clothed in the rags of mortality; for your sake he experienced hunger and thirst and sat weary beside the well; for your sake he slept the sleep of exhaustion in the boat; for your sake he heard unmerited insults; for your sake he did not turn away from spittle; for your sake he endured blows on the face; for your sake he hung on the cross; for your sake he gave up his life, and for your sake he was laid in the tomb" (*Sermon on Christian Discipline* 15).

> How is it that Christ says, *You have torn up my sacking, and have girded me with joy* (Ps 30:11)? His sacking was *the likeness of the flesh of sin* (Rom 8:3). Don't regard his talking about *my sacking* as cheap stuff; that's where your price was being kept. *You have torn up my sacking.* It's to this sacking that we have fled for refuge. *You have torn up my sacking.* It was in his passion that the sack was torn open. So how can it be said to God the Father, *You have torn up my sacking?* . . . because *he did not spare his own Son, but handed him over for us all* (Rom 8:32).

> Through the Jews, you see, who were quite unaware of it, he achieved what would redeem them when they were fully aware of it, and would confound them when they denied it. I mean, they are quite unaware of the good they wrought for us by their evil act. The sack was hung up, and it's as though the godless rejoiced. The persecutor tore open the sack with his lance, and the redeemer poured out the price he paid for us. Let Christ the redeemer sing, let Judas the seller groan, let the Jews, the buyers, blush for shame. Look, there you are; Judas sold him, the Jews bought him, they made a bad bargain, both lost out on it, both seller and buyers ruined themselves by it. You wanted to be buyers; how much better to have been bought and redeemed! He sold, they bought; a truly luckless transaction. They didn't have the price, and he didn't have Christ. To him I say, "Where is the money you received?" To them I say, "Where are the goods you bought?" To him I say, "When you sold, you cheated yourself." Jump for joy, Christian, at the deal struck by your enemies; you are the one who gained by it. What that man

sold and they bought, you, yes you, have acquired. Let our head, then, say, let the head slain for the body, dedicated for the body, say; let him say, let us listen: *You have torn up my sacking, and have girded me with joy*; that is, you have torn up my mortality and girded me with immortality and imperishability (Sermon 336, 4-5).

Christ is the Mediator

In your unfathomable mercy you first gave the humble certain pointers to the true Mediator, and then sent him, that by his example they might learn even a humility like his. This Mediator between God and humankind, the man Christ Jesus, appeared to stand between mortal sinners and the God who is immortal and just: like us he was mortal, but like God he was just. Now the wage due to justice is life and peace; and so through the justice whereby he was one with God he broke the power of death on behalf of malefactors rendered just, using that very death to which he willed to be liable along with them. He was pointed out to holy people under the old dispensation that they might be saved through faith in his future passion, as we are through faith in that passion now accomplished. Only in virtue of his humanity is he the Mediator; in his nature as the Word he does not stand between us and God, for he is God's equal,[2] God with God,[3] and with him one only God (*Confessions* X, 43, 68-69).

Our Lord and Savior Jesus Christ, in whom lies all our hope of eternal salvation, though he was God became man for this reason, that man, having put himself far away from God, should not think he had been left far off and deserted. So he became our mediator, and thus after a fashion brought to an end the time of the distance which separated us from God, so that through him we might not remain far off, but could even draw near. Nothing, you see, is so closely joined together as the Word and God; again, nothing is so closely joined together as flesh and man. So, since the Word and God was a long way away from flesh and man, the Word became flesh, and joined man to God (Sermon 313E, 1).

To taste the sweetness of God was beyond your powers, for it was distant from you and too far above you, while you were too far down and lying in the depths. Into this immense distance the mediator was sent. You, being human, could not reach God; therefore God became human, so that you, as human beings, who could not reach God, might reach another human being and through him come to God. He who was sent became *the mediator between God and humanity, the man Christ Jesus* (1 Tm 2:5). If he had been but a human being, you would be following one like yourself and would never reach God. If he were only God, you would not understand what you are not and so would never reach God. But God became human, so that by following a human being, which you could do, you might reach God, which you could not. He is our mediator (*Expositions of the Psalms* 135, 5).

"*For there is one God, and one mediator of God and men, the man Christ Jesus* (1 Tm 2:5). If you weren't lying there, half dead, you would have no need of a mediator; but because you are lying there, and cannot get up, God has somehow stretched out his arm to you as a mediator" (Sermon 156, 5).

According to Paul, Christ as mediator is our peace. *Seek peace, and follow it* (Ps 94:13-14).

Where is it? Where am I to follow? Which way has it gone by? Which way has it gone, for me to follow?" It has gone your way, but it didn't stay with you. Who am I talking to? To the human race, not to any one of you , but to the human race. Peace itself passed by way of the human race. As it passed by, the blind man cried out in yesterday's reading. And where did it go? First see what peace is, then see where it has gone, then follow it. What is peace? Listen to the apostle, he was talking about Christ: *He is our peace, who made both into one* (Eph 2:14) So peace is Christ. Where did it go? *He was crucified and buried, he rose from the dead, he ascended into heaven.* There you have where peace went. "How am I to follow it?" Lift up your heart. Listen how you should follow; every day you hear it briefly when you are told *Lift up your heart*. Think about it more deeply, and there you are, following. Listen also, however, more widely, in order to follow true peace, your peace, the peace which for your sake endured war, the peace which while enduring war for your sake prayed for the enemies of peace, and said as it hung there, *Father, forgive them, for they do not know what they are doing* (Lk 23:46). It was war, and peace was flowing from the cross. It was flowing, but what about afterward? He ascended into heaven. Seek peace — and how are you to follow? Listen to the apostle: *If you have risen with Christ, seek the things that are above where Christ is, seated at God's right hand; savor the things that are above, not those that are on earth. For you are dead, and your life is hidden with Christ in God. When Christ appears, your life, then you too will appear with him in glory* (Sermon 25, 7).

Christ Is the Priest

[Father all-kind], how you loved us, for whose sake he who deemed it no robbery to be your equal was made subservient, even to the point of dying on the cross! Alone of all he was free among the dead, for he had power to lay down his life and power to retrieve it.[4] For our sake he stood to you as both victor and victim, and victor because victim; for us he stood to you as priest and sacrifice, and priest because sacrifice, making us sons and daughters to you instead of servants by being born of you to serve us. With good reason is there solid hope for me in him, because you will heal all my infirmities[5] through him who sits at your right hand[6] and intercedes for us. Were it not so, I would despair. Many and grave are those infirmities, many and grave; but wider-reaching is your healing power. We might have despaired, thinking your Word remote from any conjunction with humankind, had he not become flesh and made his dwelling among us (*Confessions* X, 43, 69).

What did the Lord receive from you? Flesh. What was he who came? The Word of God, who existed before all things and through whom all things were made. But in order to receive something from you *the Word became flesh and made his dwelling among us* (Jn 1:14). He received from you what he would offer for you, just as a priest receives a gift from you to be offered for you, when you wish to appease the Lord for your sins. It has already happened, and that is how it happened. Our priest received from us the gift he would offer for us. For he took flesh from us, and in that flesh became a victim, a holocaust, a sacrifice. In his passion he became a sacrifice; in his resurrection he gave new life to what had been slain and then offered it to God as your first fruits. He says to you: "All that is yours is now consecrated, once these first fruits of yours are given to God." Have hope, therefore, that what happened in your first fruits will happen in you as well (*Expositions of the Psalms* 130, 7).

"The true mediator, in taking the *form of a slave* (Phil 2:6), became *mediator between God and men, the man Christ Jesus* (1 Tm 2:5). In the form of God he received sacrifice along with the Father with whom he is one God; in the form of a slave he wanted to be a sacrifice as well as receive it, so that henceforth no one could attempt to justify sacrifice offered to any creature. Consequently he, the offerer, is priest as well as offering. He willed that the daily sign of this reality should be the sacrifice of the Church which, being the body of that head, learns to offer itself through him" (*The City of God* X, 20).

Christ Is Physician and Medicine

The law was given, you see, as I have already explained, and as you must hold onto firmly, and as I must ever more insistently and tirelessly urge upon you; it was given so that we human beings might discover ourselves; it wasn't given to cure the disease, but to aggravate it with transgression, so that the doctor would be asked for. And who can this doctor be, but the one who said, *It is not the healthy who need the doctor, but those who are ill* (Mk 2:17)? So those who won't acknowledge the Creator are proudly denying their maker, while those who deny their sickness don't acknowledge the necessity of a savior. So let us both praise the Creator for our nature, and for the flaw in it which we have inflicted on ourselves, let us seek a savior. . . . Human nature was capable by free will of wounding itself; but once wounded and sickly, it is not capable by free will of healing itself. After all, if you want to live so intemperately that you get ill, you don't require a doctor to help you; you yourself are all you need for falling down. But when by your intemperate behavior you have begun to get ill, you cannot deliver yourself from sickness in the same way as you were able by your excesses to ruin your health (Sermon 156, 2).

Because human beings were unable by their own powers to fulfill the law, they became guilty under the law and begged the help of a liberator; guilt deriving from the law became a sickness in the proud. But what was a sickness in the proud became a confession of sins in the humble. The sick admit they are sick; let the physician come and heal them. Who is the physician? Our Lord Jesus Christ. And who is our Lord Jesus Christ? The one who was seen even by those who crucified him; the one who was taken prisoner, struck, flogged, smeared with spittle, crowned with thorns, hung on a cross, slain, pierced by a lance, taken down, and put in a tomb. That is who our Lord Jesus Christ is. And he is the sole physician who heals our wounds: the crucified one whom they insulted, before whom his persecutors tossed their heads and said: *Come down off that cross if you are God's Son!* (Mt 27:40). He alone is our physician. . . . There he healed your wounds where he bore his own for so long; there he saved you from eternal death where he deigned to suffer death in time (*Homilies on the Gospel of John* 3, 2-3).

Your graces know as will as I do that our Lord and savior Jesus Christ is the doctor responsible for our eternal health or salvation; and that the reason why he took upon himself the sickness of our nature was to prevent that sickness of ours being eternal. I mean, he assumed a mortal body in order by means of it to slay death (Sermon 88, 1). *It's not the healthy,* he said, *who need the doctor, but the sick* (Mt 9:12). When we were healthy we ignored his orders, and we learned by experience how totally disastrous it was for us to ignore his orders. We have already begun to get ill, we are feverish, we are lying on a bed of sickness — but we mustn't despair. Because we were unable, you see, to go to the doctor, he was quite prepared to come to us (Sermon 88, 7).

The word is faithful and worthy of total acceptance, that Christ Jesus came into the world to save sinners, of whom I am the first (1 Tm 1:15). There was no reason for Christ the Lord to come, except to save sinners. Eliminate diseases, eliminate wounds, and there's no call for medicine. If a great doctor has come down from heaven, a great invalid must have been lying very sick throughout the whole wide world. This invalid is the whole human race (Sermon 175, 1).

We were being shown [by the incarnation] how weak human beings had become by their own fault and from what weakness divine help would rescue them. This is why the Son of God took human nature to himself and in it suffered what human beings suffer. Here there is a medicine for them, so great we cannot comprehend it. What pride can be curable if it is not cured by the humility of God's Son? What avarice, that is not cured by his poverty? What anger, that is not cured by his patience? Finally, what fear, that is not cured by the resurrection of his body? Let the human race raise its head in hope and recognize its true stature, seeing what a place it has among God's works. . . . O medicine that is a cure for all: allaying every swelling, healing every infection, cutting away all that is superfluous, preserving all that is vital, repairing all losses, and straightening all that is crooked! (*The Christian Combat* 12).

Christ Is the Head

Without him [Christ] we are nothing, but in him we are both Christ and ourselves. Why? Because the whole Christ is head and body. He is the head, the Savior of the body,[7] and has already entered heaven; the Church suffering on earth is the body. If this body were not united to its head in the bonds of love so as to form a single being made up of body and head, then a persecutor would not have been reproached by the heavenly voice: *Saul, Saul, why do you persecute me?* (Acts 9:4). He was already seated in heaven where no human could touch him; how, then, could Saul, in striking out at Christians on earth, have

injured him? Christ did not say: "Why do you persecute me?"
— that is, my members. The head cried out for the sake of the
members; the head transformed the members into himself (*Expositions of the Psalms* 31, II, 1, 3).

Saul, he said, *Saul,* yes, still Saul, *why are you persecuting me?* (Acts
9:4). What a tremendous honor, my brothers and sisters! In the
Lord's words we are to recognize ourselves. Who could still be
persecuting Christ, when he was seated in heaven at the right
hand of the Father? But while the head was reigning there, the
members were still toiling away here. *The teacher of the nations*
(2 Tm 1:11) himself, the blessed apostle Paul, has taught us what
we are in relation to Christ: *But you,* he says, *are the body of
Christ and his members* (1 Cor 12:27). So the whole Christ is
head and members (Sermon 299C, 2).

God could give no greater gift to humankind, than to give them
for their head his own Word through who he had made all
things, and to unite them to him as his members. He is Son of
God and son of man, one God with the Father, one man with
other human beings. Consequently, when we speak to God in
prayer, we do not set the Son apart from him, and when the
Son's body prays, it does not separate itself from its head. Our
Lord Jesus Christ is the only Savior of his body;[8] he prays for us,
he prays in us, he is prayed to by us. He prays for us as our
priest; he prays in us as our head; he is prayed to by us as our
God. Let us therefore recognize our voice in him and his in us
(*Expositions of the Psalms* 86, 1).

Christ our head is present and acting in us as he was in Paul. And
yet all the same, when was he enduring this? Wasn't it rather
the one who couldn't fall away that was enduring it all in him and
with him? I've not the slightest hesitation in saying that it wasn't
Paul who was enduring it. Yes, he was the one enduring it, because the strength of Christ was dwelling in him. Christ was
controlling him, Christ was providing him with power, Christ
was not abandoning him, Christ was running in the runner,
Christ was guiding him through to the winning post. So I'm not
doing him any wrong, when I say that he wasn't the one who
was enduring. I say it definitely, I say it with absolute confidence,
and I can confirm my words with him as my witness. I won't
allow the holy apostle to flare up at me, when I quote his own
words to him. Tell us, Paul, tell us, holy man, tell us, apostle; let
my brothers and sisters hear that I have done you no wrong at
all. So what does he say, when he compares himself and his
labors with his fellow apostles? He wasn't afraid to say, *I have*

worked harder than all of them. Here I now get the answer straightaway, "Certainly not himself." So say what comes next, in case this delay should give me a swollen head: *I have worked harder than them all.* You had already all begun to get angry with me, but he intercedes for me, and somehow addresses you all: Don't be angry: *not I, however, but the grace of God with me* (1 Cor 15:10) (Sermon 299C, 4).

The body must follow the example of the head. "Let the body not scorn to endure what the head first endured, so that the body may remain united to the head. Your Lord was insulted; do you want to be honored by those who are cut off from the saints? Do not claim for yourself what he did not first have. *No pupil outranks his teacher, no slave his master* (Mt 10:24)" (*Expositions of the Psalms* 56, 8).

The union of the Christian with Christ the head by means of faith and love is a promise and pledge of union with him in eternal life. "*The Word became flesh* (Jn 1:14) in order to become head of the Church. The Word in himself is not part of the Church; he became flesh that he might become head of the Church. Something of ours, which he took here below where he died and was crucified, is now in heaven. Your first fruits, as it were, have gone before you; do you doubt that you will follow?" (*Expositions of the Psalms* 149, 8).

Christ Is the Teacher

"It is Christ who is doing the teaching; he has his chair in heaven, as I said a short while ago. His school is on earth, and his school is his own body. The head is teaching his members, the tongue talking to his feet. It is Christ who is doing the teaching; we hear; let us fear, let us act" (Sermon 399).

"So, since the Word and God was a long way away from flesh and man, the Word became flesh, and joined man to God. So this Lord and Savior of ours, the Son of God, the Word of God who became flesh, not by changing into flesh but by assuming flesh, taught those who believe in him how to live, taught them how to die; to live without greed, to dies without fear. He taught us how to live, so that we might not die for ever; he taught us how to die, so that we might live for ever (Sermon 313E, 1).

"He did nothing by force, everything by persuasion and teaching. The old slavery had passed, and the time of freedom had dawned. The moment had arrived, therefore, for persuading human beings, for their salvation, how they had been created with free will" (*True Religion* 31).

Christ brings light, and he is himself the light.

In this night of our mortal human life human beings experience both light and darkness: the light is prosperity, the darkness adversity. But when Christ the Lord comes and dwells in them through faith, he gives another light; he inspires and bestows patience, while warning them not to delight overmuch in prosperity lest he falter in adversity. Then people of faith begin to be detached in their use of this world's goods, not becoming enthusiastic in prosperity nor cast down in adversity, but in all things blessing the Lord (*Expositions of the Psalms* 139, 16).

"Let us walk, therefore, while it is day, that is, while we have the use of reason, so that we may be converted to the Lord and be enlightened by his Word, who is the true light, and not be overtaken by the darkness.[9] 'Day' means the presence of that light *which enlightens all human beings as they come into this world* (Jn 1:9)" (*True Religion* 42, 79).

"So let the blind run to Christ and by receiving their sight be enlightened. Christ, after all, is light in the world, even among the worst of people" (Sermon 126B).

Christ is the truth and fills with joy the hearts of those who seek him.

See how true all this is, and *let the heart of those who seek the Lord rejoice*. The Lord, after all, is Truth itself at the source. So meaning stays in my heart, emigrates to yours, and doesn't leave mine. However, when there is a meaning or idea in my mind, and I want to plant it also in your mind, I look for sound as a kind of vehicle by which it can pass over to you. And I take a sound, and load a meaning on it so to say, and utter it, and lead it along, and I teach you something and I don't lose it myself. If my idea can do this with my voice, couldn't the Word of God do it with his flesh? That's the kind of way, you see, in which the Word of God, Word with God, the wisdom of God abiding unchangeably with the Father, in order to proceed to us, looked for flesh as a kind of sound, inserted himself into it and proceeded to us and did not recede from the Father. Understand and savor wisely what you have heard. Consider how great and wonderful it is, and take care to think even more grandly, not meanly, about God. He surpasses all light, he surpasses all sound, he surpasses all meaning and all understanding. He is to be desired and longed for with love, that *the hearts of those who seek the Lord may rejoice* (Sermon 28, 5).

Christ Is Our Model

Human beings wanted riches which are the attendants upon pleasure, and did so to their own harm; he [Christ] willed to be poor. They yearned for honors and power; Christ refused to be a king. They regarded children of their body as a great blessing; he rejected marriage and offspring. Filled with pride, they regarded insults as a terrible thing; he endured every kind of insult. They judged injuries to be intolerable; what greater injury could there be than for a just and innocent person to be condemned? They regarded physical pain as a curse; he was flogged and subjected to every torment. They feared death; he was condemned to death. They considered crucifixion the most shameful kind of death; he was crucified. . . . . Thus his whole life on earth in the human nature he deigned to make his own was an instruction in how to live (*True Religion* 16, 31-32).

Christ the Lord, when he became a man, made little of earthly things in order to show us that we should make little of them. He willed that he himself should endure all the earthly ills which he bade us endure, so that we might not seek our happiness in them nor fear to be made unhappy by them. . . . He also became poor, although all things are his and were made by him; he did so in order that anyone who believes in him may not take pride in earthly riches. He refused to let others make him a king, for his intention was to show the way of humility to the wretched whom pride had separated from him: this, even though all creation bears witness to his everlasting lordship.

He who feeds all hungered; he experienced thirst who is the creator of all liquids and is the spiritual bread of the hungry and drink of the thirsty. He who is in his own person our way to heaven grew weary from walking the earth. He who makes the mute speak and the deaf hear was like a one deaf and mute before those who insulted him. He who loosens the bonds of weakness was bound; he who drives all the scourges of illness from human bodies was scourged; he who puts an end to all our crosses was crucified; he who raises dead men died. But he himself also rose, never more to die, so that while we learn from him to scorn death, we might not think our life was ending forever (*The Instruction of Beginners* XXII, 40).

Christ is a model of incomparable beauty, as Augustine exultantly tells us in commenting on Psalm 45, which is an epithalamium for the marriage of Christ and the Church.

The beautiful spouse meets us everywhere, once we have believed. He is beautiful as God and *as the Word with God* (Jn 1:1).
He is beautiful in the virgin's womb where he took our humanity
without losing his divinity; beautiful when born as the Word
who is a speechless baby, for even when he was but an infant
and sucked the breast and was carried in his mother's arms, the
heavens spoke, the angels sang praises, a star directed the wise
men, and the child who is the food of the humble was adored in
the crib. Thus he was beautiful in heaven and beautiful on earth;
beautiful in his mother's womb and beautiful in his parents'
arms; beautiful when working wonders and beautiful when being
scourged; beautiful when he invites human beings to life and
beautiful when he scorns death; beautiful when he lays down his
life and beautiful when he takes it up again; beautiful on the
cross, beautiful in the tomb, beautiful in heaven (*Expositions of
the Psalms* 45, 3).

Christ Is Our Brother

Brothers and sisters, God has so abundantly blessed us in the
name of Christ that he fills the earth with his children, adopting
them as fellow-heirs of his own Son and taking them into his
kingdom. He begot but one Son, but did not wish him to be the
only child; he begot but one Son but did not wish him to be
alone. He gave him brothers and sisters and fellow-heirs, not by
generation but by adoption. He first made his own Son share
our mortality, so that we might believe it possible for us to
share his divinity *(Expositions of the Psalms* 67, 9).

Christ Is Our Food

He is praised just as he ought to be by all his angels, whose
eternal food he is, nourishing them on imperishable fare: because he is the Word of God, on whose life they live, on whose
eternity they live for ever, on whose goodness they live for ever
in bliss. . . . They then praise him suitably; we should praise him
obediently. They are his messengers, we are his cattle. He has
loaded their table in heaven, he has filled our manger on earth.
He is the fare on their table, because *in the beginning was the
Word, and the Word was with God, and the Word was God* (Jn 1:1).
He is the fodder in our manger, because *the Word became flesh
and dwelt among us* (Jn 1:14). In order that man, you see, might
eat the bread of angels, the creator of angels became man (Sermon 194, 2).

CHRIST IS OUR FOOD

Now it's obvious that of the objects presented to our various senses, each one gives pleasure to a distinct sense. Sounds don't give pleasure to the sense of sight, nor colors to the sense of hearing. But for our hearts the Lord is both light and voice and fragrance and food. And the reason he is all these things is that he is none of them. And the reason he is none of them is that he is the creator of them all. He is light for our heart, since we say to him, *In your light we shall see light* (Ps 36:9); he is a sound for our hearts, since we say to him, *To my hearing you will give exultation and gladness* (Ps 51:8); he is fragrance for our hearts, since it is said of him, *We are the sweet fragrance of Christ* (2 Cor 2:15). Now if you are seeking food, because you have been fasting, *Blessed are those who hunger and thirst for justice* (Mt 5:6). But it is said of the Lord Jesus Christ himself that he has become for us justice and wisdom. There you have the banquet that has been provided. Christ is justice, nowhere is he in short supply; he is not provided for us by cooks, nor is he imported by merchants from overseas, like exotic fruits. He is a food that appeals to everyone whose inner man has a healthy appetite. He is the food which recommends itself to us by saying, *I am the living bread, who came down from heaven* (Jn 6:51). He is the food which nourishes without perishing; he is the food which doesn't disappear when it is taken; he is the food which fills the hungry and remains whole (Sermon 28, 2).

That's why he put those five stones in a milk can, because milk signifies grace, because it is given gratuitously, freely. The woman has taken food; what is necessary for the support of her body is transferred to the juices of the flesh, the rest that is superfluous is carried off by the proper channels, the milk-forming juice flows to the breasts in order to feed the hungry little ones freely, gratuitously. The mother's breasts, you see, are full, and she is looking for lips into which she may pour the milk, which is burdensome to the mother if there is nobody to suck it. In the same sort of way God's saints have their bosoms full of the grace of God; they are looking out for people into whom they can milk themselves. And just notice what the Lord himself did in order after a fashion to suckle us. His wisdom, which none of us could grasp with the mind as solid food, but the angels are capable of it, because the angels live on that very food; human beings, though, cannot use such food, because they are weak; so what did God do, but what a loving mother does? Because the tiny infant is unable to take in solid food, the mother transforms the solidity of the food into flesh, and after a fashion incarnates it, so that it may be suitable to the infant. That's the way God incarnated the Word, so that it might be suitable for us little ones. Here's the solid food: *In the beginning was the Word, and the Word was with God, and the Word was God. All things were made through him, and without him was made nothing. What was made is life in him; and the life was the light of men,* and the light shines in the darkness, and the darkness did not comprehend it (Jn 1:1.3-5). What human weakness can approach anything as solid as that? What faculty of ours can grasp it? But don't panic, you crowd of tiny babies! *The Word became flesh, and dwelt amongst us* (Jn 1:14) (Sermon 335K, 4).

Christ Is Our Judge

There is a prophecy about our Lord Jesus Christ in this psalm, where we heard and sang *God will come openly, our God, and he will not be silent* (Ps 50:3). For it is the Lord Christ himself, our God, the Son of God, who came hiddenly at his first advent, that will come openly at the second advent. When he came hiddenly he only made himself known to his servants; when he comes openly he will make himself known to the good and the bad. When he came hiddenly he came to be judged; when he comes openly he will come to judge (Sermon 18, 1).

"He will come at the end of time, and as it is written, *God will come openly* (Ps 50:3); not as he came the first time, disguised; but as it says, *openly*. He had to come disguised, you see, in order to be judged. But *he will come openly*, in order to judge" (Sermon 263, 1).

"So from his sublime dwelling in heaven, where his body, already immortal, is now, our Lord Jesus Christ is going *to come to judge the living and the dead*, according to the plainest evidence of the angels, as it is written in the Acts of the Apostles. As his disciples, you see, were gazing at him ascending into heaven, and trying to bring him down again with their anxious looks, they heard the angels say, *Men of Galilee, why are you standing here? This Jesus, who has been taken away from you, will come in the same way as you have seen him going into heaven* (Acts 1:11). Christ will judge in the same form as that in which he was judged" (Sermon 214, 9).

"Our Lord Jesus Christ, who came once to be judged, will come again to judge. The first time he came in lowliness; later he will come in glory. He came the first time to give us an example of patience; later he will come to judge all people, good and evil, according to their deserts" (*Expositions of the Psalms* 63, 1).

Our Duties toward Christ

Faith

The medicine for all the wounds of the soul, and the one way of atoning for all human delinquency, is to believe in Christ; nor is it in the least possible for any people to be cleansed, either of original sin which they have contracted from Adam, in whom all have sinned, and become children of wrath by nature, or of the sins which they have added themselves by not resisting the lust of the flesh, but by following it and serving it in shameful and outrageous behavior, unless they are by faith joined and fitted to the body of him who was conceived without any hankering of the flesh or death-dealing pleasure . . . By believing in him they become children of God, because they are born of God adoptively by the grace which consists of faith in Jesus Christ our Lord (Sermon 143, 1).

You heard the story when the gospel was read; a great storm burst, the boat was being tossed about and the waves breaking over it. Why? Because Christ was asleep. When does Christ go to sleep in your heart, if not when you forget your faith? Faith in Christ in your heart is like Christ in the boat. You hear nasty stories about yourself, you lose heart, you get upset; Christ is asleep. Wake Christ up, wake up your faith. You've something you can do, even when you are upset; stir up your faith. Let Christ wake up and talk to you: "Does abuse and nasty talk upset you? What didn't I myself hear first for your sake!" That's what Christ says to you, that's how your faith talks to you. Listen to it, and just see that it does talk to you like that — unless of course you've forgotten that Christ suffered for us, and that before he suffered such dreadful things for us, he heard a lot of abuse and nasty talk. . . . Believe what is said, and a great calm will settle in your heart (Sermon 163B, 6).

Confidence

If we look to ourselves, what are we? If we look to him, he is God and all-powerful. Will he who made human beings out of nothing not make angels out of human beings? Or do you think God sets little value on humanity, even though he wanted his only Son to die for it? Consider the proof of God's love. We have received so many pledges of God's promises; we have the death and the blood of Christ. Whose death? The death of the only Son. For whom did he die? "Oh, for those who are good;

surely for the just!" But what do we read? *Christ died for us who are godless*, says the Apostle (Rom 5:6)! If he bestowed on the godless the gift of his death, what gift has he left for the just, except his life?

Let the weak, therefore, raise their heads and not despair, not be downhearted or turn away or say: "We shall cease to exist." He who promised is God, and he came in order to make his promise. He appeared among us, came to make our death his own and promise us his life. He came to the land where we were exiled, in order to take what abounds here: insults, flog-gings, blows, spittle in his face, outrages, death, the cross. Such things exist in plenty in our country, and this was the kind of exchange for which he came. What then did he give, and what did he receive? He gave exhortation, teaching, the forgiveness of sins; he received insults, death, the cross. He brought bless-ings from his own country and endures evils in ours. But he promised us that someday we would be where he comes from: "Father, all those you gave me I would have in my company where I am" (Jn 17:24). Such is the love that has anticipated us! Where we were, he was with us; where he is, we too shall be (*Expositions of the Psalms* 148 8).

Even in our thoughts of Christ coming as judge, fear should not be unaccompanied by confident desire.

Let us fear the day of judgment, for the Lord is indeed coming. He who came in lowliness will come in glory. He who came to be judges is coming to judge. Let us acknowledge him in his lowliness and we shall not be terrified by him in his glory. Let us embrace him in his lowliness and we shall desire him in his glory. His coming will be one of mercy for those who yearn for him. Who are the ones who yearn for him? Those who remain faith-ful to him and keep his commandments (*Expositions of the Psalms* 67, 10).

Anxiously, therefore, and greatly fearful (who do not fear, if they really believe?), I have discoursed at length, as best I could, on what the life and ways of you and all of us should be, so that we may not only look forward calmly to that day but even long for it. For, if we love Christ, we should yearn for his coming. It is wrong (if indeed the thing is even possible) to fear the coming of someone we love; to pray, "Thy kingdom come" and to fear being heard! But why should there be that kind of fear? Because he is coming to judge? . . . But who is it that is thus coming? Why do you not rejoice at his coming? Is not the one who is coming to judge you the one who came before in order to be judged for your sake? (*Expositions of the Psalms* 147, 1).

Love

What praises, then, should we be singing to God's love, what thanks should we be expressing! I mean, he loved us so much that for our sake he came to be in time, though all times were made through him; and he was prepared to be younger in age than many of his servants in the world, though he is older in eternity than all the world. He loved us so much that he became man though he had made man; that he was created from a mother whom he had created, carried in arms he had fashioned, sucked breasts which he himself filled; that he lay squalling in a manger wordless in infancy, though he is the Word without whom human eloquence would be at a loss for words (Sermon 188, 2).

Love Christ; long for the light which Christ is. If that man longed for the light of the body, how much more ought you all to long for the light of the heart? Let us cry out to him, not with our voices, but with our behavior. . . . Love your children, love your wives, even if it's only in worldly matters and a worldly way. Because of course you ought to love them with reference to Christ, and take thought for them with reference to God, and in them love nothing but Christ, and hate it in your nearest and dearest if they don't want to have anything to do with Christ. Such, you see, is that divine sort of charity. What good, after all, would be done them by your fleeting and mortal charity? Still, when you do love them in a human way, love Christ more. I'm not saying you shouldn't love your wife; but love Christ more. I'm not saying you shouldn't love your children; but love Christ more. Listen to him saying it himself, in case you should suppose these are just my words: *Whoever loves father or mother more than me, is not worthy of me* (Mt 10:37). When you hear *is not worthy of me*, aren't you afraid? The one about whom Christ says he is not worthy of me is not with him; where will the one be who is not with him? If you don't love being with him, you should be afraid of being without him (Sermon 349, 5, 7).

Live in Christ

Faith and heartfelt love for Christ will cause Christ to be formed in the Christian and will bring about a vital, fruitful union with him. "For this reason he also says: *My children* (desiring us to imitate him like a parent), *you put me back in labor pains until Christ is formed in you* (Gal

4:19). Paul is here speaking rather with the voice of Mother Church; elsewhere he says: *While we were among you we were as gentle as any nursing mother fondling her little ones* (1 Thes 2:7). Now, Christ is formed in the believer through faith which dwells in the interior self[10] that is called to the freedom grace gives and to be meek and humble of heart. . . . Christ is formed in those who receive the form of Christ; they receive the form of Christ who are united to Christ in spiritual love (*Explanation of the Letter to the Galatians* 38).

The important thing, then, is to correspond with the hidden life-giving and formative action of Christ who dwells in us. "I mean to say, can Christ enter the heart in the flesh and with the flesh? It's in his divinity that he possesses the heart (in the flesh he speaks to the heart through the eyes, and instructs it from outside); dwelling within, so that we may be converted inwardly and be brought to life from him, and formed from him, because he is the unformed form of everything there is" (Sermon 264, 4).

NOTES

1. Rom 7:24.
2. See Phil 2:6.
3. See Jn 1:1.
4. See Jn 10:18.
5. See Ps 103:3; Mt 4:23.
6. See Ps 110:1; Mk 16:19; Heb 1:3.
7. See Eph 5:23.
8. *Ibid.*
9. See Jn 12:35.
10. See Eph 3:16.

CHAPTER 6

THE CHURCH

The Mystery

The reality of the Church as both visible entity and mystery is figuratively expressed by the moon.

> The moon is an allegory of the Church: in its spiritual part the Church is luminous but in its fleshly part overcast. Sometimes the spiritual element manifests itself to human beings in the form of good works; at other times it remains hidden in their consciences and is known to God alone, showing only its bodily element to the gaze. The same kind of thing happens when we pray in our hearts and seem outwardly to be doing nothing, for our hearts are directed, as the scripture bids us direct them, not to earth but to the Lord. . . . The moon stands for the Church inasmuch as the Church has its light not from itself but from the only Son of God, who in the scriptures is frequently given the allegorical name "sun of justice" (*Expositions of the Psalms* 11, 3).

The various aspects of the mystery of the Church can be illustrated by biblical images; there is an easy transition from each to the next.

Temple of God

"After the mention of the Trinity comes the mention of the holy Church. We have spoken of God; now we speak of his temple. *The temple of God is holy, and you are that temple* (1 Cor 3:17). This temple is the Church: holy, one, true, and catholic" (Sermon 398, 14).

> Proper order in professing our faith requires that mention of the Trinity be followed by mention of the Church; thus we mention first the dweller, then his house; First God, then his temple; first the founder, then his city. The Church is here to be taken in its full reality: not only the part which is in pilgrimage on earth, praising *the name of the Lord from the rising to the setting of*

the sun (Ps 113:3) and, after its captivity, now singing a new song, but also that part which has always remained united to God in heaven (where the Church was founded) and never experienced the disastrous fall. This is the blessed Church of the holy angels; when necessary, it comes to the aid of the part still on pilgrimage. Between the two parts there will be one fellowship in eternity, just as now there is a unity through love, for the Church as a whole was established in order to worship the one God. . . .

[The Holy Spirit] does have a temple of which the Apostle speaks: *You must know that your body is a temple of the Holy Spirit who is within you — the Spirit you have received from God.* And in another passage the Apostle says: *Do you not see that your bodies are members of Christ?* (1 Cor 6:19.15). . . . God therefore dwells in his temple: I mean not only the Holy Spirit but also the Father and the Son, who says of his own body (by reason of which he became head of the Church as it exists among human beings, *so that primacy may be his in everything* [Col 1:18]): *Destroy this temple, and in three days I will raise it up* (Jn 2:19). The temple of God, then, that is, the temple of the supreme Trinity as a whole, is the holy Church in its entirety: the Church in heaven and on earth (*Handbook* 15, 56).

Ark of salvation

"None of us doubts that the ark of Noah, in which the just were saved from the flood while sinners perished thereby, was both a historical reality and a figure of the Church. This admittedly might seem nothing more than an ingenious piece of exegesis, had not Saint Peter told us the fact in his letter" (*Baptism* 6, 78).

Spouse and mother

Let Israel be glad in their maker, let the children of Zion rejoice in their king (Ps 149:2). "Israel" refers to the children of the Church. Zion was an earthly city and it fell; in its ruins the saints dwelt in their time on earth. But the true Zion and the true Jerusalem (Zion and Jerusalem are one and the same) is eternal in heaven and it is our mother. It begot us; it is the Church of the saints; it nourished us; it is partly on pilgrimage, but in great part dwells in heaven. The part that dwells stably in heaven is the source of the angels' blessedness; the part that is on earth is the hope of the just. Of the former it was said: *Glory to God in the high heaven*; and of the latter: *and peace on earth to those on whom his favor rests* (Lk 2:14). Therefore those who groan in the present life and yearn for their native land run to it with love (*Expositions of the Psalms* 149, 4, 34).

"If we assume that only those born of the same parents are neighbors, let's turn our attention to Adam and Eve, and we are all brothers and sisters; brothers and sisters, indeed, insofar as we are human — how much more so in that we are Christians? As regards your being human, your one father was Adam, your one mother Eve; as regards your being a Christian, your one father is God, your one mother the Church" (Sermon 399, 3).

This explains Augustine's impassioned invocation of the Church in his debate with Faustus, the Manichean:

> To you, then, Catholic Church, true spouse of the true Christ, I address myself with what abilities I have, as your son and servant (a humble one, indeed) and entrusted with distributing food to my fellow servants within your communion. . . . Even the dangers I passed through helped me come to you, and to you I dedicate my services, now that I am free. If your true and trustworthy spouse, from whose side you emerged, had not provided the forgiveness of sins in his own true blood, the maelstrom of deceit would have swallowed me up; I would have become dirt, and the serpent would have devoured me beyond rescue.[1] Let the name of truth not deceive you; you alone possess the reality in your bread and your milk. In a sect, on the contrary, there is but the name of truth, not its reality. You are sure of your grown-up sons; I turn now to your little ones, my brothers and sisters, my sons and daughters, and my masters. Do you protect them under your wings like the hen, or nourish them like babes with your milk, O virgin mother, fruitful yet untouched (*Answer to Faustus* XV, 3).

The Church is a virgin mother insofar as she keeps unsullied the faith of her children.

> Such is the Catholic Church, our true mother, the true consort of that bridegroom. Let us honor her, because she is the bride of so great a Lord. And what am I to say? Great and unheard of is the bridegroom's gracious generosity; he found her a whore, he made her a virgin. She mustn't deny that she was once a whore, or she may forget the kindness and mercy of her liberator. How can she not have been a whore, when she used to go fornicating after idols and demons? Fornication of the heart was there in all her members, fornication of the flesh in some of them; of the heart in all. And he came, and made her a virgin; he made the Church a virgin. In faith she is a virgin; in the flesh she

has a few virgins, the nuns; in faith she should have all of us virgins, both women and men. In that sphere, you see, there should be universal chastity, purity and sanctity. . . . So the Church is virgin; let her be virgin (Sermon 213, 8).

Augustine often develops this concept by drawing a parallel between the Church and Mary. He does this in speaking to the faithful generally as well as in speaking to consecrated virgins who are called to imitate Mary and the Church more closely.

Thus, in a homily for Christmas:

And so the virgin holy Church celebrates today the child-bearing of the virgin. It is to the Church, you see, that the apostle says, *I have attached you to one husband, to present you as a chaste virgin to Christ* (2 Cor 11:2). How could it be a *chaste virgin* in so many communities of either sex, among so many, not only boys and girls, but also married fathers and mothers? How, I repeat, could it be a *chaste virgin*, except in the integrity of faith, hope, and charity? Hence Christ, intending to establish the Church's virginity in the heart, first preserved Mary's in the body. In human marriage, of course, a woman is given to her husband so that she ceases to be a virgin anymore; the Church on the other hand could not be a virgin unless she had found that the husband she had been given to was the son of a virgin (Sermon 188, 4).

In Mary's womb the only-begotten Son of God was pleased to join human nature to himself, in order to link to himself as undefiled head an undefiled Church: a Church which the apostle Paul calls a virgin, contemplating not only those in it who are virgins also in the Body, but craving the uncorrupted minds of all its members. *For I have betrothed you,* he says, *to one husband, to present you as a chaste virgin to Christ* (2 Cor 11:2). So the Church imitates the Lord's mother — not in the bodily sense, which it could not do — but in mind it is both mother and virgin. In no way, then, did Christ deprive his mother of her virginity by being born, seeing that he made his Church into a virgin by redeeming her from fornication with demons. It is from the Church's uncorrupted virginity that you holy virgins have been begotten. Setting at nought earthly marriages, you have chosen to be virgins also in the flesh, and you rejoice in solemnly celebrating today the one whom the virgin bore. He indeed was born of a woman, without being begotten by a man of a woman. Since he brought you the gift you would cherish, he certainly did not deprive his mother of this gift that you do cherish. As he heals in you the hurt you have derived from Eve, perish the thought that he should spoil what you have valued in Mary (Sermon 191, 3).

This is the Lord our God, this is the mediator between God and men, the man our Savior, who, born of the Father, also created his mother; created of his mother also glorified the Father; the only son of his Father without female parturition; the only son of his mother without male embrace. This is the one, fairest in form above the sons of men, the son of holy Mary, the bridegroom of holy Church, which he has restored to be like his mother; because he has both made her a mother for us, and kept her a virgin for himself. . . . So the Church too, like Mary, enjoys perpetual virginity and uncorrupted fecundity. What Mary, you see, was found worthy to possess in the flesh, the Church has preserved in the mind, except that the former gave birth to one, the latter gives birth to many, who are, however, to be gathered together into one through that one (Sermon 195, 2).

So the Church is virgin; let her be virgin; let her beware of being seduced, or she will find herself corrupted. The Church is a virgin. You're going to say to me, perhaps, "If she is a virgin, how does she give birth to children? Or if she doesn't bear children, how is it we gave in our names to be born of her womb?" I answer: she is both virgin, and she gives birth. She imitates Mary, who gave birth to the Lord. Didn't the virgin, Saint Mary, both give birth and remain a virgin? So too the Church both gives birth and is a virgin. And if you really think about it, she gives birth to Christ, because those who are baptized are his members, parts of his body. *You*, says the apostle, *are the body of Christ, and members of it* (1 Cor 12:27) (Sermon 213, 8).

Come on now, friends, think of how the Church, which is plain enough, is the bride of Christ; what's more difficult to understand, but is true all the same, is that she is the mother of Christ. The Virgin Mary came first as a representative figure of the Church. How, I ask you, can Mary be the mother of Christ except by giving birth to the limbs and organs of Christ? You people, to whom I'm speaking, you are the limbs and organs, the members, of Christ. Who gave you birth? I hear you answering to yourselves, "Mother Church." This holy and honorable mother is like Mary in that she both gives birth and is a virgin (Sermon 72A, 8).

I intend to deal in this book with virginity. May Christ help us, for he is son of the Virgin and spouse of virgins, born bodily of a virginal womb and joined to virgins in spiritual marriage. Now, since the entire Church is a virgin espoused to one man, Christ, as the Apostle tells us,[2] how especially deserving of honor those of her members are who preserve even in their bodies what the entire Church preserves in faith, as she imitates the mother of her husband and Lord! For the Church too is both virgin and mother. If she is not a virgin, then whose integrity are we watching over? If she is not a mother, then whose are the children to whom we are speaking? Mary gave bodily birth to the head of this body; the Church gives spiritual birth to the members of this head. In both, virginity does not hinder fruitfulness, nor fruitfulness exclude virginity. Since then the entire Church is holy in body and spirit, though not all members are virginal in body, how much more holy she is in those members who are virginal in both body and spirit! (*Holy Virginity* 2).

The birth which the one holy Virgin experienced is the glory of all holy virgins. Along with Mary they too are the mothers of Christ if they do the will of his Father. In fact, for this latter reason Mary herself is mother of Christ in a more praiseworthy and more blessed way, as the words of Christ himself tell us: *Whoever does the will of my heavenly Father is brother and sister and mother to me* (Mt 12:50). He secures all these relationships for himself on the spiritual level in the people he redeemed. Holy men and women are his brothers and sisters, for they are fellow heirs of his heavenly inheritance. The entire Church is his mother because by the grace of God she gives birth to his members, that is, the faithful. So too every devout soul is his mother, inasmuch as it does his Father's will in fruitful love of those to whom it gives birth, until Christ be formed in them.[3] Consequently, Mary is, in bodily terms, only the mother of Christ, but by doing the will of Christ she became both his sister and his mother.

That one woman, therefore, is both mother and virgin, not only in the spirit but in the body too. She is mother in the spirit, but not of our head as such, for he is the Savior and it is rather she that is born of him, spiritually speaking, since all who believe in him — and she is one — are rightly called the children of the bridegroom.[4] She is, however, clearly the mother of his members, that is, us, for she cooperated with his love so that believers, the members of that head, might come to birth in the Church. In the body, on the other hand, she is mother of the head himself. For it was necessary that in order to have an outstanding miracle our head should be born in the flesh of a virgin, thus signifying that his members would receive spiritual birth from the virgin Church. Only Mary, therefore, is mother and virgin in both spirit and body; she is both mother of Christ and virgin of Christ. The Church on the other hand, in those holy people who will possess the kingdom of heaven, is in her entirety the mother of Christ in the Spirit, and in her entirety a spiritual virgin of Christ; in the body, however, she is, not in her entirety but in some members, a virgin of Christ, and in some members a mother, but not of Christ (*Holy Virginity* 5-6).

With a realism of expression that is not rare in Augustine the preacher reminds those who are drawing close to the baptism which will make them children of the Church that the Church is indeed a mother.

Hope in him, you whole assembly of the new commons, you, a people being born, which the Lord has made. Strive to be brought forth in health, not fatally aborted. Look, mother Church is in labor, see, she is groaning in travail to give birth to you, to bring you forth into the light of faith. Do not agitate her maternal womb with your impatience, and thus constrict the passage to your delivery. You, a people now being created, praise your God; praise him, you that are now being created, praise your Lord. Because you are being suckled, praise him; because you are being nourished, praise him; because you are being reared, advance in wisdom and age. . . . Gladden your father, as it is written, by your progress in wisdom, and do not sadden your mother by your want of it. Love what you will be. What you will be, you see, is children of God, and sons by adoption. This will be given you free, conferred on you for nothing, at his pleasure. In this you will be the more abundantly and richly and plentifully endowed, the more pleasing you are to the one from whom you have received all this. . . . You have, or had, parents of your flesh in the world, who bore you to toil and pain and death. But each one of you, more happily bereaved, can say about them *My father and my mother have forsaken me* (Ps 27:10); therefore, Christian, acknowledge that Father who, when they forsook you, took you up from your mother's womb, the Father to whom a faithful man trustingly says, *From my mother's womb you are my protector* (Ps 22:10). God is Father, the Church mother (Sermon 216, 7-8).

Body of Christ

This image is closely connected with the image of the Church as spouse.

That you may know Christ the head and his body to be one, he says when speaking of marriage: *The two shall become as one; thus they are no longer two but one flesh* (Mt 19:5). But perhaps Christ is speaking of any marriage whatsoever? Then listen to the apostle Paul: *The two shall be made into one. This is a great foreshadowing; I mean that is refers to Christ and the Church* (Eph 5:31). Of the two, then, there is made, as it were, one person: head and body; husband and wife. The prophet Isaiah also affirms this wonderful and sublime unity of person; speaking in Isaiah as he prophesies, Christ says: *He has put a crown on my head as a husband, and he has adorned me as a wife* (Is 61:10). Thus he speaks of himself as both a husband and a wife. Why so, unless husband and wife become not two but one flesh? But if two in one flesh, why not two with one voice? Christ can speak in this way, because in Christ the Church speaks and in the Church Christ speaks: the body in the head and the head in the body.

Listen to the Apostle as he states all this with perfect clarity: *The body is one and has many members, but all the members, many though they are, are one; and so it is with Christ* (1 Cor 12:12). He does not say: "So it is with the members of Christ," even though he is speaking of the members, that is, the faithful; rather he calls them all simply "Christ." For as a body is one and has many members, yet all the members of the body, despite their multitude, form one body, so Christ is many members, yet one body. Therefore all of us together with our head are one Christ, and without our head we are nothing. Why so? Because with our head we form a vine; without our head — God keeps us from that! — we are branches that have been cut away, not good anymore to be worked on by the vinedresser, but destined only for the fire. There Christ tells us in the Gospel: *I am the vine, you are the branches; my Father is the vinegrower* and *Apart from me you can do nothing* (Jn 15:5. 1. and 5). Lord, if we can do nothing apart from you, we can do everything with you. For whatever he does in us, we also seem to do. He can do much, indeed everything, without us, but we can do nothing without him (*Expositions of the Psalms* 31, Exposition 2, 1, 4).

In the body of Christ the members and their functions differ but the love that inspires them is one and the same.

He fashioned the heart of each (Ps 33:15). With the hand of his grace and mercy he fashioned their hearts. He fashioned our hearts, fashioned them one by one, and gave each of us our own heart but did not thereby destroy the unity between us. All the members of a body are formed separately and each has its own function, yet they live in the unity of the body: the hand does what the eye cannot; the ear does what the eye and the hand cannot. Yet all these members work in unity; hand and eye and ear each fulfills its own function, and there is no opposition between them.

So too in the body of Christ individual persons are members each with his or her own gifts, because he who chose a people as his inheritance[5] *fashioned the heart of each. Are all apostles? Are all prophets? Are all teachers? Do all work miracles or have the gift of healing? Do all speak in tongues, all have the gift of interpretation of tongues? To one the Spirit gives wisdom in discourse, to another the power to express knowledge. Through the Spirit one receives faith; by the same Spirit another is given the gift of healing* (1 Cor 12:28-30. 8-9). Why? Because *he fashioned the heart of each.* As in our members the functions vary but the health is one, so in all the members of Christ there are various gifts but a single love (*Expositions of the Psalms* 33, Exposition 2, II, 2, 21).

The Existential Reality

Though it embodies a mysterious divine plan, the Church is also a concrete visible reality, which began in history and carries out its mission in time.

"The holy Church is what we are; but I don't mean 'we' in the sense of just those of us who are here, you that are listening to me now; as many of us as are here by the grace of God Christian believers in this Church, that is in this city, as many as there are in this region, as many as there are in this province, as many as there are also across the sea, as many as there are in the whole wide world, since *from the rising of the sun to its setting the name of the Lord is praised* (Ps 113:3). Such is the Catholic Church, our true mother, the true consort of that bridegroom" (Sermon 213, 8).

The Church has developed in a way that is quite clear from history. The development originates in Christ himself and is an essential element in his salvific work.

Listen to Paul: *Not only so,* he says, *but we also glory in our afflictions, knowing that affliction leads to patience, patience to approval, approval though to hope; and hope does not disappoint, because the charity of God has been poured out in our hearts* (Rom 5:3-5). Where has the charity of God been poured out from in our hearts? Where from? What were you crediting yourself with? Why were you presuming it came somehow from your own

resources? *For what do you have that you have not received?* (1 Cor
4:7). So where from, if not as it goes on, *through the Holy Spirit
who has been given to us* (Rom 5:5)? . . . So consider, brothers
and sisters, what it is that you should love supremely, what you
should hold on to with all your strength. The Lord, glorified by
rising again, commends the Church to us; on the point of being
glorified by ascending into heaven, he commends the Church to
us. When he rises again, after all, what does he say to his disciples? *These are the things I told you while I was still with you, that it
was necessary for everything to be fulfilled that is written about me
in the law and the prophets and the psalms. And then he opened their
minds to understand the scriptures, and he said to them: Since thus
it is written, and thus it was necessary for the Christ to suffer, and to
rise again from the dead on the third day.* Where is the commen-
dation of the Church? *And for repentance and the forgiveness of
sins to be preached in his name.* And where was that to be?
Through all nations, with you beginning from Jerusalem (Lk 24:44-
47). That's when he was glorified by his resurrection. What
about when he was on the point of being glorified by his ascension? What you heard: *You shall be witnesses to me in Jerusalem,
and in the whole of Judea and Samaria, and as far as the ends of the
earth* (Acts 1:8). What about with the coming of the Holy Spirit?
The Holy Spirit came; those whom he first filled started speaking in the tongues of all nations. Each man speaking all languages
— what else could it mean but unity in all languages? (Sermon
265, 10-12).

Brought into existence by the apostles and built upon them, the
Church now has as its fathers the bishops who are the successors of
the apostles.

The place of your fathers your sons shall have (Ps 45:17). The apostles begot you; they were sent, they preached, they became
fathers. But was it possible for them to remain with us perma-
nently in the flesh? Of course not — even though one of them
said: *I long to be freed from this life and to be with Christ, for that is
the far better thing; yet it is more urgent that I remain alive for your
sake* (Phil 1:23). That is what he said, but how long was he able
to remain on earth? Until the present day? Until some future
date? No! Well then, was the Church abandoned when the
apostles departed? By no means! *The place of your fathers your
sons shall have.* The apostles were sent as fathers, and in their
place sons were born to you: bishops were established. For in
fact, of whom were the bishops born who now live around the
world? The Church calls them fathers; but the Church herself

gave birth to them and established them in the place of their fathers. Do not regard yourself as abandoned, then, because you do not see Peter or Paul or those others who brought you into existence; for in fact from your own offspring you have acquired a greater number of fathers. . . .

This then is the Catholic Church: her children are princes over all the earth, her children have taken their fathers' places. Let those now cut off from unity acknowledge what I have been saying, and return to unity; let them be brought into the temple of the king. God has set up his temple everywhere, and everywhere set it firmly on the foundation of the apostles and prophets. The Church has brought forth sons and set them in their fathers' places as princes over all the earth (*Expositions of the Psalms* 45, 32).

The Catholic Church, as a visible historical reality, manifests a set of marks which fully justify faith in her.

The Catholic Church possesses a genuine, unalloyed wisdom such as only a few spiritual persons reach in this life so as to know it without any admixture of doubt, even if the degree of wisdom achieved be small (since they are human beings, after all). (As for the others — the crowd — we do not find in them intellectual insight but a simple faith which gives them full security.) But since you refuse to believe that this wisdom exists in the Catholic Church, I leave it aside and remind you of the many other reasons which fully justify me in staying within her embrace.

I am moved by the consensus of peoples and nations and by her authority which was provided in the beginning by wonders, nourished by hope, increased by love, and confirmed by antiquity. I am moved by the succession of bishops, starting with the apostolic see of the apostle Peter, to whom the Lord after his resurrection gave the task of feeding his flock, down to the episcopal body of today. I am moved, finally, by the very name "Catholic," which amid so many heresies was justifiably preserved by this Church alone, to such a point that although all heretics would like to call themselves Catholic, when a foreigner inquires where the Catholic body holds its meetings, none of the heretics dares direct the person to his own basilica or house. Such are the numerous and important bonds which bind Christians together and which rightly keep the believer in the Catholic Church, even though because of our slow minds and our sins the truth is not yet manifested to us with full clarity (*Answer to the Letter of Mani: Known as "The Foundation"* 4).

The Gifts of the Church

The Holy Spirit

The Church now speaks the languages of every people. Initially indeed the Church was located amid a single people, but even there it spoke the tongues of all. By speaking in the tongues of all, it made known the fact that it would spread throughout the nations and speak every language. If any are not within this Church, they do not receive the Holy Spirit. For if they are cut off and separated from the unity of the members, a unity which speaks all languages, let them show that they have the Spirit. If they have the Spirit, let them give the sign that was once given: let them speak all tongues! They may answer: "And what of you? Do you speak all tongues?" I do, because every tongue that belongs to the body of which I am a member belongs to me. The Church spread throughout the nations speaks every tongue. The Church is the body of Christ and you are one of its members. Since you are a member of a body which speaks all languages, believe that you speak them too.

"The unity of the members is achieved by love, and the unity itself speaks now as long ago a single man spoke. We too therefore receive the Holy Spirit if we love the Church, if we are bound together in love, if we find our joy in the Catholic name and faith. Believe it, brothers: to the extent we love the Church of Christ, to that extent he has the Holy Spirit. . . . We have the Holy Spirit therefore if we love the Church, and we love her if we remain in the bonds of charity" (*Homilies on the Gospel of John* 32, 7-8).

The word of God in sacred scripture

The Church guarantees us that a book belongs to the canon of the Bible and is therefore to be accepted as the word of God.

As far as the canonical scriptures are concerned, the student should follow the authority of the majority of the Catholic Churches; among these, evidently, are those Churches which were apostolic sees and were favored with Letters. In the matter of scripture, then, the student will follow this norm: those writings accepted by all the Catholic Churches are to be given priority over those accepted only by some; among those not accepted by all, priority goes to those accepted by the greater number of Churches and by Churches of greater authority, over those accepted by fewer Churches and Churches of lesser authority (*Teaching Christianity* II, 12).

It is the Church's tradition that guarantees, for example, the authenticity of Matthew's gospel.

> When I begin to read to you from the gospel of Saint Matthew, one of his apostles, the part where the events of his hidden life are set out in order, you will tell me straight out that this account is not by Saint Matthew. But the whole Church, which links today's bishops by sure succession with the apostolic sees, says that is by Saint Matthew! Just as I believe that the book you have is by Manes because since the time when he lived on earth it was preserved and handed on by his disciples through a clear succession of leading men, so too you should believe that this book is by Matthew because the Church has passed it on from Matthew's time to our own, through an uninterrupted series of ages, with the links in the chain of succession all clearly established (*Answer to Faustus* XXVIII, 2).

"I would not believe in the Gospel, if the authority of the Catholic Church did not persuade me" (*Answer to the Letter of Mani*).

The Church teaches and reads the scriptures. The Creed is explained to catechumens "through the scriptures and sermons in church" (Sermon 212, 2).

The people themselves, of course, listen to God's word in the inspired books. But because the Church proposes that word to them, the bishop does not hesitate to say: "When you assemble in church, put aside silly stories and concentrate on the scriptures. We here are your books" (Sermon 227).

The word of God in preaching

The Church in the person of its ministers uses preaching for building the spiritual house of God.

> *Unless the Lord build the house, they labor in vain who build it* (Ps 127:1). The Lord therefore builds the house; the Lord Jesus Christ builds his own house. Many toil at the building, but unless the Lord build it, *they labor in vain who build it*. Who are those who toil at building? All those in the Church who preach the word of God, all the stewards of his mysteries. All of us are running and toiling and building today. . . . We speak outside, the Lord builds within. We tell you how you should listen, but what you actually think only he knows who sees your thoughts (*Expositions of the Psalms* 127, 2).

The Church is the school "in which we learn of the Father and the Son and the Holy Spirit, one God" (Sermon 215, 9), and to live as Christians. "The word of God has spoken to us and provides the material for our exhortation, as the scripture bids: *Receive discipline in the house of learning* (Sir 51:23). The word "discipline" derives from *discere*, meaning "to learn." The house of learning is the Church of Christ. What is learned here and why is it learned? Who learn and from whom do they learn? They learn to live well; they do this in order to live forever. Christians learn; Christ teaches (Sermon 399, 1).

The daily bread which we ask of the heavenly Father "is the very word of God, which is doled out to us every day. That's our daily bread; it's not our bellies, gents, that live on it, but our intelligence . . . is the word of God, which is always being served up in the Churches; our wages when the work is finished is called eternal life (Sermon 56, 10).

The sacraments

The passage just quoted continues: "Again, by this daily bread of ours you can understand what the faithful receive, what you are going to receive when you have been baptized; for this too we do well to ask, and say, *Give us this day our daily bread*, that we may live in such a way as not to be excluded from the altar."

The word of God is thus closely connected with the sacraments. St. Augustine likes to present the mission of the Church and its ministers under the two linked rubrics of word of God and sacrament. We have already seen this linking in an earlier passage. It occurs again in a letter to Bishop Valerius shortly after the latter had ordained Augustine a priest. He says there that the priest is a human being "who administers to the people the sacrament and the word of God" (Letter 21, 3).

Baptism and the forgiveness of sins

The explanation of the article of the Creed: "I believe in the forgiveness of sins," provides Augustine with the occasion for teaching the catechumens that pardon can be obtained only in the Church, and this initially through baptism.

> *In the forgiveness of sins*. If this were not to be had in the Church, there would be no hope. If the forgiveness of sins were not to be had in the Church, there would be no hope of a future life and eternal liberation. We thank God, who gave his Church such a gift. Here you are; you are going to come to the holy font, you will be washed in saving baptism, you will be renewed in *the bath of rebirth* (Ti 3:5), you will be without any sin at all as you come up from that bath. . . . But since we are going to go on

living in this world, where nobody can live without sin, for that reason the forgiveness of sins is not confined only to the washing clean of sacred baptism, but is also to be had in the Lord's prayer which is also a daily prayer, and which you are going to receive in eight days' time. In it you will find, as it were, your daily baptism. So you must thank God for having granted his Church this gift, which we confess in the creed; so that when we say *in the holy Church*, we join onto it *in the forgiveness of sins* (Sermon 213, 9).

Also *the holy Church*; honor, love, proclaim her as your mother, the Jerusalem which is above, the holy city of God. She it is who, in this faith which you have heard, bears fruit and grows in the whole world, *the Church of the living God, the pillar and buttress of the truth* (1 Tm 3:15); who tolerates the wicked in the communion of the sacraments, knowing that they are due to be separated from her at the end, and withdrawing from them meanwhile in the dissimilarity of her morals. This Church has received *the keys of the kingdom of heaven* (Mt 16:19) for the sake of her grains of corn now groaning among the chaff, but destined to be piled manifestly in the granaries at the final winnowing. This is so that in her, through the blood of Christ, by the working of the Holy Spirit, there may be had *the forgiveness of sins*. In this Church the soul which had been dead in its sins comes to life again, in order to be made alive with Christ, by whose grace we have been saved (Sermon 214, 11).

The Church, our mother, in her anxious concern provides baptism for infants. "Well, they too are carried along to the Church; even if they can't trot along on their own feet, they do so on other people's, in order to be cured. Mother Church lends them other people's feet to come by, other people's hearts to believe with, other people's tongues to confess with; thus since they are burdened with their sickness through another person sinning, it is right that when they recover health here they should be saved by another person confessing on their behalf" (Sermon 176, 2).

It is within the Church that the forgiveness of sins is obtained, both in baptism and later on. "So sins are forgiven in the Church in three ways: by baptism, by prayer, and by the greater humiliation of penance" (*Sermon 398, 16*).

The eucharist

After the gift of baptism the children of the Church receive from their mother the further gifts of confirmation and especially of the Eucharist. This last gift is given daily and has the effect of welding the faithful more closely together in the unity of the Church. I haven't forgotten my promise, Augustine says at the beginning of a sermon to the newly-baptized.

I had promised those to you who have just been baptized a sermon to explain the sacrament of the Lord's table, which you can see right now, and which you shared in last night. You ought to know what you have received, what you are about to receive, what you ought to receive every day. That bread which you can see on the altar, sanctified by the word of God, is the body of Christ. That cup, or rather what the cup contains, sanctified by the word of God, is the blood of Christ. It was by means of these things that the Lord Christ wished to present us with his body and blood, which he shed for our sake for the forgiveness of sins. If you receive them well, you are yourselves what you receive. You see, the apostle says, *We, being many, are one loaf, one body* (1 Cor 10:17). That's how he explained the sacrament of the Lord's table; one loaf, one body, is what we all are, many though we be.

In this loaf of bread you are given clearly to understand how much you should love unity. I mean, was that loaf made from one grain? Weren't there many grains of wheat? But before they came into the loaf they were all separate; they were joined together by means of water after a certain amount of pounding and crushing. Unless wheat is ground, after all, and moistened with water, it can't possibly get into this shape which is called bread. In the same way you too were being ground and pounded, as it were, by the humiliation of fasting and the sacrament of exorcism. Then came baptism, and you were, in a manner of speaking, moistened with water in order to be shaped into bread. But it's not yet bread without fire to bake it. So what does fire represent? That's the chrism, the anointing. Oil, the fire-feeder, you see, is the sacrament of the Holy Spirit. Notice it, when the Acts of the Apostles is read; the reading of that book begins now, you see. Today begins the book which is called the Acts of the Apostles. Anybody who wishes to make progress has the means of doing so. . . .

So pay attention, and see how the Holy Spirit is going to come at Pentecost. And this is how he will come; he will show himself in tongues of fire. You see, he breathes into us the charity which should set us on fire for God, and have us think lightly of the world, and burn up our straw, and purge and refine our hearts like gold. So the Holy Spirit comes, fire after water, and you are baked into the bread which is the body of Christ. And that's how unity is signified.

Augustine then explains the Mass ritual point by point, and end his sermon in this way:

"So receive the sacrament in such a way that you think about yourselves, that you retain unity in your hearts, that you always fix your hearts up above. Don't let your hope be placed on earth, but in heaven. Let your faith be firm in God, let it be acceptable to God. Because what you don't see now, but believe, you are going to see there, where you will have joy without end" (Sermon 227).

Augustine uses the crossing of the Red Sea to illustrate the way in which baptism prepares for the eucharist.

When did the Israelites eat the manna? After they had crossed the Red Sea. The Apostle tells us what the Red Sea symbolizes: *Brothers, I want you to remember this: our fathers were all under the cloud and all passed through the sea.* Why did they pass through the sea? As if he heard you asking the question, Paul continues: *By the cloud and the sea all of them were baptized into Moses* (1 Cor 10:1). If the sea was so efficacious, then, how much more the outward sign of baptism? And if the prefigurative action in the sea brought the people, once across, to the manna, what will Christ show us by means of his truly efficacious baptism, once his people have passed through it?

By means of baptism he brings all his believers across, slaying their sins like so many pursuing enemies, just as all the Egyptians were slain in the sea. Whither does he bring us across, brothers? Whither does Jesus bring us through baptism, which was prefigured in Moses' action when he brought the Israelites across? Whither does he bring us? To the manna. But what is this "manna"? *I am myself the living bread come down from heaven* (Jn 6:51). The faithful who have crossed their "Red Sea" receive the "manna." Why "Red Sea"? We have seen what the "sea" is, but why "red"? The original Red Sea symbolized the baptism Christ gives. In what sense is the baptism of Christ red, except that it is consecrated by the blood of Christ? (*Homilies on the Gospel of John* 11, 4).

As a gift which comes to us from Christ through the Church, the eucharist builds up the Church and strengthens the body's life by deepening unity and fostering love.

If anyone eats this bread he shall live forever; the bread I will give is my flesh, for the life of the world (Jn 6:51). . . . The faithful recognize the body of Christ, provided they not neglect to be the body of Christ, and they become the body of Christ if they decide to live by the Spirit of Christ. Only the body of Christ lives by the Spirit of Christ. . . . It is evident that my body lives by my spirit. Do you want to live by the Spirit of Christ? Then be in Christ's body. My body does not live by your spirit, does it? No: my body lives by my spirit, and your body by your spirit. So too the body of Christ can only live by the Spirit of Christ. This is why in explaining this bread to us the apostle Paul says: *Because the loaf of bread is one, we, many though we are, are one body* (I Cor 10:17).

O sacrament of love, sign of our unity, bond of our brotherhood and sisterhood! Any who long for life have here its very source. Let them come near and believe, unite with you and live. Let them not shrink back from being woven into the tissue of members; let them not be rotten members that deserve to be cut off; let them not be deformed members that cause the body shame. Let them rather be beautiful, becoming, and healthy: united to the body and living for God by the power of God. Let them now toil on earth, so that afterwards they may rule in heaven (*Homilies on the Gospel of John* 26, 13).

In other passages besides Sermon 227 (quoted just above), the unity of which the eucharist is symbol and bond is expressed by means of an image derived by ancient tradition (beginning with the *Didache*) from the material used for the sacrament.

My flesh, he tells us, *is real food and my blood real drink* (Jn 6:55). People seek food and drink so that they may stop being hungry and thirsty. But this happy result comes only from the food and drink that make them immortal and incorruptible. This will happen in the fellowship of the saints where peace and unity will be full and perfect. Therefore, as men and women of God have come to understand long before us, our Lord Jesus Christ left us his body and blood in the form of elements in which unity is achieved out of multiplicity. The one element is made of many grains, the other of many grapes (*Homilies on the Gospel of John* 26, 17).

The eucharistic sacrifice establishes bonds of love between the children of the Church that is still in exile on earth, and the dead.

It is not to be doubted, though, that the dead can be helped by the prayers of holy Church, and the eucharistic sacrifice, and alms distributed for the repose of their spirits, so that God may deal with them more mercifully than their sins have deserved. The whole Church, I mean, observes this tradition received from the Fathers, that prayers should be offered for those who have died in the communion of the body and blood of Christ, whenever their names are mentioned at the sacrifice in the usual place, and that it should be announced that the sacrifice is offered for them (Sermon 172, 2).

Good example

Augustine exhorts the faithful who were baptized long ago to give a good example to the newly baptized. Knowing, however, that not all will do their duty, he urges the new Christians to draw inspiration from the examples of virtue which are certainly not lacking in the Church.

They are called infants because they have just now been born to Christ, having previously been born to the world. What ought to be growing strongly in you has been started afresh in them; and you that are already the faithful must set them good examples which can help them to make progress, not bad ones that may cause their ruin. Being newly born, you see, they look to you to observe how you live, who were born a long time ago. That's what we all do, when born of Adam's line; first we are babies, and then, once we've begun to notice the habits of grown-ups, we watch out for things to imitate. And since the younger follows where the elder leads, it is to be hoped that the elder will proceed along a good road, or else by following along a bad one younger and elder may perish together. And so you, brothers and sisters, who are after a fashion, in virtue of your age, parents of rebirth, I am addressing you and urging you so to live, that you may rejoice with those who imitate you and not perish with them. . . .

I am now going to address them, telling them to be grain on the threshing-floor, not to follow the chaff which is whirled around by the wind, and with which they would be lost; but to stay put on the floor with the weight of charity, so that they may eventually reach the kingdom of immortality. So you then, brothers and sisters, you, sons and daughters, you, the new offspring of mother Church, I beg you by what you have received to fix your eyes on the one who called you, who loved you, who went looking for you when you were lost, who enlightened you when you were found, and not to follow the ways of the lost, for whom the name of "faithful" is just a mistake; I mean, we're not asking what they are called, but whether they fit their name. If they have been born, where is their new mode of life? If they are of the faithful, believers, where is their faith? I hear the name, let me also recognize the reality.

Choose for yourselves the ones to imitate; those who fear God, who enter the church of God with reverence, who listen carefully to the word of God, commit it to memory, chew over it in their thoughts, carry it out in their actions; choose them for your imitation. And don't let a little voice say to you, "And where are we to find such people?" Be such people yourselves, and you will find such people. Like always sticks to like; if you live an abandoned sort of life, only abandoned people will attach themselves to you. Start living a good life, and you'll see how many companions surround you, what a wonderful brotherhood you can rejoice in. Finally, you can't find anyone to imitate? Be the sort of person someone else should imitate (Sermon 228, 1-2).

The Church a universal educator

In providing the gifts of enlightenment and grace of which I have been speaking, the Church gives the Christian the means of knowing the truth and advancing in virtue.

How many there are who, seeking self-exaltation apart from this tent that stands by the Lord's winepress, that is, apart from the Catholic Church, and too much in love with their honorable positions [referring to clergy of the Donatist sect], refuse to acknowledge the truth! If they would only take to heart the verse: *I had rather lie at the threshold of the house of my God than dwell in the tents of the wicked* (Ps 84:11), would they not cast aside their honorable positions and run to the vale of tears, thence to rise up within their hearts to God and to advance from strength to strength[6] by putting their trust in Christ and not in some fellow or other? . . . The Psalmist preferred to be lowly in the house of the Lord; but he who had invited him to the banquet, seeing him choose the lowest place, calls him to a higher: *Come up higher!* (Lk 14:10). But the Psalmist's choice was simply to be in the house of the Lord; the place did not matter, provided he was not outside the door! (*Expositions of the Psalms* 84, 15).

The blessings brought by the Catholic Church not only in relation to eternal life but even in the temporal sphere are lauded by Augustine in a well-known invocation to the mother of Christians.

O Catholic Church, true mother of Christians, rightly do you preach that pure and holy worship is to be given to God, the possession of whom means the happiest life possible to man. No creature are we to worship and serve. From that incorruptible and inviolable eternity, to which alone human beings should be subject and to which alone the rational soul must be united if it is not to be unhappy, you exclude all created, changeable, temporal reality. You do not confuse what eternity, truth, and peace itself distinguish, nor separate what the unique majesty unites. Moreover you embrace our neighbor in loving charity so that in you is to be found every effective medicine for curing the varied ills to which souls are subject because of sin.

You instruct and educate children in a simple way, the young with a strong hand, and the old in peace, thus respecting each one's age of soul no less than of body. You bid wives be subject in chaste and faithful obedience to their husbands, not to serve their lust but to beget children and for the companionship of family life. You give husbands authority over their wives, not that they may take advantage of the weaker sex but that they may follow the precepts of heartfelt love. You subject children to their parents in a kind of free servitude, and give parents a loving dominion over their children. You bind brother to brother and sister to sister in a religious bond that is stronger and closer than the bonds of flesh. You respect the bonds of nature and feeling but add those of mutual love in order to unite relatives and neighbors of every degree even more closely.

You teach servants to watch for their master's interests not only because of their subordinate condition but also from a love of duty. You make masters benevolent to their servants by urging the thought of God most high, who is Lord of both, and more ready to care for them than to coerce them. Reminding people of their common first parents, you unite citizen to citizen, nation to nation, and indeed all to each other, not only in the bonds of society but even in a kind of brotherhood and sisterhood. You teach the king to provide for his people, and you urge the people to be subject to their king. You make it clear to whom honor or affection, reverence or consolation, admiration or exhortation, teaching or rebuke or petition, is due, showing that not each of these is due to every person, although love is due to all and no one may harm another (*The Catholic Way of Life* I, 62-63).

Duties toward the Church

Live in the Church

"If persons are separated from this Catholic Church, then, however much they may think they lead a praiseworthy life, nonetheless by the simple fact that they are separated from the unity of the Church, they will not have life and the wrath of God will be heavy upon them" (Letter 141, 5).

> Let us therefore guard our unity, brothers and sisters! Apart from that unity, even the miracle-worker counts for nothing. . . . Peter drove out devils. Any aged widow, any layperson, can have charity and integral faith, yet not do what Peter did. For Peter is an eye in the body, while a widow or layperson is a finger; but the latter belong to the same body as Peter does. A finger may be less important than an eye, but it is not therefore cut off from the body. It is better to be a finger and attached to the body than to be an eye that is separated from the body (*Homilies on the Gospel of John* 13, 17).

> So believing then in the divine Trinity and the threefold unity, take care, dearly beloved, that no one seduces you from the faith and truth of the Catholic Church. . . . You can certainly see, my dear friends, even in the very words of the holy Symbol, how at the conclusion of all the articles which belong to the sacrament of faith, a kind of supplement is added, which says, *through the holy Church.* So shun as best you can the many and various deceivers, the multitude of whose sects and names it would take far too long to explain now. You see, we have many things to say to you, but you cannot bear them now. One thing only I urge you to take to heart, and that is by every means possible to turn your minds and your ears away from the person who is not a Catholic, so that you may be able to lay hold of *the forgiveness of sins* and *the resurrection of the flesh and life everlasting* through the one, true, and holy Catholic Church, in which we learn of the Father and the Son and the Holy Spirit, one God, to whom is honor and glory for ever and ever (Sermon 215, 8-9).

Have Confidence in the Church

> Meanwhile the vessel carrying the disciples, that is, the Church, is being tossed about and battered by the storms of temptations and trials; and there's no easing up of the contrary wind, that is, of the devil's opposition to her, but he goes on making every

effort to prevent her from reaching calm waters. But the one who is interceding for us is greater than he is. For in this turbulent situation in which we find ourselves struggling, he gives us confidence by coming to us and reassuring us. The one thing he has to do is stop us from shaking ourselves loose in our agitation in the boat, and hurling ourselves into the sea. Because even if the boat is being agitated and tossed about, still it is a boat. It alone carries the disciples, and receives Christ on board. Sure, it's in distress and danger in the sea, but without it we all perish immediately. So keep yourself in the ship, and turn to God with your requests. With sailors, you see, when every other plan fails, when the vessel doesn't answer the helm, and cramming on more sail is more dangerous than useful, when all human efforts and endeavors have been tried and found unavailing, then all that's left to them is the urgent pouring out of their voices to God in prayer. Well now, if God enables seafarers to come safely to port, is he going to leave his Church to her fate, and bring her through to the final haven of rest? (Sermon 75, 4).

Love the Church

"How many seek Jesus only for their temporal advantage! One individual has a piece of business in hand and looks for the good word of the clergy; another is oppressed by someone more powerful and takes refuge in the Church; others want the Church to intervene in their behalf with someone over whom they have no influence. The Church is daily filled with this kind of people" (*Homilies on the Gospel of John* 25, 10).

Instead we should love the Church with the sincere and unselfish love of children for their mother. "Let us love the Lord our God, let us love his Church: him as a father, her as a mother; him as master, her as his servant. . . . What good is it not to offend your Father, when he avenges any offense to your mother! What good is it to praise the Lord, to honor God and preach his name, to acknowledge his Son and profess that he sits at the Father's right side, if you blaspheme against his Church? . . . Be of one mind, then, dear brothers and sisters, in regarding God as your Father and the Church as your mother" (*Expositions of the Psalms* 89, 11).

"Love your father, but not above your Lord; love the one who begot you, but not above the one who created you. . . . Finally, from the love you have for your parents weigh up how much you ought to love God and the Church. After all, if those who bore you, only to die in due course, are to be loved so much, with how much charity are those to be loved who have borne you in order to enter eternity, in order to remain in eternity?" (Sermon 344, 2).

Our love for the Church must be an active love. The fruitless trees which grew only after the first sin are a taunt addressed to human beings "so that they may realize how shameful it is for them to be without good works in the Lord's field, that is, in the Church, and may fear lest God abandon them, just as they abandon the sterile trees in their fields and do not tend them" (*On Genesis: A Refutation of the Manicheans* I, 13, 19).

It is the duty of the faithful to heed the anxious exhortations of their pastors. "So it's our business, those of us, whatever sort of people we are, whom the Lord has appointed laborers in his field, to say these things to you: to sow, to plant, to water, even to dig round some trees and put on a basket or two of manure. It's our business to do all this faithfully, yours to receive it faithfully, the Lord's to help us in our work, you in your faith, all of us in battling away, but overcoming the world in him" (Sermon 101, 4).

The faithful must not only receive, but also give, especially by watching over the religious and moral climate of their own homes, where the father of the family has the position of a bishop.

> You heard in the gospel all about the reward of the good servants and the punishment of the bad ones. And the sum of that servant's wickedness, the one who was condemned and so severely sentenced, was this, that he was unwilling to invest. He kept intact what he had received; but his master wanted some interest on it. God is greedy for our salvation. If one who merely failed to invest is given a sentence like that, what should people expect who squander the capital?

> So we up here are stewards, we make the investments, you receive them. We want to collect the interest and the profits: lead good lives. That, you see, is the interest on our investments. But please don't assume that making investments has nothing to do with you as well. You can't lay out investments, dispense loans, from this particular high counter. But you can do it wherever you happen to be. If Christ is attacked, defend him; answer the grumblers, rebuke the blasphemers, distance yourselves from their company. In this way you make investments, in this way you earn some of them as interest. Do my job in your own homes. A bishop is so called because he supervises, because he has to watch over those in his care. So everyone of you in his own house, if he is the head of the household, the job of bishoping, supervising, ought to belong to him, how his people believe, seeing none of them drift into heresy, not his wife, nor his son, nor his daughter, nor even his slave, because he was bought for such a high price. The apostle laid down rules setting

the master over the slave and the slave under the master; Christ, though, paid one and the same price for them both. Don't disdain the least of your household. If you do that, you are investing what you have received; you won't be slothful slaves, you won't have to fear so appalling a sentence (Sermon 94).

NOTES

1. See Gn 3:14.
2. 2 Cor 11:2.
3. See Gal 4:19
4. See Mt 9:15.
5. See Ps 33:12.
6. See Ps 84:7.

CHAPTER 7

LOVE

Love, the Center of Christian Life

"A body gravitates to its proper place by its own weight. This weight does not necessarily drag it downward, but pulls it to the place proper to it: thus fire tends upward, a stone downward. Drawn by their weight, things seek their rightful places. If oil is poured into water, it will rise to the surface, but if water is poured onto oil it will sink below the oil: drawn by their weight, things seek their rightful places. They are not at rest as long as they are disordered, but once brought to order they find their rest. Now, my weight is my love, and wherever I am carried, it is this weight that carries me" (*Confessions* XIII, 9, 10).

For Augustine, then, love is a force which gives vital impulse and direction to all human activity. And if, in the context from which the words just quoted are taken, it is divine love that acts in us, then it is the Holy Spirit ("your gift," says Augustine a moment later) who impels us upward, toward the peace of the mystical Jerusalem. The passage continues: "Your gift inflames us and carries us upward; we are on fire and we rise up. We climb *the ascents that are in our hearts* (Ps 84:6) and we sing *a song of ascents* (Ps 120:1). Your fire, your good fire, inflames us and we arise: we rise on high toward the *peace of Jerusalem* (Ps 122:6). For *I rejoiced because they said to me, We will go up to the house of the Lord* (Ps 122:1). There good will shall establish us, so that we will want nothing else but to abide there forever."

The central importance of love is thus, for Augustine, an elementary datum of psychology. The action of grace gives a new dimension of potency to a thrust that is part of our essential structure and orients us to a transcendent goal.

If faith in the resurrection of Christ is what distinguishes the Christians from pagans and Jews, then what distinguishes them from the devils, who in their own way are also believers, is good works and, above all, love.

Just as we are distinguished from others by faith, so let us also be distinguished by morals, be distinguished by works, on fire with charity, which the demons never had. It's the fire those two also were burning with on the road. When Christ, you see, had been recognized and had left them, they said to each other, *Were our hearts not burning within us on the road, when he opened the scriptures to us?* (Lk 24:32). Burn, then, in order not to burn with the fire the demons are going to burn with. Be on fire with the ardor of charity, in order to differentiate yourselves from demons. This ardor whirls you upward, takes you upward, lifts you up to heaven. Whatever vexations you suffer on earth, however much the enemy may humiliate Christian hearts and press them downward, the ardor of love seeks the heights.

Here's a comparison for you. If you're holding a burning torch, holding it upright with its head on top, the flame, like hair, surges up toward the sky; lower the torch, the flame goes up to the sky; turn the torch upside down, do you also push the flame down to the earth? Wherever the burning brand is turned, the flame knows no other road, but to seek the sky. *Fervent in spirit* (Rom 12:11), set yourselves alight with the fire of charity; get yourselves white-hot with the praises of God and the excellence of your morals. One person's warm, another cold; let the warm person kindle the cold; and let the one who is lacking in ardor desire an increase, pray for assistance. The Lord is always ready to give; let us choose to receive with open, expansive hearts (Sermon 234, 3).

It is already clear that love cannot be simply one of the various virtues that must find a place in the life of Christians. It has a far deeper and more essential significance, for it determines the very direction of their life; it determines their attitudes and confers authentic value upon them at every moment. If it be love that carries me wherever I go, then my going acquires its meaning and value from the sincerity and direction of the love which gives rise to my desires, actions, and sufferings.

But we must not expect from Augustine, or from the Fathers of the Church generally, a theory of morality that is based solely or primarily on data from psychology or speculative thought. For Augustine the word of God is the lamp that illumines our path. Consequently his teaching on love, too, is based on scripture.

"It's the one topic, you see, for which, if anyone wishes to speak about it, he doesn't have to choose a special reading to provide him with an opportunity for his sermon; every page of the scriptures, after all, wherever you open them, rings of this subject" (Sermon 350A, 1).

> So if there's no time or leisure to pore over all the sacred pages, to leaf through all the volumes of the words they contain, to penetrate all the secrets of the scriptures, hold on to charity, on which they all depend. In this way you will hold onto what you have learned there; you will also get hold of what you haven't yet learned. I mean, if you know charity, you know something from which that also depends which perhaps you don't yet know; and in whatever you do understand in the scriptures, charity is revealed, while in the parts you don't understand, charity is concealed (Sermon 350, 2).

In fact, according to the words of Jesus which Augustine had just cited, on the two commandments of love *the whole law is based, and the prophets as well* (Mt 22:40).

If readers keep these basic affirmations in mind, they will not be tempted to make an inventory of the biblical texts which Augustine quotes and comments on, in order to find a short synthesis of his teaching on love. If every page of scripture speaks of love, readers would likely be overwhelmed by the mass of material they would turn up. I shall, therefore, limit myself to pointing out some aspects of Augustine's doctrine on love and to presenting them in an order which, while not attempting to fit his teaching into patterns imposed from without, will enable us to advance without confusion through a vast and complex material. The biblical bases of the teaching will emerge from Augustine's own words.

In many passages Augustine speaks of love without specifying its object: God or neighbor. In any event, the distinction is not very important to Augustine, since he maintains the basic unity of love even with regard to its object which is, in the last analysis, always God-who-is-Love.

The greatest praise possible for love, in Augustine's view, is given in the scriptural words to which I have just alluded: *God is love* (1 Jn 4:8.16). "Brief praise, but how great! Brief in words, great in what is said. How quickly we say: *God is love!* It takes but a moment. Count the words: they make but a little sentence. Weigh them: then how great they are!" (*Homilies on the First Letter of John* 9, 1).

"So many precepts are given us concerning faith and hope! Who can gather them all and number them? But listen to the Apostle: 'Love is the fulfillment of the law' (Rom 13:10). Therefore, where there is love, what can be lacking? And where it is not, what else can be of any use?" (*Homilies on the Gospel of John* 83, 3).

Since love is *the fulfillment of the law*, then, even though it takes its place in the list of virtues alongside faith and hope, it is in fact identical with "justice," that is, with the Christian life in its totality. Therefore Augustine can offer the following list of equivalences: "Love in its beginnings is justice in its beginnings; love as it advances is justice as it advances; great love is great justice; perfect love is perfect justice" (*Nature and Grace* 70, 84).

Augustine throws light on the value of love by highlighting the many marvelous effects love has in the person whose outlook and action it inspires.

Love lightens the burden of the Christian life. "Is anything a burden to one who loves?" Augustine lists the discomforts — heat and cold, impassable roads through woods and over mountains — which the dedicated hunter willingly endures, and he observes: "But love makes all these things, not just tolerable, but even actually pleasant, so pleasant, that if you were to prohibit hunting, he would then endure torments indeed, he would suffer hideous boredom of spirit; he can't stand quiet. All that and more they will put up with in order to get at a boar, and how difficult they find it to endure anything, in order to get at God!" (Sermon 68, 12)

The same thought occurs in the treatise on the *Excellence of Widowhood* 21, 26: "Toils are not a burden to those who love; they even find delight in them, as does the hunter, the fowler, the fisherman, the grape-gatherer, the merchant, and the athlete. The important thing, then, is: What do you love? For, when we love we experience no weariness or else we love the weariness itself."

This psychological observation is confirmed by a saying of Christ,[1] to which Augustine alludes as he recapitulates what was said in a passage we read just above: "Everything becomes easy when one loves; that is why the burden of Christ is light. We might say that the only burden is love itself, and that is light" (*Nature and Grace* 69, 83). "Do you feel you have a driver? "Yes, I do," you say. Then say to him, *Direct my steps according to your word* (Ps 119:133). He directs you under his yoke and under his burden. For his burden to be light for you and his yoke easy, he himself inspired you with love. It's easy and comfortable for one who loves; for one who doesn't, it's difficult and rough (Sermon 30, 10).

The allusion to the gospel is accompanied, in the following passage, by the image of wings in which Augustine sees the two commandments of love. "The wings are the two commandments of love on which the whole law and the prophets depend. The light burden is the love which comes to fulfillment by obedience to the two commandments. If there is any difficulty met in observing the precepts, it is light to the lover.

Intensify my love that I may fulfill the commandment!" (*Expositions of the Psalms* 68, 18).

"It is charity, after all, that renews man; because just as cupidity makes a man old, so charity makes him new. . . . He both called this commandment new, and he came here to renew us, and he made us into new men, and he promised us a new, and, what's more, eternal, inheritance" (Sermon 350A, 1). It is not hard to see why love is presented as the source of an interior renewal. If love is the deepest and most decisive motive for human action, the one that determines its direction and gives it its value, then it is clear that a life which until yesterday was marred by indifference or distorted by the passion that weakens the will is renewed in its depths by the revelation of true love. For this revelation draws the veil from a new goal, points out new ideals, and inspires new energy. Love is the secret of spiritual youthfulness, since it shows life at every state in the light of an ideal for the sake of which it is worth the effort to live without the compromises suggested by egoism and without the conventions imposed by a deadly servitude. The history of holiness is marked by the presence of perennially youthful men and women to whom boredom and lassitude are unknown and who radiate joy and hope to those around them.

It is love that sharpens the soul's sense of mystery and thus makes it experience God in a new way, awakening within it a song of praise and gratitude.

> God is everywhere present, and present in his entirety. His wisdom *reaches from end to end mightily, and governs all things well* (Wis 8:1). What God the Father is, that his Word, his Wisdom, also is: light from light, God from God. What, then, do you long to see? What you long to see is not far from you! Indeed the Apostle says that he is not really far from any one of us. *In him we live and move and have our being* (Acts 17:27). What wretchedness, then, to be far from him who is everywhere!

> Become like him through devotion, be attentive to him in your thoughts, for *his invisible realities have become visible, recognized through the created things he has made* (Rom 1:20). Look upon creation, admire it, seek its author. If you are unlike him, you will be repelled; if you are like him, you will exult. And when, being like him, you begin to draw near him and to have a clearer perception of him in proportion to your growing love (for God too is love), you will come to a new understanding with regard to something you used to say. For before you shall have had this new perception of God, you used to say that you could speak of God. But now you will begin to perceive God, and will realize that what you perceive cannot be expressed. But when you

learn this, are you to fall silent and not praise God? Are you to be mute when it comes to praise? Are you not to thank him who willed to make himself known to you? You used to praise him when you were seeking him; will you fall silent, when you find him? By no means! You will not be an ingrate! (*Expositions of the Psalms* 100, 5-6).

Love is the source of peace. There is no room for anxieties and fears (except as a trial permitted by the heavenly Father in his wisdom) in those who no longer seek themselves but are advancing in the way of love which seeks only to give and to give itself. "As love grows the soul acquires assurance, and where there is full assurance there is no fear. The apostle John says the same: *Perfect love casts out all fear* (1 Jn 4:18)."

Love is freedom. Love proceeds from a choice which is a genuine exercise of freedom. Those who act out of love affirm that he is free not only from external coercion but also from the servile fear of punishment and from the movements of egoism and passion that impel them to do what reason and their sense of truth and justice tell them they should not do. "*The love of God has been poured out in our hearts* not through the letter of the law, but *through the Holy Spirit who has been given to us* (Rom 5:5). This is the law of freedom, not of slavery, precisely because it is the law of love, not of fear" (*Nature and Grace* 67). Love expands the heart and makes it find joy in the freedom of the children of God. Augustine, who was much more sensitive to spiritual teaching than to the enchantment of biblical poetry, discovers this truth in the great passage in which Job describes the horse who trembles as he sniffs the smell of battle: "When he comes out into the light of freedom, he easily performs good works and prances exultantly in the vast field of love" (*Notes on Job* 39).

Love is the root of all good works. "Just as *greed*, after all, *is the root of all evil* (1 Tm 6:10), so charity is the root of all good things. *So the fullness of the law is charity* (Rom 13:10)" (Sermon 179A, 5).

One of Augustine's sermons ends thus: "None of God's other gifts make anything have the slightest value, unless they are tied together with the bond of love" (Sermon 209, 3). Love "is the only thing, you see, which both surpasses all things, and without which all things are worth nothing, and which draws all things to itself" (Sermon 354, 6).

Therefore, brothers and sisters, pursue after charity, the sweet and salutary bond of our minds, without which the rich man is poor, and with which the poor man is rich. This it is that endures in adversity, is moderate in prosperity; brave under harsh sufferings, cheerful in good works; utterly reliable in temptation, utterly open-handed in hospitality; as happy as can be among true brothers and sisters, as patient as you can get among the false ones. . . . It is the one thing that is not cast down by another's good fortune, because it is not jealous. It is the one thing that its own good fortune does not puff up, because it is not conceited. It is the one thing that is not pricked by a bad conscience, because it does not act boastfully. It is steady and unshaken amid reproaches, it is well-disposed in the face of hatred; calm in the face of anger, innocent in the midst of intrigues, groaning in the midst of iniquity, breathing again in the presence of truth.

This sermon ends in a fervent exhortation.

So pursue after charity, and by thinking holy thoughts about it bring forth the fruits of justice. And whatever you can find in the praises of charity that is grander than what I have been able to say, let it appear in your behavior. It is right, after all, that an old man's sermon should be not only weighty, but brief (Sermon 350, 3).

Love of God and Love of Neighbor

Augustine's teaching on love acquires new clarity and depth when his theological reflection and pastoral solicitude (two attitudes which more often than not fuse into one) are brought to bear concretely on the love of God or the love of neighbor.

So I think, but it's only what I think, that the reason the Holy Spirit was given twice was to impress on us the two commandments of charity. There are two commandments, you see, and there's one charity: *You shall love the Lord your God with your whole heart, and with your whole soul*; and, *You shall love your neighbor as yourself. On these two commandments depend the whole law and the prophets* (Mt 22:37-40). One charity, and two commandments; one Spirit and two givings. I mean, it wasn't one given first and another given later on, because it is not a different charity which loves the neighbor from the one which loves God. So it's not another charity. With the same charity as we love our neighbor with, let us also love God. But because God is one thing, our neighbor another, they are loved with one charity, and yet they are not one thing being loved. So while love of God is the great commandment that first has to be impressed on us, love of neighbor the second, one begins all the same from the second in order to attain to the first: *For if you do not love the brother whom you can see, how will you be able to love God, whom you cannot see?* (1 Jn 4:20) (Sermon 265, 9).

Love of God is the central focus of Christian life; it is also in a sense the synthesis of that life, since it implicitly includes the love of self and of neighbor. "In loving God you love yourself and are enabled to love your neighbor as yourself, in a salutary way" (*Expositions of the Psalms* 119, XXVII, 6). This evidently does not mean that the love of God becomes secondary to love of self and of neighbor. Rather, the true love of self exists only when one loves God more than self. As the martyrs have taught us, it is in denying ourselves, according to the teaching of Christ, that we love ourselves in a true way.[2]

Why love God? Because he is the supreme value and deserves an incomparably greater love than any other value. "Love God; you can't find anything better to love. You love silver, because it's better than iron or brass; you love gold more, because it's better than silver; you love precious stones more, because they exceed even the value of gold. . . . Love Christ; long for the light which is Christ!" (Sermon 349, 5)

God should be loved out of gratitude, since he has anticipated us with his own love, the supreme manifestation of which is the mystery of the redemptive Incarnation. "We, for our part, love [God] because *he first loved us* (1 Jn 4:19). Listen to the apostle Paul: *It is precisely in this that God proves his love for us because, when we were still sinners, Christ died for us* (Rom 5:8), the just for the unjust. . . . In taking flesh he also took what we might call your ugliness, that is, your mortality, so that by becoming like you and putting himself on your level he might spur you to love interior beauty" (*Homilies on the First Letter of John* 9, 9).

How are we to love God? With our words, certainly, as we sing his praises. But still more with our deeds and holiness of life.

> Love is a pleasing word but still more a pleasing deed. We cannot always be speaking of love. We have a great deal to do; our various actions are a distraction that prevents our mouths from constantly speaking of love, although there is nothing they can more profitably do. But even though we cannot always speak of love, we can always live it. For example, we cannot always be singing Alleluia, as we sing it this morning. We sing it, not even for a whole hour, but only for some little moment of that hour, and then we occupy ourselves with something else. Now, Alleluia, as you know, means "Praise God!" We cannot always be praising God with our tongue, but we can constantly praise him by our life. The works of mercy, the impulses of love, a holy and pious way of life, spotless purity, temperance and moderation — these are always to be observed. Whether we are in public or at home, with others or alone, speaking or remaining silent,

these are always to be observed, for all the virtues I have named are interior (*Homilies on the First Letter of John* 8, 1).

In another passage Augustine stresses the necessity and efficacy of the love which, rooted in the heart, inspires and directs our life at every moment, provided God be truly the object of our love.

An unclean love inflames the soul to a lust for earthly things and summons the soul, set now on the road to perdition, to the quest for perishable reality; it plummets the soul downward and sinks it in the depths. A holy love, on the contrary, elevates the soul to a higher world, inflames it with a longing for eternal things, spurs it to seek what does not pass away or die, and lifts it out of the depths of hell into heaven. Every love has its own inherent energy; it cannot remain inert in the soul of the lover but must lead the lover. Do you want to know what kind your love is? See where it leads you. Therefore, I do not bid you not to love. I bid you not to love the world, so that you may be free to love him who made the world (*Expositions of the Psalms* 122, 1).

If love of God necessarily includes love of neighbor, it is nonetheless true that there is a definite hierarchy of value among the two. From an objective viewpoint, priority undoubtedly goes to love of God. Concretely, however, we begin with love of neighbor, and in loving our neighbor our eye is purified so that we become capable of loving God.

Reflect with me on these two commandments. You ought to know them extremely well, for it is not enough what you think of them only when I mention them; rather, they ought to be indelibly written in your hearts. Think at every moment that you must love God and your neighbor: *God with your whole heart, with your whole soul, and with your whole mind*, and your *neighbor as yourself* (Mt 22:37-39; Lk 10:27). You must always be thinking of these commandments, meditating on them, keeping them before you, acting on them, carrying them out.

Love of God takes priority in the order of command, love of neighbor in the order of execution. He who gave you the two commandments of love did not put your neighbor first and God second, but God first and neighbor second. But you do not see God yet, and it is by loving your neighbor that you merit to see God. In loving your neighbor you cleanse your eye so that it can see God. As John expressly says: *If you do not love your neighbor whom you can see, how can you love God whom you cannot see?* (1 Jn 4:20). . . . Therefore, love your neighbor, and look within yourself for the source whence love of neighbor comes; within yourself, you will, as far as it is possible to you, see God (*Homilies on the Gospel of John* 17, 8).

There are, then, two ways of conceiving the relationship between love of God and love of neighbor. One way is more attentive to the evidence of psychology; the other is based on a consideration of co-existent values that must be integrated with each other.

But Augustine has still other ways of presenting the relationship. *Those who love their neighbor have fulfilled the law* (Rom 13:8). These words of Paul, says Augustine, raise a difficulty. There are two commandments of love, are there not? How, then, can it be enough to observe one of them and yet observe the whole law? The answer is suggested by two considerations, one psychological, the other theological. We can fool ourselves, Augustine notes, in believing that we love God, because such love is rather infrequently tested. On the other hand, we cannot love our neighbor as ourselves without also loving God, from whom come both the command to love our neighbor and the grace to fulfill the command.[3]

The same point is made in another passage: Those who love God cannot spurn him when he bids us love our neighbor. On the other hand, when we love our neighbor in a holy and spiritual way, what are we loving in him but God himself? Here we have a love that is different from every worldly love. To point up the distinction, the Lord added: *such as my love has been for you* (Jn 13:34). And indeed what did Christ love in us but God? (*Homilies on the Gospel of John* 65, 2).

"Human beings become spiritual. . . . by loving the Lord their God with their whole heart and soul and mind, and by loving their neighbor not in a fleshly way but as they love themselves. And they love themselves in a spiritual way if they love God with their whole being. *On these two commandments the whole law depends, and the prophets as well*" (Mt 22:40) (*True Religion* 12, 24).

The basic motive for love of neighbor is essentially theological in character. Augustine finds it expressed in a doctrine with which he is especially at home and makes the center of his ecclesiology: the doctrine of the mystical body. "On this point the apostle himself gave the example of charity, when he was urging us to love one another in the same way as the members of the body love each other in the body. *If one member suffers, he said, the other members also suffer with it; and if one member is honored, all the members rejoice with it. You are the body of Christ and his members* (1 Cor 12:26-27). If the members of a body which have their head on earth love each other, how should members love each other whose head is in heaven?" (Sermon 162A, 5)

Augustine comments thus on the meeting at Emmaus:

They listened, they were filled with joy, they breathed again, and as they declared themselves, they were on fire; and still they didn't recognize the presence of the light. But what a mystery, my brother and sisters! He goes in with them, he becomes their guest; and while he hadn't been recognized all along the way, he is now recognized in the breaking of bread. Learn to take in strangers as guests, where Christ can be recognized. Or didn't you know that if you take in any Christian, you are taking in him? Didn't he say himself, *I was a stranger, and you took me in?* And when he's asked, *Lord, when did we see you a stranger?* he answers, *When you did it to one of the least of mine, you did it to me* (Mt 25:35.38.40). So when a Christian takes in a Christian, members are serving members; and the head rejoices, and reckons as given to himself whatever has been lavished on a member of his. So here let Christ be fed when he's hungry, be given a drink when he's thirsty, clothed when he's naked, taken in when he's a stranger, visited when he's sick. Such are the needs of the journey; that's how we have to live in this wandering exile, in which Christ is in want. He's in want in his people, he's replete in himself (Sermon 236, 2-3).

The practice of fraternal love in turn deepens the union of Christians with one another and thus makes the reality of the mystical body ever more effective. "Let us therefore love one another as far as we are able and by our love draw one another to possess God within us. . . . Christ loved us in order that we might love one another; by loving us he has given us the help we need to unite ourselves with one another in mutual love and, being united by such a sweet bond, to be the members of so great a head" (*Homilies on the Gospel of John* 65, 2).

Augustine becomes lyrical when he sings the greatness of brotherly and sisterly love and its beneficent effects. "This love renews us, so that we are truly new people, heirs of the old covenant, and singers of the new song. This love, dear brothers and sisters, once renewed the holy men and women of ancient times, then the patriarchs and prophets, as it later did the blessed apostles. This same love now renews the peoples of the earth and gathers the human race, scattered though it is throughout the world, into a new people, the body of the new spouse who is wed to the only Son of God" (*Homilies on the Gospel of John* 65, 1).

Active love of neighbor is a ladder for climbing to the delights of contemplation. "Let us break our bread for the hungry and bring the homeless poor under our roof, let us clothe the naked and not spurn our own kin. When these fruits are burgeoning on earth, take heed and see that it is good.[4] Then may swift dawn break for us, so that

rising from this lowly crop of active works to the delights of contemplation, we may lay hold on the Word of Life above, and appear like
luminaries for the world, firmly set in the vault that is your scripture"
(*Confessions* XIII, 18, 22).

But if the love of neighbor is to produce these marvelous effects, it
must take for its model Christ himself and rise above every impulse of
passion and every purely natural and human sentiment. A passage
quoted just above continues as follows: "The members hear, and keep,
the words: *I give you a new commandment: Love one another* (Jn 13:34),
not as those love who corrupt one another, not as people love one
another because they are human, but as people love one another because they are all gods and sons and daughters of the Most High and
in order to be brothers and sisters to his only Son. They love one
another with the love with which he has loved them, intending to bring
them to a goal which will suffice them and where their desire for good
things shall be fulfilled" (*Homilies on the Gospel of John* 65, 1).

In particular, Christ is presented as the model of love for enemies.
"Love one another, you that love Christ; love your friends, love your
enemies. Don't think of it as being hard for you. . . . Notice the bridegroom hanging on the cross for you, and begging the Father for his
enemies: *Father*, he says, *forgive them, for they do not know what they are
doing* (Lk 23:24). . . . I taught my guardsmen this lesson. Let me recruit
you as well into my fight against the devil. Otherwise, you cannot possible fight without being defeated, unless you have prayer for your
enemies" (Sermon 90, 9).

> Here and now turn your attention to your master and Lord, not
> seated on his magisterial chair, but hanging on the tree, gazing
> all round him at the crowd of his enemies, and saying, *Father,
> forgive them, because they do not know what they are doing* (Lk
> 23:34). Observe the master, listen to one who imitated him.
> The Lord Christ was hardly praying at that moment, was he, for
> those who had asked him for pardon? You, on the contrary, are
> no doubt going to say, "And when can I do what the Lord was
> able to do?" Why should you say this? Notice where he did this;
> notice that he did it on the cross, not in heaven. After all he is
> always God in heaven with the Father; but on the cross he was
> man for you, where he offered himself as an example to be
> followed by all. It was for your sake, you see, that he uttered
> those words, so as to be heard by all. I mean, he could have
> prayed for them silently, but then there would have been no
> example for you to follow (Sermon 386, 2).

The Journey of Love

In the preceding pages we have already been hearing some of Augustine's teaching on the stages that make up the journey of love. He regards love of neighbor as a means of purifying the eye of the soul and preparing it to see and love God. The theme is of such interest that it is worth inquiring further of Augustine on this matter.

Grace of God

If readers have in mind even just the essentials of Augustine's teaching on grace, they will know that grace makes possible the first step to salvation and that human beings can do absolutely nothing on their own initiative; they must be anticipated and sustained by the grace of God. The same principle holds true in the order of practical love, in which Augustine, as I have noted, sees the reality of "justice," that is, Christian virtue and holiness.

A text of Saint Paul teaches this truth in a more explicit way: *The love of God has been poured out in our hearts by the Holy Spirit who has been given to us* (Rom 5:5). Augustine comments on this text in a sermon:

> Have you got charity? "I have," you say. Where from? "From myself." You are a long way from sweetness, if you've got it from yourself. But I will prove that you haven't got it. It is precisely because you think you get such a great thing from yourself that I don't believe you've got it. After all, if you had it, you would know where you got it from. . . . So you get your eyes and nose from God, and get charity from yourself? If charity, which beats them all, is something you have given yourself, you have made God cheap for yourself. What more can God give you? Whatever he gives you, it's bound to be less. Charity, which you have given yourself, conquers all things. But if you do really have it, you haven't given it to yourself. *For what do you have that you did not receive?* (1 Cor 4:7). To me, to you, who is it that has given anything and everything? God. Acknowledge the giver's generous donation, in order to avoid experiencing the judge's condemnation. By believing on the authority of the scriptures, God has given you charity, a great boon, charity that surpasses everything else. God has given it to you; because *the charity of God has been poured out in our hearts* — by you, perhaps? perish the thought — *through the Holy Spirit who has been given to us* (Rom 5:5) (Sermon 145, 4).

"So let charity, my brothers and sisters, insofar as it is present among you, be exercised by your living good lives, while insofar as there is little of it there, let it be obtained by your praying for it" (Sermon 209, 1).

Fear of God

Fear of God is a first step toward love: "True piety begins with fear but is made perfect in love" (*True Religion* 17, 33). If God were not to see you, Augustine asks, would you commit adultery?

> If you would, it means you are afraid of punishment, you don't yet love chastity, you don't yet have charity. You are afraid like a slave; it's dread of the bad, not yet love of the good. But go on being afraid, all the same, so that this dread may keep guard over you, may lead you to love. This fear, you see, with which you are afraid of gehenna, and that's why you don't do wrong, is restraining you; and in this way, though your mind inside wants to sin, it won't let it. Fear, you see, is a kind of warder, it's like the pedagogue of the law; it's the letter threatening, not yet grace assisting. All the same, let this fear keep guard over you, while being afraid stops you doing wrong, and in good time charity will come. It enters your heart, and to the extent that it comes in, fear goes out. Fear, you see, was ensuring that you didn't do it; charity is ensuring that you don't want to do it, even if you could entertain the idea with impunity. I have said what you should be afraid of, I have said what you should be desirous of. Set your sights on charity, let charity come in. Open the door to her by being afraid to sin, open the door to love that doesn't sin, open the door to love that lives uprightly. When she comes in, as I had started so say, fear begins to get out. The more she enters, the less fear becomes. When she has come in completely, there will be no more fear left, because *perfect love casts out fear* (1 Jn 4:18) (Sermon 161, 8-9).

Fear is a servant whose function is to prepare a place for the master, love:

> Those, you see, who only do good still because they are afraid of punishment, don't love God, are not yet counted among his sons; at least it's something, though, that they are afraid of punishment. Fear is a slave, charity a free lady; and let us say that fear is the slave of charity. To prevent the devil from taking possession of your heart, let the slave come ahead first into your heart, and keep a place for his lady who is coming. Do it, do good at least out of fear of punishment, if you can't yet do it out of love and justice. The lady will come, and the slave will withdraw, because *perfected charity casts out fear* (1 Jn 4:18) (Sermon 156, 14).

However, as Augustine notes in the continuation of the passage quoted above from Sermon 161, there is also a noble, holy fear, that of displeasing God; such a fear is not incompatible with love and is even, in fact, its constant companion.

> So charity comes in and drives out fear. She doesn't come in, however, without a companion of her own. She has her own fear with her, and brings him in herself; but he is a chaste fear, *abiding for ever and ever* (Ps 19:9). . . . A good man, though, a just man, a free person — because only the just are really free; everyone, you see, *who commits sin is the slave of sin* (Jn 8:34) — a free person takes delight in justice in itself; and if he could sin without anybody seeing and being a witness, he dreads God too as a witness. And if he could hear God saying to him, "I can see you when you sin, I won't sentence you to damnation, but you displease me;" he doesn't want to displease the eyes of a father, not of a fearsome judge, and so he's afraid, not of being damned, not of being punished, not of being tortured, but of spoiling his father's joy, of displeasing the eyes of someone who loves him. You see, if he himself loves, and is aware of his Lord loving him, he doesn't do what would displease the one who loves him (Sermon 161, 9).

Here is the program Augustine outlines for the consecrated virgin, who is able to understand his teaching. "Love God for his goodness, fear him for his severity; both sentiments will keep you from pride. If you love you fear offending your beloved loved. And what greater offense could there be than to displease by your pride him who for your sake displeased the proud? Where should that pure *fear of the Lord that endures forever* (Ps 19:10) be found in greater measure than in you whose thoughts are centered not on the world and how to please a husband, *but on the Lord and how to please him* (1 Cor 7:32-34)? That other [servile] fear is not to be found where love is, but this pure fear is inseparable from love. If you do not love, fear being lost; if you do love, fear to displease [God]. Love casts the former fear out; when love hastens into your soul, it brings this pure fear with it" (*Holy Virginity* 39).

Creatures

What is the function of creatures, all creatures, in relation to the love of God? Augustine, along with the whole Christian ascetical tradition, recognizes the danger that lurks in creatures, for they can capture our heart and claim from it an exclusive love that should in fact be directed to God alone as the ultimate end. On the other hand, Augustine is confident of the help God's creatures can offer us as we move toward the Creator. This accounts for the fervent exhortation which ends his reflections on the death of a twenty-year-old friend who had inflicted an incurable wound on his heart. "If bodies delight you, praise God for them and turn your love to their maker lest in what pleases you, you displace him. If souls delight you, love them in God, for they too are subject to change and it is only in him that they acquire stability; otherwise they would pass and perish. Love souls in him, then; carry with you up to him all of them that you can, and say to them: 'Let us love him! He made all things and is not far from us'" (*Confessions* IV, 12, 18).

Order and progression

In love, as in every virtue which limited, imperfect human beings can practice, there is an order and progression. As I have already observed, Augustine finds in zealous love of neighbor and in the exercise of charitable works the means and way of reaching love of God. I may quote here a passage from Caesarius of Arles which is regarded as a reworking of a sermon by Augustine. "So if you want to keep the order of true charity, act justly, love mercy, shun self-indulgence; begin, according to the Lord's instruction, to love not only friends but also enemies. And when you strive to maintain these standards faithfully with your whole heart, you will be able to climb up by these virtues, as by a flight of steps, to being worthy to love God with your whole mind and your whole strength" (Sermon 368, 5).

It is the Christian's duty to strive daily to climb the ladder of love, with the help which God gives in answer to trusting, persevering prayer. Augustine writes to Boniface, a general in the army: "Advance daily in this love through prayer and right action so that, with the help of him who commands and gives power to fulfill, your love may be nourished and may grow until it becomes perfect and makes you perfect" (Letter 189, 2).

"What gift does God give, in his grace, to those whom he has undertaken to lead? The writer continues and says: *Ascents in their heart* (Ps 84:6). God gives them steps by which to ascend. Where? In the heart. Therefore, the more you love, the higher you will rise" (*Expositions of the Psalms* 84, 10).

"So if my sermon has found in your hearts just a spark of such spontaneous love of God, nurse it carefully. Tell yourselves urgently to increase it by prayer, humility, the pain of repentance, the love of justice, good works, sincere sighs, a praiseworthy way of life, loyal friendship. Fan this spark of good love in yourselves; nourish it in yourselves. When it grows, and bursts into flame with a glorious, satisfying blaze, then it burns up the straw of all the greedy desires of the flesh" (Sermon 178, 11).

Drawing Closer

In this way the Christian will draw ever closer to the heights of love: that wholly disinterested, freely given love that seeks God alone. "If you love him, love him freely; if you love him truly, let the one you love be himself the reward" (Sermon 165, 4). "Let us love, let us love freely and for nothing. It is God, after all, whom we love, than whom we can find nothing better. Let us love him for his own sake, and ourselves and each other in him, but still for his sake. You only love your friend truly, after all, when you love God in your friend, either because he is in him, or in order that he may be in him. That is true love and respect; if we love ourselves for any other reason, we are in fact hating rather than loving" (Sermon 336, 2).

"Let us love God in a pure and holy way. Our heart is not pure if it worships God for the sake of a reward. *Shall we therefore go unrewarded for the worship we give God?* No: we shall surely have a reward, but the reward will be God himself whom we worship. He himself will be our reward, because *we shall see him as he is* (1 Jn 3:2). . . . However greedy you may be, God is enough for you. In this life your greed sought to lay hold of the whole earth, and even the heavens. But he who made heaven and earth is more than they" (*Expositions of the Psalms* 56, 17).

"So God must be loved, to the point that for love of him we even forget, as far as this is possible, ourselves. So what exactly is this about-turn? The soul has forgotten itself, but by loving the world. Now let it forget itself, but by loving the architect of the world" (Sermon 142, 3).

Once Christians reach these heights of love, they will be able to make their own the impassioned cry that breaks forth irresistibly from the heart of Augustine when he praises the love of the martyr (think how the souls of his hearers must have been shaken!): "It loves, is full of ardor and fervor; tramples on everything that delights it, and passes on; comes to things that are rough, fearsome, grim, threatening; tramples on them, breaks them, and passes on. Oh, to love like that, like that to advance, to die to oneself, to come to God!" (Sermon 159, 8).

In another sermon the song of love takes the form of the desire and intention that will inspire the whole activity of the pastor: to kindle in the hearts of the brethren the flame that burns in his own. Augustine is commenting on Psalm 34:4. "I do not want to be the only one to embrace the Lord. . . . Rouse love within yourselves; cry each to the other and say: *Let us together extol the Lord.* Have that kind of fervor in you! Why else do I read these words to you and explain them? If you love God, carry with you to that love all those who are united to you and all who are in your house. If you love the body of Christ, that is, the unity of the Church, draw them all to taste this joy, and say: *Let us together extol the Lord.* . . . Draw all whom you can, by exhorting, supporting, praying, discussing, giving account, and this with meekness and gentleness. Draw them to love!" (*Expositions of the Psalms* 34, II, 6-7).

Augustine trusts in the truth: "The truth always wins out!" (Sermon 296). "The truth can be hidden for a time, but it cannot be overcome" (*Expositions of the Psalms* 62, 16). The victory profits the one who is overcome: "The good for human beings does not consist simply in their being overcome; it is good for them that truth should overcome them with their consent, and bad that it should overcome them against their will. But the truth necessarily conquers, whether the conquered refuse it or accept it" (Letter 238, 29). It is in the name of truth, to which final victory is assured and in comparison with which it matters little that this or that person overcomes, that Augustine speaks in public and in private, writes, and seeks to meet his adversaries in debate.

The victory of truth is important, but it is all the more valuable if it leads to the victory of love. It is in this light that Augustine views the struggle against the Donatists who deny unity and thus are the enemies of love. It is in regard to such a struggle, whatever be the means used in carrying it on, that he proclaims as the sure rule of Christian action: "Love, and then do what you will!" (The fact that objectively speaking, in the second phase of the long conflict, Augustine, like the other people of his time, forgot certain essential rights of freedom does not deny the sincerity of his heart which always shows itself inspired by love.) At a decisive moment of change in the relations between Catholics and Donatists, on the eve of the history-making conference at Carthage in May, 411, Augustine gives voice to his firm trust in the victory of truth. But this victory in turn will have as its purpose and result another victory which completes and heightens the value of the first: the victory of love. "Those, you see, who refuse to be defeated by truth, are defeated by error. Oh, if only charity rather than animosity could overcome them! Isn't it good for him to lose the case, because if he loses he will hold onto the whole, while if he wins, he will be left with the part — or rather if he appears to win, because it's only truth that ever wins. The victory of truth is charity" (Sermon 358, 1).

NOTES

1. See Mt 11:30.
2. See Sermon 330, 1-2.
3. See Augustine, *Explanation of the Letter to the Galatians* 45.
4. See Is 58:7.

CHAPTER 8

GRACE AND PRAYER

There is an historical reason for Augustine's insistence on affirming and proving the need human beings have of God's grace if they are to do the good and win salvation, and, consequently, the necessity and duty of prayer for obtaining from God his helping grace. Pelagian propaganda, which denied the necessity of grace as understood by the Catholic Church, obliged the bishop of Hippo to engage in strenuous polemics over a period of twenty years. The defense of orthodoxy during this period led Augustine to a clarification and deepening of understanding which represented a permanent gain for theology and spirituality.

The Pelagian denial was undoubtedly the occasion that spurred Augustine to assert and develop the doctrine of grace. But we must not forget that his meditation on the word of God, which was his daily food, must inevitably have reminded him of the need for and efficacy of God's help, for these are proclaimed on every page of scripture. This teaching was indeed already clearly present in those of Augustine's writings which antedate the rise of Pelagian propaganda in Africa.

We must, moreover, take into account another factor which played a part in making Augustine so zealous in his defense and further penetration of the doctrine on grace and prayer: his personal experience of sin, struggle, conversion, and daily temptation. His own past life, narrated in the *Confessions*, was always present in Augustine's mind. He finds in that life an experiential confirmation of what he has learned from the word of God: namely, that human beings cannot shake off the yoke of sin, overcome temptation, and be united to God, unless God anticipates and supports them with his grace.

Necessity of Grace

Given the purpose of this book, which is to present not so much the doctrinal positions of Augustine as the pointers for the spiritual life which arise from those positions, I shall limit myself here to a few texts which have a rather clear practical bearing.

> Human nature was capable by free will of wounding itself; but once wounded and sickly, it is not capable by free will of healing itself. After all, if you want to live so intemperately that you get ill, you don't require a doctor to help you; you yourself are all you need for falling down. But when by your intemperate behavior you have begun to get ill, you cannot deliver yourself from sickness in the same way as you were able by your excesses to ruin your health. . . . *Therefore, brothers*, as you have been reminded today, *we are debtors, not to the flesh to live according to the flesh* (Rom 8:12). This is what we have been helped for, what we have received the Spirit of God for, this is why we also beg for help every day in our difficulties. . . . *Therefore, brothers*, having received this help, this divine help, the arm of the Lord reaching down to us from above, and the help of the Holy Spirit extended to us by this very arm of the Lord, *we are debtors, not to the flesh to walk according to the flesh*. Because faith cannot work well, except through love . . .

> So the faith to be admired, the true faith of grace, is the sort that works through love. Now to have love, and to be able to have good works as a result of it, is that something we can give ourselves, seeing that it is written, *The love of God has been poured out in our hearts through the Holy Spirit which has been given to us* (Rom 5:5)? So entirely is love or charity the gift of God that it is even called God, as the apostle John says: *Charity is God,* and whoever remains in charity remains in God, and God in him (1 Jn 4:16). . . .

> *For if you live according to the flesh, you shall die* (Rom 8:13). Not the death when you depart from the body, because you will die that death even if you live according to the Spirit; but that death about which the Lord says so terrifyingly in the gospel, *Fear him who has the power to destroy both soul and body in the gehenna of fire* (Mt 10:28). So, *if you live according to the flesh, you shall die. But if with the spirit you put to death the doings of the flesh, you shall live* (Rom 8:13). That is our work in this life, with the spirit to put to death the doings of the flesh; every day to afflict them, diminish them, rein them in, do away with them. . . . This is our

action, this our warfare. While we are wrestling in this contest, we have God as a spectator; when we are in trouble in this contest, we can ask for God as a helper. Because if he doesn't help us himself, we won't be able, I don't say to win, but even to fight. . . . So it is to be feared you may presumptuously rely on your own spirit to mortify the doings of the flesh, and so perish for pride, and find yourself withstood for being proud, not granted grace for being humble; because *God withstands the proud, but gives grace to the humble* (Jas 4:6; I Pt 5:5). . . .

So to prevent this kind of pride creeping up on you, notice what follows. After saying, *If with the spirit you put to death the doings of the flesh, you shall live*; to stop the human spirit swaggering and boasting that it is fit and strong for this work, he went on to add, *For as many as are led by the Spirit of God, these are God's sons* (Rom 8:14). So why were you ready straightaway to start swaggering, when you heard *If with the spirit you put to death the doings of the flesh, you shall live?* Yes, I know, you were going to say, This is what my will can do, this is what my freedom of choice can do. What will? What freedom of choice? Unless he's in control of you, you fall; unless he picks you up, you lie there . . . The Spirit of God, you see, who is leading you or acting on you, is your helper in your own action. He gave you this very word "helper," because you too have to do something.

You must realize what you are asking for, realize what you are admitting, when you say, *Be my helper, do not forsake me* (Ps 27:9). You are, of course, calling on God as your helper. None are helped if they don't do anything themselves. *For as many*, he says, *as are led by the Spirit of God, these are God's sons*; not led by the letter, but by the Spirit, not by the law commanding, threatening, promising, but by the Spirit urging, enlightening, helping. *We know*, says the same apostle, *that for those who love God all things work together for the good* (Rom 8:28). If you weren't working, he wouldn't be working together with you.

But you must be very determined to keep wide awake, in case perhaps your spirit starts saying, "If God's cooperation and God's help is withdrawn, my spirit can still do this; even though with trouble, even though it can only do it with considerable difficulty, still it can fulfill the task." It's as if somebody said, "We can of course get there by rowing, though with considerable trouble; oh, if only we had some wind, we would get there so much more easily!"

That's not what God's help is like, that's not what Christ's help is like, that's not what the help of the Holy Spirit is like. If it's completely lacking, you won't be able to do anything good whatsoever. You can indeed act by your free will without him helping; but only badly. That's what your will, which is called free, is fit for; and by acting badly it becomes a slave deserving to be condemned. When I tell you, "Without God's help you can do nothing," I mean nothing good. Because without God's help you have free will to act badly; although it isn't in fact free. . . .

It's easier sailing, harder rowing; and yet even just by rowing you can get there. It's easier riding, harder walking; yet even on foot you can arrive. That's not what it's like. I mean, what does the true master say, who flatters no one, deceives no one, the honest and reliable teacher who is also the savior, to whom we have been brought by that tiresome, nagging pedagogue? When he was speaking about good works, that is about the fruit carried by the twigs and branches, he didn't say, "Without me you can indeed do something, but it will be easier through me," he didn't say, "You can bear your fruit without me, but a better crop through me." That's not what he said. Read what he said; it's the holy gospel, treading on the proud necks of one and all. This isn't what Augustine says, it's what the Lord says. What does the Lord say? *Without me you can do nothing* (Jn 15:5) (Sermon 156, 2-13).

One of the Pauline texts used in the foregoing passage comes up, more briefly, in another sermon to confirm the need of divine grace in order to do good.

But any who resist bad ways of loving become Christians with good ways of living. And they battle every day in their consciences, so that they may request the prize, when they win, from the one who sees them. But surely they wouldn't win, would they, if they were battling by themselves? Leave them there alone by themselves, and they're defeated. So when it's in relying on yourself that you don't consent to the lusts of the flesh, you are on your own, and because you are trusting in yourself, you are acting alone. But when you take no account at all of your own powers, and hand yourself over totally to God, *God is the one who is working for you both the willing and the acting on your good will* (Phil 2:13).

And that's why he said, *If with the spirit you put to death the deeds of the flesh, you will live* (Rom 8:13). Human frailty should claim nothing for itself, attribute nothing to its own efforts and nothing to its own powers, because if it attributes anything to itself, it makes room for pride, and pride makes room for a mighty fall. But those who attribute whatever progress they make entirely to God are making room for the Holy Spirit. And that's why the apostle says, For as many as are being led by the Spirit of God, these are the children of God (Rom 8:14). So if we are the children of God, the Spirit of God is leading us, the Spirit of God is ruling us. Whatever evil we do is ours, while whatever good we do is God's, who works in us both the willing and the acting on our good will (Sermon 335J).

Redemption, or the work of salvation, says Augustine in another sermon, is a new creation. As God alone can create, so God alone can save. "It is not you but I who am God. I created, I create anew; I formed, I reform; I made, I make again. If you could not make yourself, how can you remake yourself?" (*Expositions of the Psalms* 46, 14).

The grace of salvation is thus even greater than the grace of creation. "So apart from that grace by which human nature was established — which is common to Christians and pagans alike — the greater grace is this, not that we were created human beings through the Word, but that through the Word made flesh we were made believers" (Sermon 26, 7).

Therefore, while bending every effort to observe the law of God, Christians must put their whole trust in God's help.

> None of us, my brothers and sisters, absolutely none of us should be engaging in combat with some vice in our hearts, and presumptuously relying on ourselves. Don't be careless and slack about fighting, but don't either be proud in relying on yourselves. Whatever it is that troubles you, whether it arises from ignorance or desire, face up to the fight; don't be slack, but call upon the spectator who is ready to help you in difficulties. In that way you can win. Put another way, you don't win, because it isn't you winning. . . . *In the name of the Lord my God I will overcome him* (1 Sm 17:45); what remains to be said in this combat, but, *Not to us, Lord, not to us, but to your name give the glory* (Ps 115:1). . . .

Whatever opposes you is easily laid low, so that the one who put you in for the contest may watch you engaging in it, help you when the going is hard, and crown you with the victor's laurels when you win (Sermon 335K, 6).

Necessity and Efficacy of Prayer

There seems no need for extensive explanation of the nature of prayer according to Augustine. The numerous texts to be quoted in regard to other aspects of the problem will make this fundamental point sufficiently clear. Here, then, I can limit myself to quoting a simple and short definition of prayer. "Your prayer is a speaking to God. When you read [the scriptures], God speaks to you; when you pray, you speak to God" (*Expositions of the Psalms* 86). I must now turn to what is highly important to us in this book: to show how prayer is absolutely necessary for the Christian and how it is certainly efficacious.

According to one of Augustine's preferred images, we are beggars before God. Only by holding out our hand to him can we obtain what we need for our daily spiritual sustenance.

> So if you want to get some justice, be a beggar to God, who a little while ago was advising you in the gospel to ask, to seek, to knock. He knew his beggar, and here he is, a great householder and rich, rich, that is, in spiritual and eternal riches, and he's urging you and telling you, Ask, seek, knock. *Whoever asks receives; the seeker finds; to the one who knocks it is opened* (Mt 7:7). He urges you to ask; will he refuse you what you ask? . . . So then, my brothers, if God has made us his beggars by advising us and urging and ordering us to ask, to seek, to knock, we too should take some notice of those who ask us for things. We do some asking ourselves. Who are we, asking for things? Who are we, that are doing the asking? What are we asking for? We are asking the good God for things; we that are doing the asking are bad people, but we are asking for justice, by which we may become good. So we are asking for something we can keep forever, something, once we are sated with it, that will put an end to all further needs. . . . We are God's beggars, remember; for him to take notice of his beggars, we in our turn must take notice of ours (Sermon 61, 4-8).

"You hear a man begging, you yourself are a beggar to God. Something is asked of you, and you are asking for something. The way you treat your petitioner is how God will treat his. You are both full and empty. Fill the empty person from your fullness, so that your emptiness may be filled from God's fullness" (Sermon 53, 5).

The statement is categorical: "If you do not pray, you will be without hope" (*Expositions of the Psalms* 104, 1, 19). And elsewhere: "So, my friends, I'm obliged to urge on both you and myself to prayer. What I mean is that in all the many evils of this present life the only hope we have is in knocking by prayer, and in believing and being firmly convinced that your Father doesn't give you what he knows is not good for you" (Sermon 80, 2).

On the other hand, everything is possible to humble, trusting, persevering prayer. The necessity and efficacy of prayer are stated in lapidary form in the words Augustine uses in speaking of the humble confession of his temptations: "Give what you command, and command what you will." Later Augustine would explain this prayer and defend it against the accusations of Pelagius.[1]

In the passages already quoted Augustine points to a sure foundation for our trust in the efficacy of prayer: God's pledge, given in an absolute freedom that is inspired by infinite love, that he will hear our prayers. This pledge is given when God invites, exhorts, and commands us to pray. Here is another passage to the point. "We have all heard our Lord exhorting us, the heavenly teacher and most trustworthy of advisers, the one who encourages us to ask being the same as the one who gives when we ask. We heard him in the gospel encouraging us to ask insistently, and to knock even to the point of bad manners."

After relating the parable of the persistent friend (Lk 11:5-8), the preacher continues:

> So at the end of this parable the Lord added an exhortation, and actually prodded and spurred us into asking, seeking, knocking, until we get what we ask for, what we seek, what we are knocking at. He had been using an example in the opposite sense, just as he did with that judge who neither feared God nor respected men, and yet when a certain widow came appealing to him every day, he was beaten by boredom, and gave her unwillingly what he couldn't give out of good will.

> Our Lord Jesus Christ, though, who petitions among us and grants requests with the Father, would certainly not have urged us to ask unless he were willing to grant. How ashamed our human inertia should be! He is more eager to give than we are to receive; he is more eager to be merciful than we are to be delivered from misery; and of course, if we are not delivered from misery, miserable shall we remain. You see, it is for our own good that he urges us to do whatever he does urge us to do. Let's wake up, and trust his encouragement, and set our sights on his promises, and rejoice in his gifts (Sermon 105, 1-2).

Prayer is, moreover, pleasing to God, who delights to hear it. "Prayer that is pure and directed to God by a faithful heart arises like incense from a holy altar. No fragrance is more pleasing to the Lord; let it rise from all who believe" (*Expositions of the Psalms* 141, 5).

Being effective by God's will, prayer assures the help we need in order to overcome the enemy of our souls. "You guard against a man by avoiding him, against the devil by praying. A visible enemy can be avoided, can't he? — wherever he is, you can take care not to be. You are avoiding someone you can see. How are you going to avoid someone you can't see? By praying. Pray against him; your weapons are those of prayer. You keep silent, that's why he waylays you; you pray and he is on fire" (Sermon 22A, 5).

Prayer is a source of joy. Augustine knows this from personal experience, as the following admission shows: "When we are filled with joy as we pray, when our souls are made serene not by worldly prosperity but the light of truth — those who have experienced this light know what I mean!" (*Expositions of the Psalms* 35, II, 6).

This pastor of souls with this wide experience is well aware of the objection that may readily be brought against anyone who claims prayer to be infallibly effective. "So why do many people ask and not receive, if *everyone who asks receives*? Or are we wrong in thinking that we ask and don't receive? Apart from the daily examples we all know about, scripture itself testifies that the apostle Paul asked that the angel of Satan should depart from him, and didn't receive. And we discover that the bad asked and received, while the good asked and didn't receive." The reason is that too often men do not ask for what they ought to ask. "I mean, the things we request on account of this temporal life are sometimes good for us and sometimes bad for us. And when God knows they are bad for those who are his, he doesn't give them to them, however much they desire and ask for them, just as a doctor doesn't give his patient whatever he asks for, and because he cares for him he refuses him what he might allow him if he didn't care for him. So he listens to all those who are his as far as eternal life is concerned. He doesn't listen to them all as far as temporal longings are concerned" (Sermon 61A, 3-4).

What Are We To Pray For?

If, then, we wish to be heard, it is very important that we know what we should be praying for.

So because Jesus Christ our God, the only-begotten Son of God, has given us the firm hope of obtaining what we ask for by encouraging us to pray, we have to know what we ought to pray for. Is there anyone, after all, who doesn't beg God for things? But you have to take care what you beg him for. The giver is all ready to give, but the petitioner needs to be but right.

You get up in the morning and request God that you may get rich. Is that something really important, that God's children ought to ask God for? The reason God has chosen to grant riches even to the worst of men is so that his children might not ask for them from their Father as something very important. In fact, by his very deeds God is addressing us after a fashion, and saying to us, "Why ask me for riches? Is that all there is of importance or value that I will give you? Just take a look at the people I do give them to, and be ashamed of asking for them; the believer asking for what the actor's got, even the Christian housewife asking for what the call girl's got." Don't ask for such things in your prayers. Let him give them if he wants, not give them if he wants.

Much less, Augustine adds at a later point, may we ask for the death of our enemies.

"What," you will say, "are we to ask for?" Worldly honors? Smoke that blows away. You were safer lower down the scale. Are you disposed to face the dangers of the heights? Honors too, in any case, are only given by God, just like riches; but to make you think lightly of riches, he reminded you of the sort of people they are also given to. They are given to good people, so that you shouldn't think they are something bad; they are given also to bad people, so that you shouldn't think they are a particularly great good. It's the same too with honors; worthy people receive them, unworthy people receive them also, to save worthy people from regarding them as important.

"So come on," you say, "tell us now what we ought to ask for." Well, I won't have you on tenterhooks with many surprises, since I have already mentioned the gospel text, *Peace on earth to men of good will* (Lk 2:14). Ask for a good will (Sermon 105A, 1-2).

Elsewhere, however, Augustine shows himself more indulgent to human weakness, by saying that we may ask God for blessings of the temporal order, provided we leave the decision to the will of the heavenly Father. "In regard to temporal goods, then, we warn and exhort you, brothers and sisters, not to ask for anything with your heart set upon it but to ask only what God knows to be useful to you. You yourselves do not know what is useful to you. Sometimes you think something is useful! You are sick; do not tell the doctor what medicines he is to prescribe for you" (*Expositions of the Psalms* 54, 5).

Reflecting on the Apostle's words: *We do not know what to ask, so as to pray as we ought* (Rom 8:26), Proba sees a greater danger in praying badly than in not praying at all; therefore she asks Augustine what we are to pray for. He says: "My answer will be a brief one: pray to have the life of the blessed. This is, at bottom, what all want. Even those who live evil and abandoned lives would not live that way unless they thought they were or could become happy thereby. What else are you to pray for, then, except what good and evil people alike desire but only the good obtain?" (Letter 130, 9).

It is permissible and even necessary, while we are passing through earthly trials and suffering, to ask God for help and comfort. "Nothing is better or more important in time of trial than to withdraw from outward noise and enter into the secret chamber of the heart,[2] there to call upon God where no one sees me groaning or God coming to my aid. We must close the door against all disturbance from outside, humble ourselves by confessing our sins, and exalt and praise God for his correction as well as his consolation. This is how we must act, whatever be the effort it takes" (*Expositions of the Psalms* 35, II, 3).

It is spiritual needs above all, however, that should drive Christians to prayer, for they know, if anyone does, that the soul is more important than the body. They will beg the help they need to overcome temptations. Augustine develops this idea at some length when he comments on the sixth petition of the Lord's Prayer: *Lead us not into temptation.*[3] In these difficult moments we should imitate the disciples who when the storm rose called upon Jesus for help.[4]

> So then, there are two sorts of benefits, temporal ones and eternal ones. Temporal ones are such things as health, wealth, honor, friends, house, children, wife and the other things of their life through which we are traveling as foreigners. . . . Eternal benefits, on the other hand, are first and foremost eternal life itself, the imperishability and immortality of flesh and soul, the company of angels, the heavenly city, unfailing titles of nobility, a Father and a fatherland, the one beyond death, the other beyond enemies. We should be longing for these benefits with infinite desire, pray for them with tireless perseverance, not with long speeches but with the evidence of our sighs. Desire is praying always, even if the tongue is silent. . . . So let us beg for these everlasting benefits with insatiable eagerness, let us seek those good things with a singleminded determination, let us ask for those good things without a scruple of anxiety. . . .

> And therefore, dear brothers and sisters, let us ask for these temporal benefits too, but in moderation, safe in the knowledge that if we receive them, the one who gives them knows what is suitable for us. You've asked, have you, and haven't been given what you asked for? Trust the Father, who would give it to you

if it suited you. Look, you can work it out from a comparison with yourself. Your small son, ignorant of the ways of the world, stands in the same relation to you as you, ignorant of the divine world, stand in to the Lord. So there's your little boy, crying at you all day long to give him a pruning knife, to play with as a sword. You refuse to give it to him, you don't give it, you ignore his tears in order not to lament his death. Let him cry, let him torment himself in a tantrum for you to lift him up on a horse; you don't do it because he can't control it; it will throw him and kill him. You are denying him a part, because you are keeping the whole for him. But so that he may grow up and possess the whole safely, you don't gave him a dangerous little part (Sermon 80, 7).

As the preceding passage indicates, Augustine identified spiritual blessings with eternal blessings or eternal life. It is on the latter, above all, that the Christian's desires and prayers should focus. "Prayer will pass away and praise take its place; tears will pass away and joy replace them. Now, in the days of our affliction, let our prayers constantly rise to God from whom we ask but one grace. Let us not cease to ask for it until by his gift and under his guidance we attain it" (*Expositions of the Psalms* 27, II, 14, 11).

The Canaanite woman was right in asking Jesus to heal her daughter. How much more ought we pray to obtain eternal life! "There is one gift, immensely great indeed, for which we ought to pray always and not grow weary, something more important by far than the cure of a daughter. I mean immortal life. That is what we must pray for constantly, as long as we live on earth, until the end when we shall have life without end, a life in which there shall be no more praying but only rejoicing" (Sermon 77B, 1).

What are we to ask God for in prayer? We still have not heard the last and highest answer. God himself should be the supreme object of our prayer to him!

"'What shall I do?' you say. 'What shall I pray for?' What shall you pray for? For what the Lord, the heavenly teacher, taught you to pray. Call upon God as God; love God as God. There is nothing better than he: desire him, long for him" (*Expositions of the Psalms* 86, 8). "So because you can see the sort of people I've given it to, ask me for better things, ask me for more excellent things, ask me for spiritual things; ask me for myself" (Sermon 311, 13).

Before God, as Augustine has already told us, we are beggars. "What does the beggar ask you for? Bread. And you, what do you ask God for, if not Christ, who says, *I am the living bread who came down from heaven* (Jn 6:51)?" (Sermon 83, 2).

How Are We To Pray?
The cry of the heart (Corde clamandum est)

Recollection and interiority are the basic conditions for entering into a genuine conversation with God in prayer.

This fact is due to the special nature of this conversation, since the latter brings us into contact with him who dwells within us and knows our heart. "When human beings speak, they use articulated sound as an outward sign of their will. God, however, is to be sought out and addressed in the hidden recesses of the rational soul or in what we call the inner self. For here he willed to set up his temple" (*The Teacher* 1, 2). "Here [in our heart] we have a voice which God hears but of which the human ear knows nothing. . . . We have an inner mouth; within ourselves we pray, with that mouth we pray. And, if we prepare a house within ourselves to welcome God, therein we speak and therein we are heard" (*Expositions of the Psalms* 138, 2).

In his commentary on the Sermon on the Mount Augustine writes:

> *Whenever you pray*, he says, *go into your room* (Mt 6:6). What is meant by this room but the heart? The Psalmist indicates the same thing when he says: *Repent in your hearts and in your chambers* (Ps 4:5). Then Jesus continues: *Close your door, and pray to your Father in private.* There is little use in entering your room if you leave the door open to troublesome visitors. Through that door outward things will boldly plunge and seek to enter our inner selves. Outside, as I said, stand all temporal and visible things; they penetrate into our thoughts through the door, that is, the bodily senses. Then a crowd of empty images distract us as we pray. We must therefore close the door, that is, resist our senses, so that we may direct to our Father the spiritual prayer that arises in the heart where the Father, who is hidden, sees (*The Lord's Sermon on the Mount* II, 11).

Augustine is evidently not ignorant of the torment and danger arising from the countless distractions which threaten to make prayer lifeless.

> At times, however, your thoughts go aside and lead you astray, frequently when you are on your knees in prayer. You prostrate your body, bow your head, confess your sins, and adore God: I see the body lying there, but where has the soul gone? I see the members prostrated — let us see if the mind is standing vigilant, eyes fixed on him whom it is adoring, if it is not tossed about by its thoughts as by a heavy sea, and carried this way and that by the wind. If you were conversing with me and were suddenly to

turn to your servant, dismissing me from your attention as a partner in dialogue (to say nothing of someone from whom you were asking a favor!), would I not rightly think that you were insulting me? Yet that is what you do every day to God! (*Expositions of the Psalms* 141, 18).

I shall speak in a straightforward way, brothers and sisters, as one human being to another. Let each of us confront his own heart and look at himself without delusion or flattery. There is, after all, nothing more stupid than such self-deception. Let each one look therefore and see the kind of things that go on in the human heart: how our prayers are often frustrated by our empty thoughts, so that the heart can hardly stand and face its God; how it wants to control itself and face God, yet flees from itself as it were, unable to find bars within which to restrain itself or weights with which to prevent its flights and wanderings, so that it may stay and rejoice in its God. Even a single such stable prayer would be hard to find among many. Individuals might think this distracted state proper to them but not to others, were it not that in God's word we find David himself somewhere praying and saying: *I found my heart, Lord, so that I might pray to you* (2 Sm 7:27). He says that he found his heart, implying that it usually evaded his control and that he had to pursue it as though it were a fugitive but could not catch it and was forced to cry out to God: *My heart has abandoned me* (Ps 40:13).

Therefore, brothers and sisters, when I think of what the psalmist says here: *Gladden the soul of your servant, for to you, O Lord, I lift up my soul; for you are good and forgiving* (Ps 86:4), it seems to me that he calls God "forgiving" because he puts up with these wretched ways of ours but nonetheless expects us to pray so that he may strengthen us. And when we have offered him that prayer, he willingly accepts it and answers it. He does not remember the many poor prayers we utter and welcomes the one good one which with difficulty we manage to offer (*Expositions of the Psalms* 86, 7).

The cause of the difficulty of which I am speaking is the natural condition: it is very difficult to break the hold of sensible things which lay siege to our souls through our bodily senses.

People stand and sing to God, perhaps at some length; their lips continue to move in song, yet their thoughts may be off following some desire or other. Our mind was ready to praise God, but then because of various desires or cares it goes wandering thither and yon. From a higher place, as it were, the mind gazes down at its affections as they move about and turns to them in their restlessness, saying to them: *Praise the Lord, O my soul!* (Ps 146:1). Why are you, O my soul, taken up with other things? Why so occupied with earthly and mortal cares? Stay with me and praise the Lord! But the soul, weighed down and unable to be stable as it should, replies to its own mind: *I will praise the Lord in my lifetime.* What does this mean: *in my lifetime?* It means: Now I am in my death-time.

Therefore, first exhort yourself with the words: *Praise the Lord, O my soul!* and let your soul give answer: *I will praise as I can: weakly, poorly, wretchedly. Why? Because as long as I am in the body, I am in exile from the Lord* (2 Cor 5:6). But why do you praise the Lord in this imperfect, unstable way? Because *the corruptible body burdens the soul and the earthen shelter weighs down the mind that has many concerns* (Wis 9:15). Take from me the body that burdens the soul, and I will praise the Lord; take from me the earthen shelter that weighs down the mind which has many concerns, so that I may pass from multiplicity to unity, and I will praise the Lord. But as long as I am in my present state, I cannot praise him for I am weighed down. Well, then, will you be silent and never praise the Lord perfectly? *I will praise the Lord in my lifetime* (*Expositions of the Psalms* 146, 6).

Attention can be fostered by using the kind of prayer which the Egyptian monks practiced. They used

frequent but very brief prayers which they shot like arrows or darts "ejaculatory"; in this kind of prayer the watchful ready attention so necessary for anyone who prays does not weaken and disappear because the prayer is too long. The monks thus show rather clearly that on the one hand our attention should not flag simply because it cannot be long sustained, and on the other, if it can be sustained, it should not be interrupted too quickly. In other words, prayer does not require a great deal of speaking, but we should do a great deal of praying if attention and fervor can be sustained (Letter 130, 20).

It matters little whether the prayer be vocal or silent. The important thing is the "cry of the heart." "How many people utter words, but their hearts are mute! And how many are outwardly mute, while their hearts cry out! It is to the heart that God's ear is bent; as the bodily ear listens to what the mouth says, so too the ear of God is directed to the human heart. Many who pray with closed lips are heard, while many who are very vocal are not heard. It is with the heart that we must pray" (*Expositions of the Psalms* 120, 9).

Augustine is not requiring extraordinarily fervent dispositions in the person who prays; he simply wants us to apply ourselves seriously when we pray.

> If the cry that goes up to the Lord in prayer issues only from the bodily mouth while the heart is not intent upon God, is there any doubt that the prayer is empty? If it comes from the heart, even though the voice is silent, then other men may not perceive it but God does. Therefore, whether we pray vocally, when there is need of it, or silently, we must cry to God from our hearts. The cry of the heart means a serious application of the mind. When that is present in prayer, it expresses the strong affective movement of persons who pray with longing and give them hope that their prayer is effective. The whole heart cries when thoughts do not wander off elsewhere (*Expositions of the Psalms* 119, XXIX, 1).

It is clear from this passage and others quoted above that the stress on interiority as essential to prayer does not mean a rejection of vocal prayer but only a demand that such prayer be a sincere expression of the soul's tension toward God.

In other passages the function of words uttered in prayer is explained and justified by the stimulus they give us ourselves and to those others with whom we are engaged in a mutually supportive communion of prayer to God, the Father of all.

"When we pray, we have no need of the spoken word, except when priests pray and must express their thoughts so that other people, but not God himself, may hear and be aided by what they hear to be united to God" (*The Teacher* I, 2). "When we pray, we must not think of God being instructed or reminded by us; our words serve to impress things of our mind or to remind or instruct others" (*The Teacher* VII, 19).

"Our signs are not hidden from him who created all things by his word and does not look for human words. Words are therefore necessary in order that we may keep before our minds the thing we are asking for, and not because we think the Lord needs to be informed or bent to our will" (Letter 130, 20-21).

There is a "hidden sigh" uttered by the "servant of God" which other people usually do not hear. "But if a person's desire so occupies the heart, that the wound felt by the interior self finds outward expression, then the other asks why this sigh is uttered." The answer, in the case of true servants of God, is that they sigh because they "remember the sabbath rest" of God's kingdom, that is, the eternal rest for which they yearn (*Expositions of the Psalms* 38, 13).

Words, then, are appropriate, but not excessive words; and among the words we use, first place goes to those taught us by Christ himself.

So the first thing our Lord did was to cut out long-windedness, to stop you presenting God with a flood of words, as though you were keen on teaching God something with your flood of words. So when you pray, it's devotedness you need, not wordiness. *But your Father knows what is necessary for you, before you ask him for it* (Mt 6:7-8). So don't talk much, because he knows what is necessary for you. Here though, I suppose, some-one may say, "If he knows what is necessary for us, why should we say even a few words? Why pray at all? He knows; let him give us what he knows we need." Yes, but the reason he wanted you to pray is so that he can give to an eager recipient, not to one who is bored with what he has given. This eager desire, you see, is something he himself has slipped into our bosoms. So then, the words our Lord Jesus Christ has taught us in his prayer give us the framework of true desires. You are not allowed to ask for anything else, but what is written here (Sermon 56, 4).

"We may utter any other words whether formulated by us our-selves in order to make our own feelings clearer to us, or followed attentively in order to make these same feelings more intense. In any case, we shall be saying nothing that is not already expressed in the Lord's prayer, if at least we are praying in a right and fitting way" (Letter 130, 22).

Purity of heart

Remove all these things [vices]; enter into your heart, and you will find joy there. When you begin to experience this joy, your very purity of heart will be a source of delight and stimulate you to prayer. You may at times stumble on a place where silence reigns and peace and cleanliness, and you may say: "Let us pray here," for the orderliness of the spot pleases you and you think God will hear you there. But if the cleanliness of a visible place thus pleases you, why are you not offended by the uncleanness of your own heart? Enter, then, and make it all clean. Then raise your eyes to God and he will immediately hear you (*Expositions of the Psalms* 34, II, 8).

If we are to give ourselves seriously to prayer, we must be detached from riches.

How can you commit yourself deeply to prayer if you do not hope in God? But how can you truly hope in him if you also hope in insecure riches and forget the Apostle's salutary advice: *Tell those who are rich in this world's goods not to be proud, and not to rely on so uncertain a thing as wealth. Let them trust in the God who provides us richly with all things for our use* (1Tm 6:17-19) (Letter 130, 2).

"Prayer of course is something spiritual, and therefore all the more acceptable the more it lives up to its nature. But it is poured out with all the more spiritual power, the more the heart that is pouring it out is withdrawn from the pleasures of the flesh" (Sermon 210, 9).

Pray with faith (Orate fide)

It is absolutely necessary to pray with faith and therefore with confidence that we will be heard. "Have faith; but in order to have faith, pray in faith. But you wouldn't be able to pray in faith, unless you had faith. It is only faith, after all, that prays. *How, you see, will they call upon one in whom they have not believed? (Rom 10:14)*" (Sermon 168, 5).

> If faith falters, prayer perishes. I mean, who are going to pray to what they don't believe? Which is why the blessed apostle, in urging us to pray, said, *Everyone that calls upon the name of the Lord shall be saved.* And to show that faith is the fountainhead of prayer, and that the stream can't run when the head of water dries up, he went on to add, *How, though, shall they call upon one in whom they have not believed? (Rom 10:13-14).* So in order to pray, let us believe; and in order that the very faith by which we pray may not fail, let us pray. Faith pours out prayer, prayer being poured out obtains firmness for faith (Sermon 115, 1).

What are the motives on which faith relies in prayer? *First, the One who has promised is greater than we.* "What human mortal would dare to desire it, if God had not so graciously promised it? Pray; it's a great thing you are praying for, but the one who promised it to you is greater" (Sermon 77B, 6).

Secondly, our Father is good.

> In the reading from the holy gospel the Lord urged us to pray: *Ask, he said, and you shall be given; seek, and you shall find; knock, and it shall be opened to you. For everyone who asks receives; and the seeker finds, and to the one who knocks it shall be opened. Or who is the man among you of whom his son asks for a loaf, will he hand him a stone? Or if he asks for a fish, will he hand him a snake? Or when he asks for an egg, will he hand him a scorpion? If you therefore, he says, bad though you are, know how to give good gifts to your children, how much more will your Father who is in heaven give good things to those who ask him? (Mt 7:7-11). Bad though you are, he says, you know how to give good gifts to your children.* It's a wonderful thing, brothers; we are bad, and we have a good Father. What could be clearer? We have heard ourselves men-

tioned: *Bad*, he says, *though you are, you know how to give good gifts to your children.* And after calling them bad, see what sort of Father he shows them. *How much more will your Father . . . ?* Whose Father? Bad people's, of course. And what kind of Father? *No one is good but God alone* (Lk 18:19) (Sermon 61, 1).

Thirdly, Christ is the pledge of the divine promise. When he promised to hear our prayer, the Father gave us a pledge: the incarnation and death of his Son.

> You think it something tremendously difficult, for a man to become an angel; doesn't it strike you as difficult, much more difficult in fact, and much more incredible, for the only Son of God to become man? That human beings can become angels is doubted by man, for whose sake God became man! Do you really doubt you can receive what you ask for, when you have a guarantee like that, one who graciously made himself your debtor for nothing? You haven't made God a loan, or invested any money in him, or put him in your debt in any way. Whatever you have, you have from him, don't you. And whatever you are going to receive, aren't you going to receive it from him? He was prepared to make himself your debtor, and what a debtor too! He wrote out a bond, he gave a guarantee. His body is the divine scripture, his guarantee is the death of Christ, his promissory note is the death of Christ. He gave the death of his Son to the ungodly; has he refused the death of his Son to the godly and the faithful? (Sermon 77B, 6).

Christ prays for us, as he did in a special way in the upper room before suffering for us. "The Lord Jesus Christ, who listens to us with the Father, was also quite ready to pray for us to the Father. Could anything be more certain than our good fortune, when the one who prays for us is the very one who gives us what he prays for? Christ, you see, is man and God; he prays as man, he gives us what he prays for as God" (Sermon 217, 1).

Faith, therefore, will lead us to pray in unison with Christ, our head.

> God could have given no greater gift to human beings than to give them as their head the Word through whom he created all things, and to give them to him as his members. Thus the Word is both Son of God and son of man: one God with the Father, one in manhood with other men. Therefore, when we speak to God in prayer, we do not separate the Son from him; and when the body of the Son prays, it does not set its head apart from itself. Rather, it is the one savior of his body, our Lord Jesus Christ, that prays for us and prays in us and is prayed to by us.

He prays for us as our priest; he prays in us as our head; he is prayed to by us as our God. Let us therefore recognize his voice in us and our voice in him (*Expositions of the Psalms* 86, 1).

Humble yourself! (Humilia te)

In admonishing those superstitious people who hurried into the hills to pray, in the belief that they would thus be nearer to God and could make him hear them better, Augustine tells them: "Do you want to make contact with God? Humble yourself; don't take it literally and materialistically, and go off down to underground vaults and there start beseeching God. Don't go seeking either caverns or mountains. Hove lowliness in your heart, and God will give you all the high altitude you want. He will come to you and be with you in your bedroom" (Sermon 45, 7).

Humility leads those who pray to recognize that they are poor and needy in every way and therefore to seek God's help.

> The salvation that flows from your face, my God, sustains me (Ps 69:30). The poor man who prays here was not abandoned, was he? When do you ever deign to bring a poor person in rags to your table? Yet the salvation that flows from God's face sustained the poor man of the Psalm! God hid in his own face the poor man's wretchedness. For it is said of God: You hide them in the shelter of your presence (Ps 31:21). Do you want to know what riches that face [presence] contains? They are the riches that provide you with food you want, when you want it; and that food will enable you never to hunger. I am poor and in pain, and the salvation that flows from your face, my God, sustains me (Ps 69:30). To what effect? That I might no longer be poor and in pain? . . . For the Lord hears the poor. He has heard the poor, but he would not, if they were not poor.
>
> Do you want to be heard? Be poor! Let pain, not distaste, utter its cry from your lips. For the Lord hears the poor, and his own who are in bonds he spurns not (Ps 69:34). When offended by his servants, he puts them in chains; but when in their chains they cry out to him, he does not scorn them. What chains are these? Mortality and the corruptible flesh: these are the chains that bind us (*Expositions of the Psalms* 69, II, 15 and 18).

Love

"But pray from your sincere and free love of God, that your prayer may reach him whom you love freely and for nothing" (Sermon 22A, 5).

Augustine lays his greatest stress, however, on the love of neighbor which must accompany prayer and make it acceptable to God. Lent, which is a season for fasting, prayer, and good works, offers him an occasion for this teaching. "Before everything else, brothers and sisters, fast from quarrels and discord. . . . If you want to shout, use the kind of shouting about which it says, *With my voice I shouted to the Lord* (Ps 142:1). That indeed is not a shout of quarreling, but of loving; not of the flesh, but of the heart. . . . *Forgive, and you will be forgiven; give, and it will be given you* (Lk 6:37-38). These are the two wings of prayer, on which it flies to God" (Sermon 205, 3).

> But to our prayers we must add, by almsgiving and fasting, the wings of loving kindness, so that they may fly the more easily to God and reach him. From this the Christian mind can readily understand how far removed we should be from the fraudulent filching of other people's property; when it perceives how similar it is to fraud when you don't give to the needy what you don't need yourself. The Lord says, *Give, and it will be given to you; forgive, and you will be forgiven* (Lk 6:37-38). Let us practice these two sorts of almsgiving, namely giving and forgiving, gently and generously; since after all we pray to the Lord that good things may be given to us, and that evil things may not be repaid us. . . . In this way, in humility and charity, by fasting and giving, by restraining ourselves and pardoning, by paying out good deeds and not paying back bad ones, by turning away from evil and doing good, our prayer seeks peace and obtains it. Prayer, you see, flies beautifully when it's supported on wings of such virtues, and is in this way more readily wafted through to heaven, where Christ our peace has preceded us (Sermon 206, 2-3).

"During these days our prayer is lifted up to the heights with the support of kindhearted almsgiving and frugal fasting; because there is no impudence in asking for mercy from God, when it is not refused by one human being to another, and when the serene aim of the heart at prayer is not deflected by the cloudy, lowering images and fancies of the pleasures of the flesh" (Sermon 207, 3).

"Therefore, if down to these holy days a shameful anger has been master in the hearts of any of you, now at least let it depart, so that your prayer may arise in peace" (Sermon 208, 1).

"But during these days our prayers should be more than usually fervent; so to help them with suitable supports, let us also be more fervent in distributing alms" (Sermon 209, 2).

Love is also urged upon those who have renounced the world and given themselves to the ascetical life.

As for those of you who also fast on other days, add during these days to what you normally do. Those of you who throughout the other days of the year crucify the body by perpetual continence, cleave to your God during these days by more frequent and more earnest prayer. All of you, be of one mind and heart, all of you faithfully faithful, all of you, in this time of exile and wandering, full of heartfelt sighs and fervent love for the one, common home country. See to it that none of you envies, none of you mocks in another the gift of God which you don't have in yourself. In the matter of spiritual goods, regard as your own what you love and admire in your brother or sister; let them regard as their own what they love and admire in you (Sermon 205, 2).

Pray with perseverance (Perseveranter oremus)

Blessed be God who refused me not my prayer or his kindness! (Ps 66:20). The speaker has reached the resurrection where we ourselves already are in hope. In fact, we are the speaker, and the words are ours. As long as we live here below, we ask God not to refuse our prayer and his mercy; we ask that we may pray with perseverance and receive his mercy without ceasing. For many grow weary of praying; when newly converted they pray fervently, but then they become tepid, cold, and finally negligent, as though they were now safe. The enemy keeps watch, but you sleep! The Lord himself tells us in the Gospel about *the necessity of praying always and not losing heart* (Lk 18:1). Augustine then gives a quick synopsis of the parable of the unjust judge, which follows in Luke upon the verse just quoted, and concludes his sermon: Therefore let us not lose heart in prayer. What God intends to give he may put off but he will not take away; we are sure of his promise and should not lose heart in prayer, though even this perseverance is his gift. This is why the Psalmist says: *Blessed be God who refused me not my prayer or his kindness!* When you see that your prayer is not refused, be at peace, for neither is his mercy refused (*Expositions of the Psalms* 66, 24).

Prayer should be continuous in the sense that our desire and our love for God should not lessen.

All my desire is before you (Ps 38:10). Let your desire be before him, and *your Father, who sees what no man sees, will repay you* (Mt 6:6). Your desire is your prayer; if your desire is unbroken, so is your prayer. For the Apostle was not talking nonsense when he said: *Never cease praying* (1 Thes 5:17). Can we uninterruptedly bend our knee, prostrate ourselves, and lift our hands, in order to obey the Apostle's words: *Never cease praying?* If that is what he means by praying, I do not see how we can pray without ceasing. But there is another uninterrupted prayer which is interior: our desire.

If you long for the sabbath peace of God, then, whatever else you may be doing, you are ceaselessly praying. If you want not to cease praying, then do not cease desiring. Your unbroken desire is your voice that never stops praying; but if you stop loving, you fall silent. Who are the ones who fall silent? Those of whom it is said: *Because evil will increase, the love of many will grow cold* (Mt 24:12). The coldness of love is the heart's silence; the warmth of love is the heart's cry. If your love abides, you are always crying out; if you are always crying, you are always desiring; if you desire, you keep before your mind the sabbath rest of God (*Expositions of the Psalms* 38, 14).

There is a further way of making our prayer continuous, although this further way is itself the spontaneous outflow of a love that ever burns brightly: to do good, to do it in every way.

Then my tongue shall recount your justice, your praise, all the day (Ps 35:28). But whose tongue can recount the praise of God all day long? Well, my sermon is already rather long, and you are getting tired. To the question: Who can praise God all day long? I therefore briefly suggest a means whereby you can praise God all day long if you want to. Perform every action well and you have praised God. When you sing a hymn, you praise God, for what is your tongue doing, unless your mind is praising God? If you stop singing and go off to eat, then do not become drunk, and you have praised God. Do you go to bed? Then do not rise to do evil, and you have praised God. Are you involved in business? Then do not be dishonest, and you have praised God. Are you a farmer? Do not get into disputes, and you have praised God. Be guiltless in all you do and you prepare yourself to praise God (*Expositions of the Psalms* 35, II, 16).

Using a fine image, Augustine elsewhere explains that good works are the instruments that accompany song, the way the psaltery accompanies the psalms.

A psalm is not just any song, but one sung to the psaltery. A psaltery is a musical instrument, like the lyre or zither or others invented for accompanying song. Those who engage in psalmody, therefore, do not use their voice alone; they also use an instrument, called the psaltery, and bring hands into harmony with voice. Do you want to sing psalms? Then let not your voice alone utter God's praises, but let your good works harmonize with your voice. When you sing with your voice, you must sometimes fall silent; sing with your life, and you never need be silent. . . . Give praise when you do business, give praise when you take food and drink, give praise when you rest on your bed, give praise when you sleep. There is not a single moment when you are not praising (*Expositions of the Psalms* 147, 2).

Is there no point, then, in setting aside fixed times for prayer in the narrower sense of the word? There is indeed, Augustine tells us, for he is well aware that to make such a program of continuous prayer a reality we must catch our breath by withdrawing from time to time from all other occupations and engaging in fervent prayer.

If we constantly feed our desire with faith, hope, and love, we are always praying. However, we also pray to God in express fashion, at fixed intervals, in order to remind ourselves, to give ourselves an account of our progress in desire, and to stir ourselves to greater fervor. The more fervent we become, the better the results in our action. For this reason the Apostle's words: *Never cease praying* (1 Thes 5:17) are to be understood thus: never stop longing for the blessed life (that is, eternal life, and it alone) and asking it of him who alone can give it.

Let us always desire this gift from the Lord our God and constantly ask for it. Occasionally, at fixed times, let us set aside the other thoughts and occupations that tend to make our desire die down, and apply ourselves anew to prayer. In this way, we exhort ourselves through the words of our prayer to move toward the object of our desire; for the desire that has begun to be tepid will become completely cold and die out, unless the flame is stirred up from time to time (Letter 130, 18).

Prayer and Life

The reader will have observed that with these considerations I have gone beyond the limits of prayer in the strict sense of the word and branched out into Christian life in its totality. The extension would not be justified were it not that in Augustine's spirituality prayer cannot be simply cut off from the rest of life. One constant duty of the Christian is this prolongation of prayer, for it is the guarantee that our prayer is in harmony with the spirit of Christ.

Augustine comments on the cry of the two blind men at Jericho: *Take pity on us, son of David!* (Mt 20:30).

But what's the meaning of crying out to Christ, brothers and sisters, if not matching the grace of Christ with good works? I say this, my friends, in case we should be making a noise with our voices, and remaining mute in our morals. Who are the ones who cry out to Christ, to have their inner blindness dispelled as Christ passes by, that is, as he administers temporal sacraments to us, by which we are reminded to lay hold of eternal realities? Who are the ones who cry out to Christ? Those who think nothing of the world are the ones who cry out to Christ. Those who scorn the pleasures of the world are the ones who cry out to Christ. Those who say, with their lives rather than their lips, *The world has been crucified to me and I to the world* (Gal 6:14), they are the ones who cry out to Christ. Those who distribute and give to the poor, so that their justice endures for ever and ever, they are the ones who cry out to Christ (Sermon 88, 12).

It is this coherence of prayer and life that gives us confidence about being heard. "Don't worry, dear brothers and sisters; you will receive. Ask, seek, knock, you will receive, you will find, the door will be opened to you. Only don't ask, seek, and knock just with your voices, but also with your morals; do good works, without which you certainly have no business to lead this life. Wipe out your sins by daily good works" (Sermon 77B, 7).

Good works are the perpetual alleluia to which the bishop exhorts us in a sermon preached during the Easter season in another cathedral than his own.

It is evidently the pleasure of the Lord our God that, finding myself present here in the flesh, I should also have been singing *alleluia* with your graces. In English that means "Praise the Lord." So let us praise the Lord, brothers and sisters, with our lives and our tongues, with hearts and mouths, with our voices and our behavior. That, surely, is how God wants *alleluia* to be sung to him, so that there is no discord in the singer. So first of all let there be harmony in ourselves between tongues and lives, between mouths and consciences. Let our voices, I repeat, be in harmony with our behavior, or else it may happen that good voices are witnesses against bad behavior. O blissful *alleluia* in heaven, where the angels are God's temple! There, I mean, supreme harmony reigns among those who are praising, because there is no anxiety about their exultant singing. That's because there is no *law in the members fighting against the law of the mind* (Rom 7:23) there; no aggressive cupidity there, to endanger the victory of charity. So here let us sing *alleluia* while still anxious and worrying, so that we may be able to sing it one day without any worry or care (Sermon 256, 1).

NOTES

1. See *The Gift of Perseverance* XX, 53.
2. See Mt 6:6.
3. See Sermon 223E, 1.
4. See *Expositions of the Psalms* 26, 4.

CHAPTER 9

THE ULTIMATE GOAL

"There we shall be still and see; we shall see and we shall love; we shall love and we shall praise. Behold what will be, in the end, without end! For what is our end but to reach that kingdom which has no end?" (*The City of God* XXII, 30)

The Passage: Death

"And so it is perfectly in order for loving hearts to grieve at the death of their dear ones, but with a sorrow that will let itself be assuaged; and to shed the tears that suit our mortal condition, but that are also prepared to be consoled. These should be quickly dried by the joy of the faith with which we believe that when the faithful die, they depart from us for only a little while, and pass on to better things" (Sermon 172, 3).

> When we celebrate days in remembrance of our dead brothers and sisters, we ought to bear in mind both what we should be hoping for and what we should be afraid of. We have reason to hope, you see, because *Precious in the sight of the Lord is the death of his holy ones* (Ps 116:15), but reason to be afraid, because *The death of sinners is very evil* (Ps 34:21). That's why, as regards hope, *The just will be kept in mind for ever,* while as regards fear, *he will not fear an evil hearing* (Ps 112:6-7). There will be something heard, you see, than which nothing could be worse, when those on the left hand are told, *Go into everlasting fire* (Mt 22:41). That is the evil hearing which the just will not fear, because he will be among those on the right hand who will be told, *Come, blessed of my Father, receive the kingdom* (Mt 22:34). In this life, though, which is spent halfway between and before ultimate good and ultimate evil things . . . we must hold onto what we heard just now in the gospel: *Whoever believes in me,* he said, *even though he dies, is alive.* He both proclaims life and does not

deny death. What does it mean, *even though he dies, is alive?* Even though he dies in the body, he is alive in the spirit. Then he adds, *and whoever is alive and believes in me will not die for ever* (Jn 11:25-26). . . . Yes, but even though he dies for a time, *he will not die for ever.* . . . So then, although we are going to die in the body, we are alive if we believe (Sermon 173, 1).

For the Christian, death is the passage of life, because Christ, who is life, by dying won the victory over death, as Augustine explains in commenting on the words of John 3:14-15: *As Moses lifted up the serpent in the desert, so must the Son of Man be lifted up, that all who believe in him may not perish but have eternal life.*

What is the serpent that is lifted up? The death of the Lord on the cross. Death came from the serpent and therefore is represented by its image. The bite of the serpent is deadly, the death of the Lord life-giving. To look upon the serpent is to make him powerless. What does that mean? It means: look upon death and death will have no power. But whose death? The death of life, if we may so put it. Yes, we may put it that way, and we are saying something wonderful. But must we not say what had to come to pass? Shall I hesitate to say what the Lord deigned to do for me? Was Christ not life? Yet he hung on the cross! Was Christ not life? Yet he died! But in the death of Christ death itself died; death was swallowed up in the body of Christ.

In our own resurrection, when we sing in triumph, we too shall say:

O death, where is your victory? O death, where is your sting? (1 Cor 15:55). Until then, brothers and sisters, let us look upon the crucified Christ so that we may be healed of sin, for *as Moses lifted up the serpent in the desert, so must the Son of Man be lifted up, that all who believe* in him may not perish but *have eternal life.* As those who looked upon the serpent did not die of the serpent's bite, so those who look with faith on the death of Christ are healed of the bite of sin. Those people, however, were restored from death to temporal life. But here we read: *so that they may have eternal life.* That is the difference between the figure and the reality: the figure gave temporal life, the reality gives eternal life (*Homilies on the Gospel of John* 12, 11).

Death, then, takes on its true meaning only if we look to the eternal life to which death leads.

The Mystery of Eternal Life

In this life we are still wandering exiles, still sighing in faith for I know not what kind of home country. And why "I know not what kind," seeing that we are its citizens, unless it is because by wandering away into a far country (Lk 15:13) we have forgotten our true native land, and so can say about it, "I know not what kind of place it is"? This amnesia is driven from our hearts by the Lord Christ, king of that country, as he comes to join us in our exile; and by his taking of flesh, his divinity becomes a way for us, so that we may proceed along it through Christ as man, and abide in Christ as God. So what now, brothers and sisters? That secret place, which eye has not seen, nor ear heard, nor has it come up into the heart of man (1 Cor 2:9) — what eloquence can be adequate for me to unfold it to you, or what eyes will enable us to see it? Sometimes we can know something which for all that we are unable to express; but what we don't know, we are not capable of ever expressing at all. So while it could be that, if I knew those things, I would still be unable to express them to you, how much more difficult must my expression of them be, seeing that I too, brothers and sisters, am walking together with you by faith, not yet by sight? . . .

So what does it matter, if the Lord was the only one who could actually know the things he said about the life that is going to be for ever; while others who follow the Lord Jesus Christ himself, who knew what he could speak about, declined for all that to say it. He said somewhere, you see, to his disciples, *I still have many things to say to you; but you are unable to take them now* (Jn 16:12). It was on account of their weakness that he put off saying what he knew, not on account of any difficulty he would have himself. We, on the other hand, on account of the common weakness of us all, make no attempt to give fitting expression to something we know; but instead we explain as best we can things that it is fitting for us to believe; and you, for your part, must grasp it as best you can. And if any of you, perhaps, can grasp more than I can express, don't waste your time on this thin little trickle, but hurry off to the abundant fountain, since with him is the fountain of life, in whose light we shall see light (Sermon 362, 4-5).

In that place [heaven] there will be no hunger, there will be no thirst, there will be no nakedness, there will be no sickness, there will be no exile, there will be no toil, there will be no sorrow. I know that none of these things will be found there, and I don't know what will be found there. After all, I'm acquainted by experience with these things that won't be found there; but as for what we are going to find there, *neither has eye seen, nor ear heard, nor has it come up into the heart of man* (1 Cor 2:9). We can love, we can desire, in this exile we can sigh for such a great good; think worthy thoughts about it and explain it in suitable words, that we cannot do. I certainly can't. So, my dear brothers and sisters, look for someone who can. If you can find such a person, drag me along with you as a disciple. What I do know is that *the one who is able*, as the apostle says, *to do far beyond what we ask or understand* (Eph 3:20) will take us through to where what is written will come true: *Blessed are those who dwell in your house; they will praise you for ever and ever* (Ps 84:4). There, our whole business will be the praise of God (Sermon 236, 3).

"Every praise can be heaped on that indescribable possession of the truth, all the more since everything we can say is inadequate. It is the light of the enlightened, the rest of the weary, the native land of returning exiles, the food of the needy, and the crown of those who overcome. All the partial, created blessings of time which unbelievers mistakenly desire, his loving sons will find in a far truer and eternal way in their creator" (*Questions on the Gospel* II, 39).

Eternal Life Is God

Presence of God

So we love life, and we have no hesitation at all about loving life; nor can we in the least deny that we love life. So let us choose life, if we love life. What are we choosing? Life. First of all, here, a good one; after this one, the eternal kind. First of all, here, a good one, but not yet a blessed one. Lead a good one here, and a blessed one is being kept for you later. . . . Truth, real Truth, is promising us life which is not only eternal but also blessed; where there's no nuisance to annoy, no toil, no fear, no grief. What you find there is full and total definitive freedom from all anxiety. Life under God, life with God, life coming from God, life which is God himself. Such is the life which is promised us for eternity (Sermon 297, 8).

"Eternal life, will there be anything more valuable for us? Will anything, I repeat, be able to make us richer, when God is the estate we possess? Or have I uttered an insult in saying that God is going to be our property? I haven't. I learned what I have just said. I found a holy man praying and saying, *O Lord, my share of the inheritance* (Ps 116:5).

Stretch wide the net of your insatiable desires, greedy, and find something greater than God, find something more precious than God, find something better than God. What won't you possess, when you possess him?" (Sermon 105A, 2).

In eternal life the presence of God will assure the elect of peace and blessedness. This is why we speak of a "spiritual body." "Why, my dear friends, would a body be called spiritual, if not because it will serve the spirit at its beck and call? . . . There will be nothing there about which the apostle groans, *The flesh lusts against the spirit, and the spirit against the flesh* (Gal 5:17). There will be nothing there of *I can see another law in my members fighting back against the law of my mind* (Rom 7:23). There won't be any of these wars there; there it will be peace, it will be perfect peace there. You will be wherever you like, but you will not draw away from God. You will be wherever you like; but wherever you go, you will have your God. You will always be with him, from whom you will draw your happiness, your bliss" (Sermon 242, 11).

"After this present life, our knowledge will become perfect, for now our knowledge is partial but when the time of perfection comes it will no longer be partial.[1] There will be perfect peace, for now another law in my members militates against the law of my mind, but then the grace of God, coming through our Lord Jesus Christ, will free us from this body of death.[2] There will be perfect health, and the body will feel no want or fatigue, for this corruptible flesh will become incorruptible in that time and that order of which the resurrection is a part" (*True Religion* 53, 103).

"When we cleave to that most pure and perfect goodness, there will be no needs requiring attention. We shall be blessed, lacking nothing, having much, requiring nothing. And what is it that we shall have, so that we require nothing? I have told you; what you now believe, you will afterward see. So what I said, having much and requiring nothing, that is, lacking nothing; what is it that we are going to have? What is God going to give those who serve him, worship him, believe in him, hope in him, love him?" (Sermon 255, 2).

"Give us peace, Lord God, for you have given us all else; give us the peace that is repose, the peace of the Sabbath, and the peace that knows no evening. This whole order of exceedingly good things, intensely beautiful as it is, will pass away when it has served its purpose: these things too will have their morning and their evening" (*Confessions* XIII, 25, 50).

Vision of God

"As regards this life, Moses is told, *Nobody has seen the face of God and lived* (Ex 33:20). You see, we are not meant to live in this life in order to see that face; we are meant to die to the world, in order to live forever to God. Then we won't sin, not only by deed, but not even by desire, when we see that face which beats and surpasses all desires, because it is so lovely, my brothers and sisters, so beautiful, that once you have seen it, nothing else can give you pleasure. It will give insatiable satisfaction of which we will never tire; we shall always be hungry, always have our fill" (Sermon 170, 9).

"*To you we owe our hymn of praise, O God, in Zion* (Ps 65:2). Zion is our native land; Jerusalem is identical with Zion, and you ought to know the meaning of the latter name. As Jerusalem means 'vision of peace,' so Zion means 'looking,' that is, vision and contemplation. An indescribably great object of vision is promised to us, and that object is God who built the city" (*Expositions of the Psalms* 65, 3).

"*Blessed the single-hearted for they shall see God* (Mt 5:8). We shall see a vision, brothers and sisters, which eye *has not seen, ear has not heard, nor has it so much as dawned on man* (1 Cor 2:9); a vision far more lovely than any earthly beauty: gold or silver, woods or fields, the beauties of sea and air, the beauties of sun and moon, the beauty of the stars and the beauty of the angels. It is lovelier by far than any or all of these, for they all have their beauty from it" (*Homilies on the First Letter of John* 4, 5).

> What, after all, are the good going to receive? Here you are, I'm telling you now, what I didn't tell you a few moments ago; and yet in telling you, I'm not telling you. I said, you remember, that there we shall be in good health, we shall be secure, we shall be alive, we shall be without hardships, we shall be without hunger and thirst, we shall be without any defect, we shall be without the deprivation of our eyes. I said all this; and I didn't say what more we shall have. We shall see God. But this will be so great, and will be such a great thing, that compared with it that "all" is nothing. I said that we shall be alive, that we shall be healthy and secure, that we shan't endure hunger and thirst, that we shan't sink into weariness, that sleep won't overwhelm us. What is all this compared to the bliss that will be ours in seeing God? So because God himself, precisely as he is, cannot be revealed to us right now, and yet we are going to see him; that's why it's *what eye has not seen, nor ear heard* (1 Cor 2:9), that the good will see, those will see who receive a good mark in the resurrection of the body, because they gave a good obedience in the resurrection of the heart. . . .

> When is he going to show himself to his lovers? After the resurrection of the body, when the godless will be removed, lest he should see the glory of God. Then, you see, *when he appears,*

we shall be like him, because we shall see him just as he is (I Jn 3:2). That is eternal life. I mean, everything we were talking about amounts to precisely nothing compared with that life. That we are alive, so what? That we are in good health, so what? That we shall see God; great! That is eternal life; he said so himself. *No this is eternal life, that they should know you, the one true God, and Jesus Christ whom you have sent* (Jn 17:3). This is eternal life, that they should know, see, grasp, know what they had previously believed, perceive what they had previously not been able to grasp. Now let the mind see what the eye had not seen, nor the ear heard, nor had it occurred to human thoughts. This is what will be said to them at the end: *Come, you blessed of my Father, perceive and receive the kingdom which has been prepared for you from the beginning of the world. So the bad shall go into eternal burning, but the just* — where? *into eternal life* (Mt 25:34. 46). And what is eternal life? *This is eternal life, that they should know you, the only true God, and Jesus Christ whom you have sent* (Sermon 127, 11-13).

Praise of God

During this exile we are afflicted; only in our settled home will we find happiness. Toil and tribulation will pass away; prayer shall cease and praise take its place. There will be the dwellings of human beings who celebrate: no sighing of desire but only the rejoicing of those who possess. Then we shall be what we now long to be: *we will be like him, for we shall see him as he is* (I Jn 3:2); then our only occupation will be to praise and enjoy God. What else could we look for, when he who made all things is enough by himself? He shall dwell in us and we in him; all things will be subject to him, so that God may be all in all.[3] *Happy, therefore, they who dwell in your house* (Ps 84:5). Why are they happy? Because they have gold and silver, a large household and many children? Why are they happy? *Happy they who dwell in your house! Continually they praise you.* They are happy in this one occupation that never wearies them.

Now that we have reached this point, brothers and sisters, let this be our one desire; let us prepare ourselves to rejoice in God and praise him. . . . Let us also praise the Lord now as best we can, even amid our sighs. For in praising him here we do not yet possess him but still long for him. When we finally possess him, all sighing shall cease, and there shall be only pure and eternal praise (*Expositions of the Psalms* 87, 9).

It is then that he will be seen most perfectly, when we are supremely at leisure. But when will we be supremely at leisure, if not when all the times of toil have passed away, all the times of the necessities we are not tied down by, as long as the earth goes on producing thorns and thistles for sinful man, so that he has to eat his bread in the sweat of his brow?[4] So when the times of the earthly man have been transacted in every respect, and the day of the heavenly man perfected in every respect, we shall see in a supreme manner, because we shall be supremely at leisure. When all decay and need, after all, is at an end in the resurrection of the faithful, there will be nothing any more for which we will have to toil and labor. It says *Be at leisure and see*, in the same way as if it said, "Recline and eat." So we shall be at leisure and we shall see God as he is; and on seeing God we shall praise him. And this will be the life of the saints, this the activity of those at rest, that we shall praise him without ceasing. We won't just praise him for one day; but just as that day has no end in time, so our praise will have no end at which it stops; and that's why we shall praise him for ever and ever. Listen to scripture saying this too to God, saying what we all desire: *Blessed are those who dwell in your house; they will praise you for ever and ever* (Ps 84:4) (Sermon 362, 31).

Fullness of Goodness and Joy

In our earthly dwellings we find satisfaction in various delights and pleasures, and everyone wants to dwell in a house where there is nothing to offend and much to delight. And if what gave us pleasure is taken away, we want to migrate to some other spot. Let us therefore satisfy our curiosity and ask the Psalmist what we, and he himself, will be doing in that house where he ardently desires and prays (the only thing he asks of the Lord!) to dwell all the days of his life. "What do you do there, I ask you? What do you want?" His answer? "That I may gaze on the joy of the Lord." That is why I love and yearn to dwell in the Lord's house all the days of my life. There is a wonderful vision to be had there: to contemplate the joy of the Lord himself! This man desires that when his night is over he may be bathed in the light of the Lord. . . . There is the absolute good, the essential good by which and from which all other good things are: that good is the joy of the Lord, and we shall contemplate that joy! Brothers, reflect! If the things which men call good delight us, if the good things delight us which are not good of themselves (nothing changeable is good of itself), then how much more shall we find delight in the contemplation of the changeless, eternal good which is ever the same! (*Expositions of the Psalms* 27, II, 8).

"Do you love riches? God himself will be your riches. Do you love a fine fountain? What more splendid and lightsome than his wisdom? No matter what you may love here on earth, the creator of the universe will replace it all for you" (*Expositions of the Psalms* 63, 14).

"Among the children of God there will be perfect peace; all will love one another and see themselves filled with God, when God will be all in all.[5] We will have but one object of vision: God; we will have one common possession: God; we will share one peace: God. All that he gives us now, he himself will then be for us, taking the place of all else that he gives; he will be our full and perfect peace" (*Expositions of the Psalms* 85, 10).

Only the carnal can be stupid enough to fear that the possession of God may not be enough to make them completely and everlasting happy.

God will give us his splendor, that we may enjoy it; but the wicked shall be swept away, that they may not see God's splendor. God himself will be the immense totality of our possession. "Greedy fellow, what were you trying to lay hold of?" What can we ask of God, if God himself is not enough for us?

But when it's said that we shall have God and be content with him alone, or rather that we shall be so delighted with him that we will require nothing else — because in the one thing which he is we shall enjoy each other, and also in each other we shall enjoy him — what are we, after all, if we don't have God, or what else but God should we love in ourselves and each other, either because we do have him or in order to have him? So when it's said that all other things will be withdrawn, and there will only be God to delight us, it's as if the soul feels restricted, because it has been used to delighting in many things; and the carnal soul says to itself, addicted to the flesh, tied up with fleshly desires, having wings stuck together with the birdlime of evil desires to stop it flying to God, it says to itself, "What will there be in it for me, where I shall not eat, I shall not drink, where I shall not sleep with my wife? What sort of joy will I have of that?" This joy of yours comes from sickness, not from good health. Certainly, this flesh of yours, in this time, is sometimes sick, sometimes in good health. . . . So we shall not be in need of anything; and that's why we shall be blessed. We shall be full, you see, but of our God; and all these things that we desire here as being so important, that's what he will be for us. Here you

look for food as something very important; there God will be
your food. Here you seek the embraces of the flesh; *For me,
however, to cleave to God is good* (Ps 73:28). Here you seek riches;
how will you be lacking anything, when you have the one who
made everything? And to give you complete assurance with the
words of the apostle, this is what he said about that life: *That
God might be all in all* (I Cor 15:28) (Sermon 255, 7).

Eternal Joy

"In God's house there is unending festivity. For nothing that is cele-
brated there passes away. The dance of the angels is a perpetual feast;
the presence of God's face is ceaseless joy. This festive day has no
beginning and no end. From that eternal unending festival we may
catch the faint echo of a song that is sweet to the heart's ears, but not
if the world's noise distracts us. To those who walk in their present
dwelling and meditate on the marvels God has done for the redemption of the faithful, the sound of that festival is sweet in their ears and
draws the heart to the fountain of water" (*Expositions of the Psalms* 42,
9).

> *With length of days I will gratify him* (Ps 91:16). What does *length
> of days* mean? Eternal life. Brothers and sisters, do not think that
> length of days means the same as when we say the days are
> short in winter and long in summer. Is that the kind of days he
> has in store for us? No, the length here is the length that has no
> end, the eternal life that is promised in the image of *long days*.
> And because this length of days is enough, God rightly says: *I will
> gratify him*. Nothing, however long in time, is enough for us if it
> has no end; what ends is really not to be called long. If we are
> greedy, then, we should be greedy for eternal life. Long for that
> life, for it is endless. That is how far our greed should reach. Do
> you have a limitless wish for silver? Then yearn without limit for
> eternal life. Do you want your possessions to have no end?
> Then seek eternal life (*Expositions of the Psalms* 91, 12).

So let us praise the Lord, who is in heaven, dearly beloved. Let
us praise God, let us say *alleluia*. Let us signify during these days
the day that has no end. Let us signify in the place of mortality
the time of immortality. Let us hasten to our eternal house and
home. *Blessed are those who dwell in your house; they will praise you
for ever and ever* (Ps 84:4). The law says it, scripture says it, Truth
says it. We are going to come to the house of God, which is in
heaven. There we shall praise God, not for fifty days, but, as it
is written, *for ever and ever*. We shall see, we shall love, we shall
praise. Nor shall our seeing come to an end, nor shall our loving

fade away, nor shall our praising ever be silent. It will all be everlasting, all without end (Sermon 254, 8).

Our Present Life in the Light of Eternal Life
Believe in eternal life

The basis of this faith is God's word. On earth there are citizens of the holy Jerusalem, mingled in body with the citizens of Babylon, but

> distinguished from them by holy desire. They have not yet gone forth inasmuch as they are mingled in body with these others, but they have begun to go forth by the disposition of their hearts. Let us listen, then, brothers and sisters; let us listen and sing and desire the place whose citizens we are. What are the joys that are sung to us? How can love of our own city be re-kindled in us after we had forgotten it because of our long exile? Our Father has sent us letters from that place, our God has provided us his scriptures; by these writings and letters the de-sire to return thither is lit in us anew, for by loving our exile we had turned our back to our native land and our face to our foe (*Expositions of the Psalms* 65, 2).

"Love him absent, to enjoy him present. Long to hold him, to em-brace him. First cling to him by faith, then afterward you will cling to him by sight. Now, as a traveler, you are walking by faith and by hope. When you arrive, you will enjoy him whom you have loved as you traveled on your journey. It's he who founded the native country to which you should be hurrying to come. He has sent you a letter from there, not to put off returning from your travels" (Sermon 22A, 4).

"Those who sigh in the present life and long for their native land, should run by love, not by the body's feet, seeking not ships but wings: the two wings of love. What are these two wings of love? The love of God and the love of neighbor. Now we are in exile, longing and sigh-ing. From our native land letters have reached us, and we read them to you" (*Expositions of the Psalms* 149, 5).

> But what's this you say, who has ever come back here from there, and who has shown people what goes on among the deni-zens of the underworld? On this point too your mouths have been stopped by the one who brought a dead man back to life on the fourth day, and himself rose again on the third day to die no more, and before he died, as being the one from whom noth-ing is hidden, described what sort of life awaits the dying, in the case of the poor man at rest and the rich man on fire. But the people who say "Who has ever come back here from there?" don't believe all this. . . . So that's why God became man, and

wanted to die and rise again, so that what the future held in store for humanity might be revealed in human flesh, and yet that we might believe God, not man. And certainly the Church of the faithful, spread throughout the world, is there now before their very eyes. Let them read how it was promised so many centuries ago to one man, who believed in hope against hope, to become the father of many nations. So we now see fulfilled what was promised to the single man Abraham as he believed; and are we to despair of what is promised to the whole world as it believes ever coming about? (Sermon 157, 6)

So in his sufferings Christ showed us one life that is laborious, full of troubles, temptations, fears and griefs, the life with which this age runs its course; while by his resurrection he demonstrated that life where nobody will grieve, nobody be afraid, nobody be reconciled because nobody will quarrel; as though to say, "Look, there's what you have to endure, and what you have to hope for; to endure sufferings, to hope for resurrection." And what a resurrection! Not the sort that was granted to Lazarus, who would die again. *Christ rising again from the dead*, as the apostle said, *dies no more, and death has no further dominion over him* (Rom 6:9). I know that you all desire such a life. Who wouldn't desire it, after all? (Sermon 335H, 1).

Christians who do not think of eternal life show that they do not have faith.

You infidel there, you look to the present, you're cowed by present dangers; think sometimes about the future. Tomorrow and tomorrow; sooner or later it will be the final and last tomorrow. Day treads on the heels of day, and never catches up with the one who made the day. With him, you see, there is a day without yesterday and tomorrow; with him, you see, there is a day without sunrise or sunset; with him there is everlasting light, *there is the fountain of life, and in his light shall we see light* (Ps 36:9). At least let the heart be there; as long as the flesh has to be here, let the heart be there. The whole of you will be there if the heart is there (Sermon 299E, 3).

This faith must be an active faith and rouse believers to prepare themselves for eternal life by facing labors and difficulties.

There is, after all, another life, my brothers and sisters; there is, believe me, after this life another life. Prepare yourselves for it; be indifferent to all the present life has to offer. If you are provided with it, do good with it; if you aren't, don't burn yourselves up with greedy longing. Transport it, transfer it ahead of you; let what you have here go on up there, where you are going to follow. Listen to the advice of your Lord: *Do not treasure up for yourselves on earth, where moth and rust ruin things, and where thieves dig through and steal; but treasure up for yourselves treasure in heaven, where a thief has no access, where moth does not spoil things. For where your treasure is, there too is your heart* (Mt 6:19-21). Every day, Christian believer, you hear, *Lift up your hearts*, and as though you heard the opposite, you sink your heart into the earth. Transport it. Have you got the means? Do good with it. You haven't got the means? Don't grumble against God (Sermon 311, 15).

Happy they who dwell in your house! Continually they praise you (Ps 84:5). That is everlasting rest. No end will it have — this rest and joy, this gladness and incorruption. You will have everlasting life and the repose that is endless. Now, what kind of toil is it that should be crowned by endless rest? If you want to make a valid comparison and judge with justice, an everlasting rest should be purchased by an everlasting labor! That is the truth! But do not be afraid, for God is merciful. For if your labor were everlasting, you would never reach everlasting rest! If you had ever to toil, when would you reach that rest which deserves to be purchased by an everlasting toil, because it is an everlasting rest? Calculate the value: an everlasting rest certainly deserves to be achieved through an everlasting toil. Yet if you had to labor forever, you would never reach any rest. Therefore, if you are to reach what you purchase, you must not have to toil forever — not because the rest is not worth it, but simply so that you may finally possess what you have bought.

It deserves to be bought by an everlasting toil, yet it must be bought by a temporary toil. The labor ought to indeed be everlasting for the sake of an everlasting rest. What are a million years of toil worth? Yet a million years have an end. "But what I give you," says the Lord, "will never end." Such is God's mercy! He does not say: "Toil for a million years." He does not ever say: "Toil for a thousand years, or five hundred years." He says only: "Toil for the few years you live. Then you will have rest, and it will be everlasting" (*Expositions of the Psalms* 94, 24).

Fear sin

The thought of death should inspire in us a salutary fear, not of bodily death but of sin which is the death of the soul.

Be afraid of the second death, where the soul is not wrenched from the flesh, but the soul is tormented with the flesh. Don't be afraid of the transitory death, be afraid of the permanent one; there is no worse death than where death doesn't die. For fear of death you were willing to sin; sin killed your inner self; sin killed the very life of your flesh. Finally, that death of the body would not have followed, unless it had been preceded by the death of the soul. The soul deserted God willingly, and deserted the flesh unwillingly. The Lord, though, did not desert the flesh unwillingly; he died when he wished, because he was born when he wished. But why all this? Just so that you wouldn't be afraid, there you have the reason it all happened. And we are afraid of death; we're afraid of death as though we were able to avoid death. Fear what you can avoid, that is to say, sin. Sin you can avoid, death you can't (Sermon 335B, 5).

Brothers and sisters, let us be wise of heart; let us fear God, who makes such wonderful promises, and such terrible threats. This life must come to an end sooner or later. You can see how people pass away from here every day. Death can be delayed, it can't be eliminated. Willy-nilly, this life must come to an end; let us long for the one that has no end, and the only way to get to that life is through death. So don't be afraid of something that is going to come sooner of later anyhow; let's be afraid, rather, of something which, if it comes and catches us in sins, can drag us off not to temporal but to everlasting death, from which may God preserve us all, both you and me. O man or woman, whoever you are, aren't you afraid of dying for eternity? You behave in such a way as to be punished or to die for endless time. Let fear of this death teach you how much to be dreaded is that future death. You are afraid of death; will you get out of dying? Willy-nilly, death must come. You're afraid of death; you ought to be more afraid of sin, because it's through sin, you see, that the soul dies; sin is the enemy of your soul (Sermon 77A, 4).

Wait in Hope

We need hope to strengthen us in this present laborious life.

What we said was, *Let us weep before the Lord who made us, for he is the Lord our God* (Ps 95:6-7). In case anyone weeping should despair of being listened to, God is reminded of a reason why in a sense he has got to listen to us: *for he is the Lord our God, who made us.* He is our God; *we are the people of his pasture and the sheep of his hands* (Ps 95:7). Men who are shepherds, or even landowners who own the flocks and herds, haven't made the sheep they own, haven't themselves created the sheep they feed. But our Lord God, because he is God and creator, made himself sheep to own and sheep to feed. It wasn't someone else who brought the sheep he feeds into beings, nor is it someone else who feeds the sheep he brought into beings. So let us weep before him. And you know, we are not in a good way while we are in this world. When we please the Lord in the region of the living, that is when our tears shall be wiped away, and we shall sing the praises of him who has delivered us from the bonds of death, our feet from slipping, our eyes from tears, that we may please the Lord in the region of the living, because it is difficult to please him in the region of the dead. Even here, though, there are ways of pleasing him, by begging him to have mercy on us, by abstaining as far as we can from sins, and in so far as we can't, by confessing and lamenting them. In this way we go through this life hoping for that other life, weeping in hope — or rather weeping now as we try to cope, rejoicing as we look forward in hope (Sermon 47, 1).

The basis for our hope of eternal life is Christ who by suffering and dying for us had made our death acceptable. Here we have a dominant motif in Saint Augustine's preaching during the Easter season.

In this life you cannot be happy. Nobody can. You're seeking a good thing, but this earth just isn't the region for the good thing you're seeking. What are you seeking? A happy life. Well, it isn't to be found here. If you were looking for gold in a place where it isn't to be found, someone who knows it's not to be found there would tell you, "What are you digging for? What are you messing up the ground for? You're making a hole you can go down, not one where you can find anything." What are you going to answer the person giving you this warning? "I'm looking for gold." "I'm not telling you," he says, "that what you're looking for is nothing. It's a good thing you're looking for, but it isn't to be found where you're looking." So also, when you say, "I want to be happy," it's a good thing you're looking for, but it's not to be found here. If Christ had it here, you will have it here too. In the region of your death, what did he find? Consider this: coming from another region, what did he find here but what there's plenty of here: toils, pains, death? There you are, that's what you've got here, that's what there's plenty of here. He ate with you what there was plenty of in your miserable hovel. He drank vinegar here, he drank gall here. That's the sort of thing he found in your hovel.

And he invited you to his splendid table, the table of heaven, the table of the angels, where he himself is the bread. So he came down and he found all these nasty things in your hovel, and he didn't disdain to share your table, nasty though it was, and he promised you his own. What does he tell us? "Believe, believe that you are going to come to the good things of my table, seeing that I did not turn up my nose at the nasty things of yours." So he took your bad things, and will give you his good things? Yes, of course he will. He promised us his life, but what he actually did is even more unbelievable; he paid us his death in advance, as though to say, "I'm inviting you to my life, where nobody dies, where life is truly happy, where food doesn't go bad, where it provides nourishment and undergoes no diminishment. There you are, that's where I'm inviting you, to the region of the angels, to the friendship of the Father and the Holy Spirit, to the everlasting supper, to be my brothers and sisters, to be, in a word, myself. I'm inviting you to my life. Are you reluctant to believe that I will give you my life? As a pledge, keep hold of my death." So now, while we are living in this perishable flesh, by a change of habits let us die with Christ, by a love of being just let us live with Christ. We are only going to receive the happy, blessed life, when we come to him who came to us, and when we begin to be with him who died for us (Sermon 231, 5).

That's how he came, came as savior. He died, but he slew death; he put an end in himself to what we were afraid of. He embraced it, and killed it. Like the greatest of hunters, he caught hold of the lion, and killed it. Where is death now? Look for it in Christ, it's no longer there; it was there, however, and it died there. Oh, what life, the death of death! Be of good heart, it will also die in us. What has first occurred in the head will also be given to the members; death will also die in us. But when? At the end of the world, in the resurrection of the dead, which we believe, and about which we have no doubts (Sermon 233, 5).

"Are you amazed that as human beings you should have eternal life? Are you amazed that as human beings you should arrive at eternal life? You should rather be amazed that God for your sake arrived at death" (Sermon 342, 5).

Christ has even been kind and thoughtful enough to suffer fear in the face of death in order that he might strengthen his weak followers.

But someone may say: "The Christian soul should not be disturbed even when death is imminent, should it? After all, the Apostle said that he longed to *depart and be with Christ* (Phil 1:23). Can the object of his desire trouble him when it comes?" The answer is easy for those who call even this trouble a joy! . . . But let us listen to the sacred scriptures and seek to resolve the problem with the Lord's help. When we read that *after saying this, Jesus grew deeply troubled* (Jn 13:21), let us not say that he was troubled by joy! He would refute such an interpretation by his own words at another point: *My heart is sad enough to die* (Mt 26:38). The same thing is meant when, as the betrayer was to leave alone and return with his helpers, *Jesus grew deeply troubled.*

Christians are courageous indeed (if there are in fact any such) who are not troubled by imminent death. Can they claim they are more courageous than Christ? Who would be silly enough to say that? If, then, even he was disturbed, it was in order to strengthen the weak members of his body (that is, of his Church) by voluntarily taking their weakness on himself. If any of his members are still troubled in soul by approaching death, they should contemplate him; for otherwise they may think themselves rejected by God because they are afraid and thus succumb to the worse death of despair. How great the blessings we should hope for and look forward to from sharing his divinity, when he calms us by his tranquility and strengthens us by his weakness! (*Homilies on the Gospel of John* 60, 4-5).

Hope brings perseverance in trials. The only song God teaches us is that of faith, hope, and love. He does this so that our faith may be strong in him, as long as we do not see him; for we believe in him whom we do not see, in order that we may have the joy of someday seeing him when the vision of his light replaces faith. When that time comes, we shall not be told: "Believe what you do not see," but "See and rejoice." Our hope, too, should be immovably fixed upon him, not wavering, fluctuating, or shaken, any more than the God in whom we hope can be shaken. Now there is hope; then there will be fulfillment, not hope. Hope is needed as long as the object of our desire is not seen; as the Apostle says: *Hope is not hope if its object is seen; how is it possible for one to hope for what he sees? And hoping for what we cannot see means awaiting it with patient endurance* (Rom 8:24). What is needed now is patient endurance, until what was promised comes. . . . Love, which joins faith and hope as a third partner, is greater than faith and hope (1 Cor 13:13). Faith has for its object things not seen, and vision replaces it when they are seen (2 Cor 4:18). Hope is for what is not yet possessed; when fulfillment comes, we will possess and no longer hope. But love can only grow more and more intense. For if we love him whom we do not see, how much more will we love him when we do see him? Let our desire for him grow greater, then! (*Expositions of the Psalms* 92, 1).

Love eternal life

Love of God and of the eternal life in which we shall see God is urged upon us in the passage just quoted and in many others. "*While we dwell in the body we are away from the Lord* (2 Cor 5:6). No matter what abundance offers itself to us here, we are still not in that native land to which we are hastening. If you find exile sweet, you do not love your native land; if the thought of that country is sweet to you, you find exile bitter" (*Expositions of the Psalms* 86, 11).

If we sincerely love Christ, we must love his coming. "*I should like you to be free of all worries* (1 Cor 7:32). Those who are without worries wait in peace for the coming of the Lord. What kind of love for Christ would it be that fears his coming? Are we not ashamed, brothers? We love Christ but we fear his coming! Do we really love him? Or do we love our sins more? Let us hate our sins and love him who comes to punish sin. He will come, whether we like it or not; the fact that he has not yet come does not mean that he will not come. He will come indeed, and at a time you do not know; but if he finds you prepared, it does not matter that you do not know" (*Expositions of the Psalms* 96, 14).

> What is it that torments the heart of Christians? The fact that they do not yet live with Christ. What is it that torments their heart? The fact that they are in exile and longing for their native land. If this is what torments your heart, then, even though this world calls you happy, you are sad. Even if you prosper on every side and the world smiles on you, you are sad because you see yourself in exile. You know you are happy in the eyes of fools but not according to the promise of Christ. You await the fulfillment of that promise and are sad; awaiting it you long for it; longing you ascend; ascending you sing a "Song of ascents" [gradual psalm]; and singing it you say: *To you I lift up my eyes who are enthroned in heaven* (Ps 123:1) (*Expositions of the Psalms* 123, 2).

"After all, this life is loved, whatever it's like; and whatever it's like, wretched, miserable, people are frightened of its coming to an end, and dread the prospect. This would help us to see, to consider seriously, how much we should love eternal life, when this miserable life, that's got to end anyhow sometime, is loved so dearly. Just think, brothers and sisters, how much you should love the life in which you never come to the end of life" (*Sermon* 84, 1).

> Let us love eternal life, and let us gauge how hard we ought to strive for eternal life, from the way in which we see people who love this temporal life that is bound to end sometime strive so

hard for it, that when the fear of death looms up they do every-thing they can, not to eliminate death, but simply to put it off. The pains a man will take, the trouble he will endure when death looms ahead, running away, going into hiding, giving everything he has, and paying his ransom, struggling, enduring all sorts of torments and vexations, bringing in doctors, and whatever else a man can do! But notice that by taking endless pains and spend-ing all his means a man can do something to live a little longer; to live always, he can do nothing. So if all that trouble, all that effort, all that expense, all that determination, all that vigilance, all that care is spent of living just a little longer, how much more should be spent on living forever? (Sermon 127, 2)

From love of this temporal life advance, if you can manage it, to loving the eternal life which the martyrs loved, while they thought nothing of these temporal things. I beg, I beseech, I implore not only you, but together with you also myself and us clergy: let us cherish eternal life. I don't want us to love it more, though it is much more; let us just cherish it in the same way as temporal life is cherished by its lovers, not as temporal life was cherished by the martyrs. They, you see, cherished it either not at all or very little, and they found it easy to put eternal life before it. So I didn't have the martyrs in mind, when I said, "Let us cherish eternal life as temporal life is cherished"; I meant, as temporal life is cherished by its lovers, so let us cherish eternal life, love of which is what Christians profess (Sermon 302, 2).

It is self-deception to want death delayed so that we may make greater spiritual progress. "Some people who profess the true faith delude themselves in wanting not to die so that they may make further progress, for genuine progress consists precisely in the desire to die. If they want to say the truth, they should not say: 'I want not to die so that I may make progress,' but rather: 'I do not want to die because I have made so little progress.' A believer's unwillingness to die does not prove an intention to make progress; it is rather proof that little progress has yet been made" (*Eight Questions on the Old Testament* 3).

Desire Eternal Life

Love of eternal life leads us to desire it and to move toward it in our heart.

"Everyone has lofty desires. But what is there lofty on earth? So if you have lofty desires, desire heaven, desire heavenly things, desire things higher than the heavens. Long to be a fellow citizen of the an-gels, set your sights on that city, yearn for that society where you will never lose a friend or endure an enemy" (Sermon 20A, 5).

Why, after his resurrection, did the Lord will to give us the Spirit who heaps the greatest blessings upon us inasmuch as through him "the love of God has been poured out in our hearts" (Rom 5:5)? What did he mean to tell us? He was telling us that in our resurrection too love should flame forth, separating us from worldly love and directing us wholly to God. On earth we are born and die; let us not love this life, but through charity emigrate and dwell in heaven, through that love, I mean, with which we love God. During this life of exile, let us think only that we shall not always be here; then by living aright we shall be preparing for ourselves a place we need never leave (*Homilies on the Gospel of John* 32, 9).

Praise the Lord from the heavens, praise him in the heights (Ps 148:1). First the psalmist speaks of heaven, then of earth, for he is praising God who made both heaven and earth. Heaven is calm and at peace; there is always joy there, no death or sickness or anxiety, and the blessed are always praising God. We, on the contrary, are still here below, but, realizing how God is praised there, let us fix our hearts upon that place and not fruitlessly hear the words: "Lift up your heart!" We lift up our heart lest it be corrupted here on earth, for we are pleased by what the angels do there. It pleases us now in hope; it will please us in full reality when we reach that place (*Expositions of the Psalms* 148, 5).

If it's the end of the world, then it's time to quit the world, not to love the world. Look, the world is in a state of turmoil, and everyone loves the world! Suppose the world were at peace? How you would cling to a beautiful world, seeing how fervently you embrace a world in a mess! How eagerly you would gather its flowers, seeing that you don't pull your hand back from its thorns! You don't want to leave the world, the world leaves you, and you follow the world. So let us purify our hearts, dearly beloved, and not give up the virtue of endurance, but rather gain wisdom and hold on to the virtue of restraint. Toil passes away, rest is coming; deceptive delights pass away, and the good is coming which the faithful soul has been longing for, and for which every pilgrim exile in the world is fervently sighing: the good home country, our heavenly home, our home with the angelic peoples, our home country where no citizen ever dies, where no hostile alien gains admittance, our home where you will have God as your everlasting friend, and where you need fear no enemy (*Sermon* 38, 11).

But the longing for eternal life must always be subordinated to God's will.

> Is the psalmist asking anything great when he says: *Lead my soul out of prison* (Ps 142:8)? After all, sooner or later the soul must necessarily go forth. Perhaps the just may say: "Let me die now! Lead my soul forth from the prison of this body." But if they are too eager, they do not love. They ought indeed to ardently desire it, as the Apostle himself says: *I long to be freed from this life and to be with Christ, for that is the far better thing* (Phil 1:23). But where is the love? Paul continues: *Yet it is more urgent that I remain alive for your sakes* (Phil 1:24). Therefore, let the Lord lead us forth from the body when he wishes to (*Expositions of the Psalms* 142, 18).

Prepare Yourself for Eternal Life

By praising God.

> Meditation during our present life should be made in the atmosphere of praise of God, since the everlasting joy of our future life will arise from the praise of God, and no one can become fit for that future life unless he practices for it now. Therefore we praise God now, but we also petition him. Our praise is tinged with joy, whereas petition is accompanied by sighs. Something has been promised us and we do not have it yet. Because he who has promised is trustworthy we have the joy hope gives; but because we do not yet possess it, we sigh with longing. It is good for us to persevere in our longing, until the promise is fulfilled and sighing is ended, being succeeded by purest praise (*Expositions of the Psalms* 148, 1).

By thinking of death.

> *Whoever perseveres to the end, that person shall be saved* (Mt 10:22). And perhaps the end of this world, this age, is a long way off, perhaps it is close. But the Lord wanted the date when it would happen to be unknown, so that people would always be prepared as they wait for something that will happen they don't know when. But whether the end of the age is close at hand or a long way off, as I said, the end of each of us as individuals, which constrains us to pass, according to our deserts, from this life to another one, cannot be a long way off, given the briefness of this mortal existence. We should all, surely, be prepared for our own end. The last day will certainly do no harm to any who always think of every day as possibly their last, and so live in

such a way that they die without a qualm and so die in such a way that they don't die an eternal life (Sermon 64A, 1).

By doing good.

Choose yourself a place, while you are in a bad place, that is, in this world, in this life full of trials, in this mortality full of groans and fears — while you are in a bad place, choose yourself a place where you can move to from the bad place. You won't be able to move to the good place from the bad place unless you do good in the bad place. What sort of place is that other? One where nobody goes hungry. So if you want to live in the good place where nobody goes hungry, in this world *break your bread to the hungry* (Is 58:7). Because in that blessed place nobody is a foreigner, and all are living in their own native land; then if you wish to be in the good place, whenever in this bad place you find a foreigner who has nowhere to go, welcome him into your home. Show hospitality in the bad place, in order to get to the place where you cannot be a "guest worker" (Sermon 217, 5).

NOTES

1. See 1 Cor 13:9.
2. See Rom 7:23-25.
3. See 1 Cor 15:28.
4. See Gn 3:18-19.
5. See 1 Cor 15:28.